C0-AYN-484

ASIA IN THE MODERN WORLD, No. 8

FOUNDATIONS OF THE CHINESE REVOLUTION, 1905-1912

(AN HISTORICAL RECORD OF THE T'UNG-MENG HUI)

BY TA-LING LEE

Published by the St. John's University Press
under the auspices of the Center of Asian Studies

Asia in Modern World, No. 8

FOUNDATIONS OF THE CHINESE REVOLUTION, 1905-1912

(AN HISTORICAL RECORD OF THE T'UNG-MENG HUI)

by

TA-LING LEE

Assistant Professor of History
Southern Connecticut State College
New Haven, Conn.

Research Associate

Center of Asian Studies, St. John's University, New York

Published by the St. John's University Press
under the auspices of the Center of Asian Studies

Library of Congress Catalog Number 78-118835

PREFACE

This study by Professor Ta-ling Lee concerns the role played by the T'ung-meng Hui (Alliance Society) in the Chinese revolution during the period from 1905 to 1912. The subject is dealt with from several angles, which roughly correspond to the number of chapters into which the study is divided.

After an examination of the setting in which the T'ung-meng Hui, headed by Dr. Sun Yat-sen, came into being in August, 1905, the author analyzes its organizational setup and the ideological guide-lines as reflected in its programs. This is followed by an investigation of the T'ung-meng Hui's expansion both at home and abroad, its relations with other groups, and the propaganda activities and military campaigns it carried out. The study of both the static and dynamic aspects of the T'ung-meng Hui leads to the conclusion that the organization played a vitally important role in guiding the revolutionary movement in China during the period under review.

The establishment of the T'ung-meng Hui came about as the result of the merger of the Hsing-chung Hui (Regenerate China Society), the Hua-hsing Hui (Rejuvenate China Society), the Kuang-fu Hui (Restoration Society), and other splinter groups. Although there were other revolutionary groups at the time, the T'ung-meng Hui since its formation had become the mainstay of the revolutionary movement in China that culminated in the Wuch'ang revolution in October, 1911.

At its inception, the T'ung-meng Hui made clear as its objectives the overthrow of the Manchu Dynasty and establishment of a republic. In the political field, the revolutionists consistently stressed nationalism and republicanism as the dual guideposts; in the economic field, they advocated moderate socialism. To defend their cause, they carried out in 1905-1907 the celebrated great debate with the royalists, headed by K'ang Yu-wei and Liang Ch'i-ch'ao, who supported the emperor and championed constitutional monarchy. The debate showed that while the royalists were primarily conservative in outlook, the revolutionists were dedicated to what they believed to be the world's most advanced political system.

The T'ung-meng Hui expanded rapidly after its formation in 1905. The revolutionists used different methods, adapted to local conditions, in organizing branches, such as wooing overseas Chinese leaders and allying with the secret societies at home. While members inside China planned and took part in revolts, overseas members played an important role in providing financial support.

Between 1907 and 1911, no less than eight revolts were staged in south China. Since the T'ung-meng Hui had no military force of its own, it relied heavily in these revolts on the secret societies and the New Army, which the revolutionists succeeded in some measure in infiltrating, particularly at the lower echelon. While their military importance may be limited, these revolts were significant as a political demonstration against the Manchu rule.

Great themes run through this book: reform and revolution, innovation and renewal, conservatism and radicalism, tradition and modernity. All relate to the foundations of the Chinese revolution, 1905-1912.

The most significant result of the revolution was the overthrow of the centuries-old monarchical system and the establishment of a republic in China. Both in providing ideological leadership and in guiding the actual course of action, the role of the T'ung-meng Hui was crucial. Indeed, it may be said that had it not been for the T'ung-meng Hui, there would not have been the outbreak of the revolution in 1911.

Professor Lee was educated in China. He earned his doctorate in History from New York University. At the present time, he serves as Assistant Professor of History at the Southern Connecticut State College, New Haven, Connecticut, and as Research Associate of the Center of Asian Studies at St. John's University. We are grateful to have his research published as No. 8 of our *Asian in the Modern World Series.*

Paul K.T. Sih
Director, Center of Asian Studies
St. John's University, New York

INTRODUCTION

This study deals with the T'ung-meng Hui (Alliance Society), the organization which was largely responsible for leading the Chinese revolution against the Manchu Dynasty from 1905-1911. Due to the fact that the term "Chinese revolution" has now frequently been used to describe the emergence of the Communist regime on mainland China in 1949, it is perhaps necessary to point out at the outset that, in this work, the term Chinese revolution will be used to denote the revolution of 1911 whenever it is not further identified.

The Chinese revolution of 1911 undoubtedly is one of the most important milestones, if not the most important, in modern Chinese history. And yet curiously enough, it has been one of the most neglected fields of study in both Chinese and Occidental literature. While there are not many serious studies on this subject in the Chinese language, apart from the orthodox Kuomintang writings, works in English and other western languages are still fewer.[1] Much about the revolution remains to be told, and indeed much remains to be done to make the significance of the revolution fully appreciated.

With the success of the Chinese Communists in 1949, the swift ascendancy of China under Communism to world power, and the vast changes brought about by the Chinese Communists, people now begin to question whether or not the revolution of 1911 had really succeeded, or indeed whether or not it should be called a revolution at all. The view expressed by O. Edmund Clubb, for example, is typical of this line of skepticism. Pointing to the fact that Yuan Shih-k'ai took over the control of the government only months after the establishment of the republic, and that Yuan's death in 1916 was followed by a decade of warlordism in China, he suggests that the revolution of 1911 was actually a failure.[2]

---

1. A fine study on this subject is Ching-tung Liang, *The Chinese Revolution of 1911* (New York: St. John's University Press, 1962).

2 O. Edmund Clubb, *Twentieth Century China* (New York: Columbia University Press, 1964), Chapters I, II.

However, I find it difficult to accept such a view, gained *ex post facto.* Until we have thoroughly examined the episode and analyzed and evaluated its complexities, it would be rash to jump to any conclusion. It may be convenient first to look at the ascendancy of Yuan Shih-k'ai immediately after the 1911 revolution and the more recent success of the Chinese Communist Party as proof that the earlier revolution had failed, and then try to tailor one's interpretation of that "failure" in the light of the later development, but this is hardly the way of doing justice to the revolution of 1911. Any understanding of the revolution must begin with the revolution itself, not the development after it. The present study will concentrate on the revolution itself.

The formation of the T'ung-meng Hui in Tokyo in 1905, unifying under its banner various revolutionary partisans, was an event of singular importance. Since that time, until the Wuch'ang uprising of October 10, 1911, the T'ung-meng Hui was no doubt the mainstay of the revolutionary movement in China. In terms of organization, size, activities and appeal, the T'ung-meng Hui was certainly the most important body among others during the period. Of the ten abortive uprisings before the birth of the republic of which Dr. Sun spoke, eight were staged during this period, under the direct leadership of the T'ung-meng Hui. There were of course other organizations, some independent, others allied with the T'ung-meng Hui, still others merged with the T'ung-meng Hui, but they were mostly local in character, often with not very clearly stated goals, and few of them carried out persistent military campaigns as did the T'ung-meng Hui. Certainly none of them can rival the T'ung-meng Hui in influence and power. With the passage of time, the T'ung-meng Hui was gaining in strength and size while others were weakening or disappearing from the horizon. Indeed on the eve of the 1911 revolution, with the exception of a few local groups, the T'ung-meng Hui had become the only all-inclusive revolutionary organization in China.

This book will study both the static and the dynamic aspects of the T'ung-meng Hui. It will seek to answer a number of questions: How was the T'ung-meng Hui formed? What was its organizational setup? Who were the important leaders besides Dr. Sun Yat-sen? Did it have a body of coherent political and social ideologies? Aside from its goals of overthrowing the Manchu Dynasty and establishing a republic, did it have more detailed objectives and concrete programs for the realization of its objectives? What were the main differences between the revolutionists and the royalists headed by K'ang Yu-wei and Liang Ch'i-ch'ao? How did they fight out over their differences? Is a judgement as to which side was superior possible? If so, what should be the criteria? How did the T'ung-meng Hui grow and how were its funds raised? In the course of its growth and particularly in its penetration of the New Army (a crucial factor behind the successful uprising in Wuch'ang in October, 1911 that spearheaded the downfall of the Manchu Dynasty) how did the T'ung-meng Hui make use of the secret societies and how important a role did the secret societies play?

This is, of course, by no means an exhaustive list of questions on the subject. Nor is it assumed that all the questions can be satisfactorily answered. But these are vital questions on the T'ung-meng Hui and indeed on the revolution of 1911. It is hoped that whatever answers are provided here will contribute to a fuller answer to a larger question, namely, how important a role did the T'ung-meng Hui play in the revolution of 1911?

TABLE OF CONTENTS

Chapter I

THE ORIGINS OF THE T'UNG-MENG HUI

THE SETTING: IMPERIALISM AND REFORM

The formation of the T'ung-meng Hui in Tokyo in 1905 came eleven years after the organization of the Hsing-chung Hui (Regenerate China Society) by Dr. Sun Yat-sen in Honolulu in 1894, the first revolutionary body in China devoted to the overthrow of the Manchu government and the establishment of a republic. The years from 1894 to 1905 had been a period of unprecedented humiliation for China and the Chinese people. Not since the days when the door of the Middle Kingdom was forced open by the guns of British warships in the Opium War of 1842 had China suffered so much at the hands of foreign powers. In particular, two events during this period, namely, the Sino-Japanese War of 1895 and the Boxer Rebellion of 1900, were of far-reaching consequences. Coming out of the war a loser, China suffered futher humiliations and the weakness of the Manchu Court was fully exposed. For the first time in the memory of the Chinese, the Middle Kingdom was soundly defeated by a small Asian neighbor, hitherto regarded as an inferior country long under China's "cultural umbrella." This defeat was followed by a period in which the great powers scrambled for privileges in China, exacting leased territories, railroad concessions and mining rights, and circling out their respective "spheres of influences." Knowledgeable persons were alarmed by talks of the danger that China might be partitioned by the powers.

The immediate result of this situation was the intensification of the reform movement advocated by K'ang Yu-wei, culminating in the fateful "one hundred days" in 1898 and the subsequent collapse of the reform movement in the face of the strong reactionary force led by the Empress Dowager, Tz'u Hsi. K'ang, a Cantonese scholar in the Confucian tradition but well-versed in Western thought, was convinced that the only way to save China in the face of foreign imperialism was not merely to imitate the foreign powers in building battleships and manufacturing guns, but to initiate a wholesale revision of the century-old institutions, which were the real hindrance to any effort at genuine modernization. However, despite a receptive and conscientious emperor, Kuang Hsu, who adopted K'ang's ideas and began a large-scale reform, the effort was soon to be put down and the emperor was himself practically deposed in the 1898 coup d'etat.

After the failure of the reform attempt, K'ang and Liang Ch'i-ch'ao, his disciple, went abroad in exile to continue preaching the necessity of reform, while the conservatives once again seemed to have the country firmly in their grip. However, the country as a whole was becoming more restive and, despite the control of the Manchu Court, the yearnings for change were finding expression in a variety of ways.

The influence of the K'ang-Liang group was by no means eliminated by virtue of the failure of the 1898 reform attempt. In their exile abroad, K'ang and Liang, whose sympathy and support for the emperor remained undiminished, continued to promote vigorously the cause of constitutional monarchy. They organized the Pao-huang Hui (Preserve Monarch Society) and K'ang, traveling in the United States, succeeded in winning many overseas Chinese to his cause either by converting the revolutionary groups organized earlier by Sun Yat-sen into branches of the Pau-huang Hui, or by establishing new branches.[1]

Meanwhile, Liang, with his widely respected literary ability and intellectual persuasion, started a fortnightly in Tokyo, the *Hsin-min Ts'ung Pao* (New Citizen's Journal), to introduce Western learning and defend constitutional monarchy. As one of the most respected journals of the day, the *Hsin-min Ts'ung Pao* was very influential among the Chinese students and served as the organ of the Pao-huang Hui. Liang almost single-handedly edited this journal, tirelessly writing long persuasive treatises in defense of constitutional monarchy. It was in the *Hsin-min Ts'ung Pao* that he later launched the celebrated great debates with the revolutionists over such vital issues as whether China should be

---

1 Feng Tzu-yu, *Chung-hua-min-kuo k'ai-kuo-ch'ien ko-ming shih* (Revolutionary History of China before the Founding of the Republic) (Taipei: Shih-chieh Book Co., 1954), Vol. I, pp. 42, 47.

a constitutional monarchy or a republic, whether some feature of socialism would be desirable for China, etc. These debates were of epochal importance to China, not only because they represented two different schools of thought, and the advocates of each were no less concerned with the destiny of the nation than those of the other, but also because the arguments of both sides are relevant to the affairs of the present day.[2]

After the triumph of the 1898 coup, the conservatives, who were so confident of the superiority of the traditional Chinese culture and set out to preserve it, were further convinced that only a strong national defense could keep China from being cut up by the powers, and they proceeded to build one. However, the defense they had built in the next two years was far from adequate. The strong foreign policy adopted by the Manchu Court after the 1898 coup, and the misuse of a spontaneous outburst of anti-foreign nationalism were to lead to the disastrous Boxer Rebellion, in which China was again brought to its knees, this time before almost all the powers of the world.

After the Boxer Rebellion, the Empress Dowager belatedly came to the realization that reform was the only way to save the nation from further foreign exploitation, and more important, to prevent a revolution against the shaky Manchu rule. Although she had ruthlessly crushed the 1898 reform attempt, she now tried to resume some of the reform measures, at least superficially. One of the measures she resumed was the sending of young students to study abroad to learn Western ways of modernization. However, the young students, once exposed to Western thought, soon became one of the most formidable forces against the Manchu Court, which had looked upon them as the hope of the future. These students were quick to absorb Western thought and even quicker to be influenced by it. The more they were exposed to the cross currents of Western thought, the more restive they grew. They invariably became radicals, and increasingly became convinced that for China to restore her past glory and to modernize in the modern world, the Manchu Court, whose incompetence had been proven, must go.

---

2 See *infra*, Chapter IV.

SUN YAT–SEN: EARLY REVOLUTIONARY YEARS

As the intellectual turmoil among the educated younger generation of China continued, an organized radical movement, with clearly stated aims, had been under way since 1894. That was the revolution led by Dr. Sun Yat-sen. Just exactly when Sun definitely began to form his revolutionary idea is hard to pin down, partly because idea itself is always in process of growth. From Sun's own writings and from studies of other source materials, Chinese historians generally agree that he first conceived of his revolutionary idea after China was defeated in the Franco-China War of 1885. However, whatever revolutionary idea he had at that time was no doubt embryonic and not clearly defined. Save for his own recollections written some thirty years later, there was little contemporary record showing how deeply he felt about the revolution at the time and what action he had contemplated. It was not until 1919 that Sun started systematically to put down his revolutionary ideas and his programs for national reconstruction in a series of books under the general title of *Chien-kuo fang-lueh* (Programs for National Reconstruction). A chapter in one of the volumes, entitled *Sun Wen hsueh-shuo* (Sun Yat-sen's Theory), contains a brief recollection of his revolutionary activities. In it, Dr. Sun wrote:

> I first made up my mind to overthrow the Manchus and to establish a Chinese Republic in 1885, when China was defeated by France in the Franco-China War. For the next ten years, when I first was a medical student and later a practitioner in Hong Kong and Macao, I have been steadfast in pushing those objectives.[3]

That Dr. Sun wanted to overthrow the Manchu government at this time seems consistent with the ideas he had entertained since even earlier days. There is little doubt that Sun started out as a nationalist and remained so throughout his life. Since his youth, he had shown deep interest in the Taiping Rebellion, an attempt by the Han people to overthrow the ruling Manchus, who were regarded as "aliens." Sun admired the Taiping leaders so much that in his medical student days in

---

3 Sun Yat-sen, "Sun Wen hsueh-shuo" (Sun Yat-sen's Theory), *Kuo-fu ch'uan-shu* (Complete Works of the Founding Father) (Taipei: National War College, 1961), p. 32. Sun's writings have been published in separate volumes and in various versions of his Complete Works. The version used here, edited by Chang Ch'i-yun, a noted historian, is the most recent.

Hong Kong, he was nicknamed by his schoolmates Hung Hsiu-ch'uan, leader of the Taiping Rebellion.[4]

Later on, as a medical practitioner in Hong Kong, Dr. Sun petitioned Li Hung-chang, viceroy of Chihli, for reform, outlining in a long letter his philosophy and proposals. The gist of his reform ideas was contained in the now famous four brief lines, namely, "human talents should be fully utilized; material wealth should be fully employed; natural resources should be fully exploited; and commodities should be circulated without hindrance."[5] It is interesting to note that his ideas at this time were not radically different from those of K'ang Yu-wei; they both were deeply concerned with the perilous position of the country under foreign aggression, and both were dedicated to the aims of saving the country. They agreed perfectly on their aims; whatever differences there were between them on the means of attaining the goals that emerged later on had not yet become clear at this time. In fact, before the 1898 coup, K'ang's younger brother, Kwang-jen, and two of K'ang's disciples, Ho Chang and Ch'en Ch'ien-ch'iu, talked with Sun about joining forces. As late as after the coup, there still appeared to be possibilities, at one time or another, of a coalition formed by Sun and the K'ang-Liang forces. When K'ang escaped to Japan after the 1898 coup, Sun, out of sympathy and admiration, sought to meet K'ang, but K'ang avoided seeing him.[6]

K'ang and Liang were helped to Japan by two Japanese friends, Miyazaki Torazo and Hirayama Shu, who were sympathetic to the Chinese revolutionary cause. They thought the K'ang-Liang group and Sun had the same goal of saving China and therefore should cooperate. In earnest they tried to bring the two groups together. Through their help, Ch'en Shao-pai one day went to see K'ang and Liang and talked for several hours about revolution. According to Ch'en, K'ang insisted

---

4 Ch'en Shao-pai, "Hsing-chung Hui ko-ming shih-yao" (Brief Revolutionary Hsitory of Hsing-chung Hui), *Hsin-hai ko-ming* (The Revolution of 1911) (Shanghai: People's Publishing House, 1957), Vol. I, p. 24. Chen was one of Dr. Sun's earliest associates.

5 *Kuo-fu ch'uan-shu,* pp. 352-57.

6 Miyazaki Torazo "Sun Yat-sen," trans. Huang Chung-huang, *Hsin-hai ko-ming,* Vol. I, p. 105.

on how virtuous the Emperor was and refused to oppose him, but Liang seemed more inclined to the cause of revolution.[7] After K'ang left Japan, Sun became closely associated with Liang and several times they talked secretly and at length. They frequently attended the same gatherings of Chinese students, and they were members of at least one patriotic organization formed by the students with the explicit aim of overthrowing the Manchu "aliens."[8] From three letters Liang wrote to Sun, there was evidence that Liang and Sun were at one time, in the autumn of 1899, near an agreement on forming a new organization with Sun as head and Liang taking the second place. Their talks came so close to bearing fruit that plans were under way to draft the regulations of a new organization.[9] However, upon hearing this, K'ang Yu-wei, who was then in Singapore, was enraged and ordered Liang to go to Hawaii immediately to form a Po-Huang Hui branch there. With Liang's departure, the talks of cooperation came to an abrupt end. After Liang's return to Tokyo the following year, he veered sharply toward monarchical constitutionalism. With the ensuing great debates, any rapprochement was out of the question. It became increasingly clear that the difference between K'ang and Sun, or between the royalists and Sun's followers, was serious and fundamental. It was primarily a difference between an evolutionist and a revolutionist, as a Western scholar so aptly puts it.[10]

If Dr. Sun during this period appeared less consistent in his avowed goal of overthrowing the Manchus, the orthodox Kuomintang historians are quick to come to his defense. According to Chang Ch'i-yun, Sun's petition to Li Hung-chang by no means indicated that Sun intended to compromise with the Manchus. On the contrary, Chang asserts, what Sun really wanted was to see Li's reaction to his proposals for possible incorporation into Sun's revolutionary blueprint.[11] On the possible

---

7 Ch'en Shao-pai, *op. cit.*, p. 57.

8 Feng Tzu-yu, *op. cit.*, p. 114.

9 *Ibid.*, p. 44.

10 Harley F. MacNair, *China in Revolution* (Chicago: Chicago University Press, 1931), p. 10.

11 Chang Ch'i-yun, *Tang-shih kai-yao* (Outline History of the Kuomintang) (Taipei: China Cultural Service, 1954), Vol. I, p. 15.

cooperation between Sun and Liang, another Kuomintang historian points out the insincerity of Liang. Showing facsimile reproductions of Liang's letters to Sun in his book, Feng Tzu-yu argues that Liang had no intention of forming a coalition with Sun in the first place.[12]

In examining whether Sun was consistent in his goals, one should not, however, overlook the fact that the Pao-huang Hui headed by K'ang Yu-wei and Liang Ch'i-ch'ao was at the time a much stronger organization than that of Sun's. As pointed out earlier, the K'ang-Liang group and Sun had the same supreme goals of saving the nation, and whatever practical difference that might exist between them had not begun to emerge at this early stage. Moreover, despite the general image of an idealist that has been given Sun by historians, Sun proved to have been no less a pragmatist. He never lost sight of the actual circumstances under which he labored at a given time. Fully aware of the limitations, he was always ready to accept the second best alternative if the circumstances so dictated. His revolutionary ideas were broad and general enough to enable him to cooperate with, and recruit, if possible, whatever partisan that by nature was under the reform banner. Thus in 1895, when he expanded the Hsing-chung Hui, taking in members of the Fu-jen Wen She (Benevolence Literary Society) in Hong Kong, an organization devoted to educating the public by introducing Western knowledge, he did not hesitate to hand over the chairmanship of the newly formed organization to Yang Ch'u-yun, who headed the Fu-jen Wen She.[13] Again in 1902, he joined the Erh-shih Shih-chih Chih-na Wang-kuo Chi-nien Hui (Twentieth Century China National Shame Memorial Society),[14] a radical group organized in Tokyo by Chang Ping-lin and others, dedicated to "radical revolution," i.e., the overthrow of the Manchus.

After his petition had met with deaf ears of the aged Li Hung-chang, Sun became disillusioned with the idea of peaceful reform and veered gradually toward revolution. In his student days in Hong Kong and later as a medical practitioner in Macao and Hong Kong, he

---

12 Feng Tzu-yu, *op. cit.*, p. 44.

13 *Ibid.*, p. 7.

14 *Ibid.*, p. 114.

became closely associated with four other radicals, Cheng Shih-liang, Yu Shao-wan, Yang Ho-ling and Ch'en Shao-pai. Cheng was connected with the secret societies and he himself was a member of the Triad Society.[15] Sun was quick to learn that the original purpose of the secret societies was to overthrow the Manchu "aliens" and restore the Ming Dynasty. This appealed to him greatly and may have strengthened his anti-Manchu conviction. At the same time, he may have begun to think of using the force of the secret societies, as he later did, to help carry out the goal of his revolution. This cross-influence is apparent, although the extent of such influence is difficult to measure. At any rate, Sun's idea about the overthrow of the Manchus crystalized in 1894, when he founded the Hsing-chung Hui in Honolulu. One of its declared goals was "to drive out the Tartars."[16]

The Hsing-chung Hui, at the beginning, had apparently only a handful of followers. Sun himself recalled that only his brother and a few others pledged full support by contributing money to it.[17] Despite the fact that the Hsing-chung Hui was far from being a force of any significance, Sun proved himself to be an impatient young revolutionist. After founding the Hsing-chung Hui and with the money he had raised, he immediately returned to Hong Kong and launched an uprising in south China in 1895. In 1900, another attempt was made. In both uprisings, the role of the secret societies was important. As many as 3,000 secret society members were said to have taken part in the first uprising.[18] The man credited with rallying the secret societies to the revolutionary cause was Cheng Shih-liang. After the failure of the first two uprisings, the revolutionary movement reached a low ebb. The next uprising did not take place until 1907, two years after the formation of the T'ung-meng Hui. Throughout this period, Sun mostly travelled abroad, preaching his revolutionary ideas and organizing supporters among the overseas Chinese.

---

15 Feng Tzu-yu, *Chung-kuo ko-ming yun-tung erh-shih-liu nein tsu-chih shih* (A History of the Organizations Connected With the Chinese Revolutionary Movement During Twenty-six Years) (Shanghai: Commerical Press, 1948), p. 4.

16 Chang Ch'i-yun, *op. cit.*, p. 20.

17 Ch'en Shao-pai, *op. cit.*, p. 29.

18 *Ibid.*, p. 30.

For Sun, these were trying years. In the overwhelmingly conservative overseas Chinese communities, he waged a courageous fight against the Pao-huang Hui, whose influence was growing. He was generally regarded as a "rebel," and was officially so designated by the Manchu government. After the failure of the 1895 uprising, he had a price on his head. The next year, he narrowly escaped death in the famous kidnapping case in London, when the Chinese legation held him and tried unsuccessfully to ship him back secretly to China to be decapitated. It was not until after 1900 that the revolution gradually began to win appreciable support.From that time on, as Sun observed later, "condemnations from the common people were seldom heard and among the intellectuals not a few began to show sympathy."[19]

Sun of course was making a general statement and he probably exaggerated a little. Actually, he was at this time still widely regarded as too radical and dangerous a person. Indeed, as late as 1901, he was still thought of as a "rebel" even by many who were themselves radicals dedicated to the cause of reform. One interesting anecdote may be cited by way of illustration. In that year, Sun was in Yokohama actively contacting those Chinese students who were most radical. Wu Chih-hui, one of the intellectual figures in contemporary China who had by then already made his name as an erudite scholar and a man of vigorous reform ideas, actually refused to see Sun when a mutual friend suggested one day that they visit Sun together. Wu did not meet Sun until 1905 when both of them were in London, where Sun called upon him. Since then, they had become close friends and Wu, admiring Sun and his ideas, later joined the T'ung-meng Hui and eventually became one of the most ardent supporters of the revolution. Recalling his refusal to see Sun in Tokyo in 1901, Wu wrote upon Sun's death in 1925: "At that time, although I was a self-styled reformist, I was still firmly in support of Emperor Kuang Hsu and thought I should keep away from the rebellious ideas of Sun's. Since he was a rebel, how could I bear to see him?[20]

---

19 Sun Yat-sen, "Sun Wen hsueh-shuo," p. 34.

20 Wu Chih-hui, "Wuo i i-chiang Chung-shan hsien-sheng" (Some reminiscences about Sun Yat-sen), *Meng Chin* (Advance), (Peiping), No. 3, March 12, 1925.

TOKYO: HAVEN OF RADICALS

For centuries, the Chinese have been taught to stay at home in order to be close to one's parents. This is considered a great virtue. Confucius said: "When parents are living, one should not travel to far away places, and should travel only when it is necessary."[21] While one was not even supposed to go too far away from one's hometown, it would be unthinkable for one to travel out of the country to an unknown land to learn from the "barbarians." But like many other deep-rooted conservative credos in China that were crumbling in the face of the onslaught of Western civilization at the turn of the century, the concept of not leaving one's own land was subjected to gradual change.

Obviously because of geographical proximity, and because of the fact that Japan had already had a head start in absorbing Western ideas for modernization, Tokyo became the natural destination of many a young Chinese student who was later to play an important role in contemporary China. In a way, Japan provided both an example for modernization and a bridge between old China and the Western world. Just when the Chinese students first began to arrive in Japan is hard to determine, but by the time of the 1898 coup, there were already some 100 of them in Japan, mostly in Tokyo.[22] Feng Tzu-yu said that in 1899-1900, fewer than 100 were in Japan, including himself, and about half of them were in favor of "radical measures" aimed at "basic changes" in order to save the country.[23] The next year, the number of Chinese students in Japan increased to some 1,500.[24] Aside from a few of them, who went there at their own expenses, the great majority were financed by the government in the form of full scholarships provided from four sources, namely, by the Pei-yang Kung-shueh (North Sea College) in Peking, and the Nan-yang Kung-shueh (South Sea College) in Shanghai, respectively established in 1895 and 1896, which were

---

21 Confucius *Analects,* Chapter I.

22 Li Shu-hua, "Wu Chih-hui hsien-sheng ts'ung wei-hsin-p'ai ch'eng-wei ko-ming-tang ching-kuo" (Wu Chih-hui, From Reformist to Revolutionist), *Chuan-chi Wen-hsueh* (Biographical Literature) (Taipei), Vol. IV, No. 3, March 1964, p. 36.

23 Feng Tzu-yu, *Chung-hua-min-kuo k'ai-kuo-ch'ien ko-ming shih,* Vol. I, p. 54.

24 Li Shu-hua, *op. cit.,* p. 36.

roughly equivalent to present day colleges; by the Chinese Legation in Tokyo, and by the provincial government of the student's native province.[25] By 1902, there were several thousands of them in Tokyo[26] and later on some 13,000 were said to have reached Japan in a single year.[27] By 1905, the total number of Chinese students and tourists in Japan could have reached 20,000.[28] The students generally fell into two categories: those studying science and liberal arts in Japanese colleges and those who entered or aspired to enter the Japanese military schools to study military science.

After the Boxer Rebellion and two abortive attempts against the Manchu Court, launched in 1900 respectively by the revolutionists and the royalists (the latter aimed specifically at toppling the Empress Dowager and restoring power to the Emperor) the students in Japan grew increasingly restive and numerous radical organizations and publications began to appear.

The earliest Chinese student organization in Japan was the Li-chih Hui (Endeavor Society). Organized in 1901, it was primarily a fraternal body. As far as can be ascertained, it did not directly participate in revolutionary activities. Whatever indirect contribution it may have made to the cause of revolution may be due to the fact that it endeavored to foster the study of Western knowledge and sponsored the translation of a number of books. It published the books in the *I-shu Hui-pien* (Translation Series), including constitutions of many countries and biographies of world figures. The next year, 1902, the society was split into two factions, one radical and one moderate. Those in the radical faction organized themselves into an independent

---

25 *Ibid.*

26 Feng Tzu-yu, *op. cit.,* p. 55.

27 Ku Chung-hsiu, *Chung-hua-min-kuo k'ai-kuo shih* (The History of the Founding of the Republic of China), (Shanghai,1914; reprint, Taipei, 1962), p. 2.

28 Li Shu-hua, *op. cit.,* p. 37. See also Hu Han-min, "Tzu Chuan" (Autobiography), *Ko-ming Wen-hsien* (Materials of the Revolution of 1911) (Taipei: Committee for the Compilation of Materials on the Party History [of the Kuomintang], 1958), Vol. III, p. 383. A more conservative estimate, however, puts the number of students at around 8,000. See Wu Hsiang-hsiang, *Sung Chiao-jen: Chung-kuo min-chu hsien-cheng ti hsien-ch'u* (Sung Chiao-jen: Forerunner of Chinese Democracy and Constitution) (Taipei: Book World Co., 1964), p. 40.

group called Ch'ing-nien Hui (Young Men's Society), and eventually became revolutionists.[29]

The first radical organization was the Kwang-tung Tu-li Hsieh-hui (Kwangtung Independence Association), set up in 1901 by a group of Cantonese students in Japan, to promote the independence of their native province from the Manchus. Sun Yat-sen, who was at the time living in Yokohama, supported the organization vigorously. This marked the beginning of close contact between Sun and the Cantonese students in Japan.[30]

In the same year, a permanent meeting place was set up in Tokyo by the Chinese students. The general sentiment of the students was probably best expressed by Wu Lu-chen, a fellow student, who in a speech at the inauguration of the Chinese student center compared it to the Independence Hall in Philadelphia.[31] The next year, a large-scale "Chih-na Wang-kuo Chi-nien Hui" (China National Shame Memorial Conference) was called in Tokyo by a number of radical student leaders, among who Chang Ping-lin and Feng Tzu-yu, who later played an important role in the T'ung-meng Hui. The meeting was barred at the last minute by the Tokyo police at the urging of the Chinese Minister in Tokyo, Ts'ai Chun.

Chang Ping-lin was a literary figure, who was at the time already well-known as an authority on Chinese classics. He was first a member of K'ang Yu-wei's Ch'iang-hsueh Hui (Foster Study Society), but eventually he refused to endorse K'ang's support of the Emperor and played practically no role in the society. For some time, he served on the editorial staff of the *Shih-wu Pao* (Journal of Contemporary Affairs) in Shanghai, published by Liang Ch'i-ch'ao. At one time, he was invited to serve on the personal brain trust of Chang Chih-tung, viceroy of Hupeh, only to be fired for his "radical views and his disrespect for the Emperor." After the 1898 coup, he was on the black list of the Manchus and he fled to Formosa, and later on to Japan, where he was first introduced to Sun Yat-sen by Liang Ch'i-ch'ao.

---

29 Li Shu-hua, *op. cit.*, p. 36.

30 Feng Tzu-yu, *Chung-hua min-kuo k'ai-kuo-ch'ien ko-ming shih,* Vol. I, p. 55.

31 *Ibid.*, p. 56.

Returning to China, he taught Chinese classics at the missionary Soochow University in Kiangsu province. There again, his radical views against the Manchus soon attracted the attention of the local magistrate, who asked the school authorities to dismiss him. He went to Japan again, and served as an editor at a publishing house, Kwang-chih Shu-chu (Broaden Knowledge Book Company), which was established by Liang Ch'i-ch'ao to translate Western books.

The theme of the memorial meeting was clear: it was to commemorate the 262nd anniversary of the "loss" of China, meaning that China by then had been ruled by the Manchus for 262 years. When invited to join the memorial meeting, both Sun and Liang agreed to have their names listed as sponsors. Liang, however asked that his name not be made public.[32] Like many others, Chang Ping-lin, the chief organizer of the meeting, was at this time a nationalist in the sense of being anti-Manchu, both because the Manchus were "aliens" and because their incompetence was responsible for China's humiliation. Whether at this time he already had identical revolutionary ideas with Sun Yat-sen about establishing a republican form of government is rather doubtful. Chang was then already a widely respected man, and he once spoke of Sun, rather contemptuously, as a man "with a little knowledge of world affairs." While in Formosa, he once wrote an article to exhort K'ang Yu-wei to sever Manchu ties, and by way of comparison, he said: "Even Sun Wen (Sun Yat-sen), with only a little knowledge of world affairs, knows the difference between the Chinese and the Manchus, and advocates revolution to overthrow the latter."[33]

On New Year's Day, 1903, a large-scale meeting was again called at the student center. This time the meeting was allowed to be held and among the over 1,000 participants was the Chinese Minister, Ts'ai Chun. Several students got up to the rostrum and, in defiance of Ts'ai, delivered fierce speeches denouncing the despotism of the Manchu Dynasty. Unless sovereignty was restored to the Han race, they declared, China would be doomed. One Manchu student, named Ch'ang Fu, who tried to speak in defense of his own race, was greeted with

---

32 *Ibid.*, p. 116.

33 *Ibid.*, p. 113.

boos and jeers from the audience and he had to leave the rostrum half way through his speech. Apparently because of his loyalty, Minister Ts'ai later recommended him for the post of consul in Yokohama.[34]

In April of that year, the Chinese students in Japan, enraged by Russia's occupation of Manchuria, translated their indignation into action. A Resist-Russia Volunteer Army was organized, with the aim of returning home to fight the Russians. Later known as the Chun-kuo-min Chiao-yu Hui (National Military Education Society), it boasted of a membership of over 1,000 persons who, in defiance of the Japanese authorities, took to daily military drills to prepare themselves for the battlefield. Meanwhile, two representatives were sent to Tientsin to see Yuan Shih-k'ai, then viceroy of Chihli, to pledge the full support of the students in Japan for strong action against the Russians. Their petition was ignored by Yuan. Upon hearing that Yuan was about to arrest them, the two students fled Tientsin. This episode aggravated the indignation of the students in Japan, who openly condemned the Manchus as traitors.[35]

In the winter of that year, a further step was taken by some Chinese students in Japan. Under Sun Yat-sen's leadership, a military school was set up secretly by a group of fourteen students in Tokyo, which Feng Tzu-yu described as the first military school established by the revolutionists. One Japanese retired army officer was hired as instructor and daily drills were conducted. The school was, however, soon closed down by the Japanese authorities.[36]

In the spring of 1904, a revolutionary society with considerable following was formed in Tokyo. It was the Hua-shing Hui, set up by students from the central China province of Hunan, with the avowed purpose of overthrowing the Manchus. The name of the society, Hua-hsing–meaning rejuvenating China–best explains its aim. Among the organizers of the Hua-hsing Hui were Huang Hsing, Sung Chao-jen and Liu K'wei-i, all from Hunan. All three played an important role later in the revolution. In the autumn of that year, members of the

---

34 *Ibid.*, p. 56.

35 *Ibid.*, p. 57.

36 *Ibid.*

Hua-hsing Hui, with the help of secret societies, launched an abortive uprising in Hunan. After the failure of the uprising, the leaders of the Hua-hsing Hui fled to Japan again.[37]

Coupled with the growth of radical organizations were publications put out by the restive students. Periodicals, journals and other publications, of varying quality, were making their appearance. Almost unanimously, these publications stressed the necessity of learning Western knowledge, they urged reform, and agitated for revolution against the Manchus. While the influence of these publications might be insignificant because of their small circulation and limited audience, they unmistakably pointed to the restiveness of the students and their burning desire to "save the country." Incomplete statistics show that at one time or another, before 1905, there were at least a dozen such publications circulating among Chinese students in Tokyo, and some of them reached China by various means. Among such publications were *I-shu Hui-pien* (Translation Series), *Kuo-min Pao* (Citizen's Journal), *Hu-pei Hsueh-sheng-chieh* (Hupeh Students), *Han Sheng* (Voice of the Han Race), *Che-chiang Ch'ao* (Chekiang Tide), *Chiang-su Hu-nan Yu-hsueh I-pien* (Kiangsu and Hunan Students Translation Series), *Erh-shih Shih-chi Chih Chih-na* (Twentieth Century China), *K'ai-chih Lu* (Enhance Knowledge), *Hsin Kwang-tung* (New Kwangtung), etc.[38]

GROWING OPPOSITION TO THE MANCHUS

Meanwhile, within China, radical organizations also made their appearance. In Shanghai, the intellectual center of China, one such organization was the Ai-kuo Hsueh She (Patriotic Institute), established in 1902 by Ts'ai Yuan-p'ei, Chang Ping-lin and others. Originally known as the Chiao-yu Hui (Education Society), it started out as a society devoted to the compilation of school textbooks and later grew to a full-fledged school, with faculty members and students espousing

37 The best book on the Hua-hsing Hui is Hsueh Chun-tu, *Huang Hsing and Chinese Revolution* (Stanford: Stanford University Press, 1961).

38 Feng Tzu-yu, "Chi Chung-kuo T'ung-meng Hui" (Reminiscences of T'ung-meng Hui), *Chung-kuo chin-tai shih lun ts'ung* (Collected Essays on Modern Chinese History), ed. Wu Hsiang-hsiang (Taipei: Cheng-chung Book Co., 1957), Ser. I, Vol. 8, pp. 31-32.

radical ideas. Meanwhile, many faculty members were on the editorial staff of *Su Pao* (Kiangsu Journal), an outspoken anti-Manchu publication. Located in the foreign concession and thus out of the jurisdiction of the Chinese authorities, the journal openly advocated the overthrow of the Manchus. After repeated negotiations, the Manchu authorities finally secured the permission from the British concession and launched a surprise raid. Several radicals were held, including Chang Ping-lin and Tsou Yung, the famous young author of *Ko-ming chun* (Revolutionary Army), a fiercely anti-Manchu tract often compared with Thomas Paine's *Common Sense.* Having gotten wind of the raid other leaders fled the country. The Ai-kuo Hsueh She and the *Su Pao* were both closed down by the Manchus, and the ensuing public trials of Chang and Tsou attracted wide attention. The *Su Pao* case had wide repercussions in the intellectual circles in China and among the Chinese students in Japan.

Another revolutionary body was the Kuang-fu Hui, or Restoration Society, which was organized in Shanghai in 1904 by students who had returned from Japan. Among its most active leaders were Hsu Hsi-lin, who directed two abortive military campaigns against the Manchus; Ch'iu Chin, the well-known heroine, who was later captured and killed by the Manchus; and T'ao Ch'eng-chang, who was instrumental in rallying the forces of secret societies. Ts'ai Yuan-p'ei, who had already made his name as the head of the Chiao-yu Hui in Shanghai, was chosen to head the revolutionary body.

The Kuang-fu Hui was active in the lower Yangtze Valley, particularly in Anhwei and Chekiang provinces. It had considerable following in the secret societies and in the New Army. Chekiang was one of the provinces where secret societies were particularly active. Even before the formation of the Kuang-fu Hui, various secret society sects had been won over to the cause of revolution through the efforts of T'ao, Hsu, Ch'iu and others. When the T'ung-meng Hui was formed in Tokyo in 1905, many leaders of the Kuang-fu Hui joined it. However, the Kuang-fu Hui continued in existence, and carried out its own anti-Manchu activities. Because of its important role, the Kuang-fu Hui will be treated in more detail in a later chapter.

Meanwhile, the royalists, under the leadership of K'ang Yu-wei and Liang Ch'i-ch'ao, continued to champion the return of power to Emperor Kuang Hsu and the setting up of a constitutional monarchy. In order that the Emperor, practically deposed, could be reinstated, they were convinced that the Empress Dowager must step aside, and be forced to do so if necessary. Thus an attempt at overthrowing the Empress Dowager was made by T'ang Ts'ai-ch'ang, financed with funds raised from among the overseas Chinese by K'ang Yu-wei. In trying to overthrow the Manchu ruler, be it the Empress or the Emperor, the revolutionists found common cause with the royalists and helped in the revolt, launched in Wuhan in central China in 1900. The revolt was a failure, due largely to the preventive measures taken by Chang Chih-tung, then viceroy of Hupeh. Chang was widely regarded as having reform ideas. T'ang first tried to persuade him to declare Hupeh independent from the Empress Dowager's court as a step towards overthrowing the Empress. However, Chang, although a progressive man, was not so progressive as to be ready to oppose the Peking government, to which his loyalty remained unchanged. He took quick action to arrest the leaders and to attack the headquarters of the Tzu-li Chun (Independent Army), organized by T'ang, before T'ang had a chance to carry out his impressive plan, which called for an army of some 200,000 men, divided into seven groups, to capture the entire Yangtze Valley. For this uprising, K'ang, through his personal influence, had raised over a million dollars from among the overseas Chinese.[39]

The Manchu Court, under the Empress Dowager Tz'u Hsi, faced opposition not only from the revolutionists, the radical students, and the royalists, but from still another source, namely, the secret societies, whose original purpose was the restoration of the Ming Dynasty. Despite the fact that the original goal of the secret societies had lost much of its meaning after long years of the Manchu rule, there was at least one uprising staged by the secret societies against the Manchus amidst the turmoil around the turn of the century, with no direct role played by either the revolutionists or the royalists.

This attempt was made at Canton in 1903. The leader in the uprising was Hung Ch'uan-fu, younger brother of Hung Hsiu-ch'uan,

---

39 Feng Tzu-yu, *Chung-hua-min-kuo k'ai-kuo-ch'ien ko-ming shih,* Vol. I, p. 79.

leader of the Taiping Rebellion. Living in retirement in Hong Kong after the failure of the Taiping Rebellion, but maintaining close connections with the secret societies, he had not forgotten his military career during the heyday of the Taiping Rebellion, and had often thought of overthrowing the Manchus. His dream seemed to have a chance to come true in 1903 when a fellow Cantonese, Li Chi-t'ang, a rich merchant in Hong Kong, agreed to donate 500,000 dollars to organize members of the secret societies for a revolt in Canton. According to the plan, the revolt was to take place on the Chinese New Year's Eve–January 28, 1903, according to the Gregorian calendar–when all Manchu officials, civilian and military, would be at the imperial temple for a ceremony to greet the New Year. The revolters were to set off an explosion at the temple to kill all officials there, and then proceed to take control of the local administrative and military centers. The plot, however, was uncovered by the Manchu authorities when a shipment of arms was seized near the Hong Kong-Macao-Canton borders. The Manchu officials, with the help of the Hong Kong authorities, soon arrested most of the leaders, thus foiling the attempt before it got off the ground. Hung first escaped to Singapore, and returned to Hong Kong later and died at the age of 69.

The ultimate goal of this revolt seemed never clearly spelled out. One source maintained that there were plans to declare the establishment of a republic after the seizure of Canton and to install Yung Wing, the first Chinese to study in the United States, who was then a widely respected intellectual leader, as provisional president.[40] In the posters intended for public display after the uprising, the revolters, however, identified themselves as belonging to the Ming Dynasty, meaning that their move was designed to restore the rule of the Ming Dynasty after the overthrow of the Manchu "aliens." The poster, seized in large quantities by the Manchus reads:

> **Public Notification to Assure Peace and Order to the Subject, Issued by the Viceroy of Southern Kwangtung of the Great Ming Dynasty:**
>
> You are all fully aware that the Manchu Dynasty is corrupt and incompetent. Through heavy taxes, it has brought untold sufferings to the people and has invited universal condemnation. The present crusade

40 *Ibid.,* p. 121-22.

is for the noble purpose of overthrowing the Manchus and restoring the glory of the Han people. Freedom of religion will be assured and merchants will be protected. With the elimination of the criminal ones, the foundation of everlasting peace shall be laid. This is to fulfill the mandate of the Heaven and the subject need not fear nor doubt.[41]

Thus around the turn of the century, the Manchu Court under the Empress Dowager Tz'u Hsi was faced with opposition from many quarters, from young students in the upper social stratum to the secret societies at the bottom of the intellectual ladder. There was no longer any question that the Manchus must go; what was needed was a rallying center to pool the various opposition forces. It was chiefly to serve this purpose that the T'ung-meng Hui came into being in 1905.

SUN'S AMERICAN AND EUROPEAN TOUR

After the failure of the uprising at Huichow in 1900, Sun alternately stayed in Japan and Indo-China. For nearly two years, he was rather inactive. In 1903, he embarked on an extended trip around the world to promote his ideals and to recruit new supporters. He first sailed for Hawaii, from where he proceeded to the American continent and then to Europe. In nearly two years of travelling, he did two things that were of particular importance, namely, he attempted to reorganize the secret societies in America and he set up revolutionary bodies among the Chinese students in several European capitals.

After his arrival in Hawaii in 1903, Sun was often invited to address overseas Chinese gatherings. He found apparent changes among the overseas Chinese since his last visit seven years before. While conservatism was predominant and most people had turned away from his radical ideas then, he now found a much more receptive, often enthusiastic audience when he spoke of his revolutionary ideas and plans.[42] For six months, he lived in Hawaii, busy mixing with the overseas Chinese. After he found that the great majority of them

---

41 Direct translation from Chinese text, *ibid.*, p. 123.

42 Kuomintang, Committee for Compilation of Party History, "Tsung-li shih-chi chien-pien kao" (Draft Brief Biography of the Leader), in Wu Hsiang-hsiang, ed., *Chung-kuo chin-tai-shih lun-ts'ung* (Collected Essays on Modern Chinese History), (Taipei: Cheng-chung Book Co., 1957), Ser. I, Vol. 8, pp. 31-32.

belonged to the Chih-kung T'ang (also known as Hung Meng), a branch of the secret society which was the counterpart in America of the San-ho Hui (Triad Society) in south China and the Ko-lao Hui (Elder Brother Society) in central China, he immediately joined it as a member.[43] The next year, he arrived on the American continent for his second visit there. Touring various cities where Chinese congregated, he soon found that the best way of rallying the overseas Chinese to the cause of revolution was through the Chih-kung T'ang. Although the Chih-kung T'ang, like its counterparts in China, was originally anti-Manchu, it had by now become for all practical purposes a kind of fraternal body among friends and clan members. There were local chapters in various cities, but they played no role as centers of political activity, and were virtually independent of the head office in San Francisco. Sun viewed the Chih-kung T'ang, with an estimated membership of over 100,000,[44] as a great asset and was determined to win it over to the cause of the revolution. Having already joined it as an active member himself, he proposed to revitalize the organization through a campaign of nationwide registration of all members. Meanwhile, he embarked on a tour of many cities to meet with local Chinese to persuade them to register with their local chapters. During his speaking tour, he tirelessly explained the original anti-Manchu objectives of the Chih-kung T'ang in an attempt to arouse the long-forgotten nationalistic sentiments among the Chinese. He wrote an eighty- article new constitution for the Chih-kung T'ang, with a long preamble, exhorting members not to forget the original goals of their organization. The preamble spoke of the Manchus as nearing total collapse and pointed out that the time for the Han race to do away with the Manchu rule was at hand. It hailed the surging revolutionary tide as a manifestation of both heavenly will and popular demand, adding that Chih-kung T'ang stood ready to follow the will of the Heaven. Calling the chance once in a millennium, it pledged the Chih-kung T'ang to the task of "recovering the mother country and saving the compatriots" from 260 years of Manchu rule.[45] Article II of the constitution clearly set forth the objectives of the revitalized organization. It said: "The Chih-kung T'ang is dedicated to

---

43 *Ibid.*

44 Feng Tzu-yu, *Chung-hua min-kuo k'ai-kuo-ch'ien ko-ming shih,* Vol. I, p. 155

45 *Ibid.*, p. 151.

the goals of driving away the Tartars, restoring China, establishing a republic and equalizing land ownership."[46]

In his ambitious attempt to convert at one stroke the Chih-kung T'ang to the cause of revolution, Sun, however, faced two difficulties. Despite what was said in the constitution, most of the overseas Chinese were occupied with their own businesses and at best only showed lukewarm interest. In addition, Sun's attempt was greatly hampered by the followers of K'ang Yu-wei and Liang Ch'i-ch'ao, who had earlier set up branches in various cities and many of the same persons heading the branches were also important officers of the Chih-kung T'ang. So the registration drive was never pushed in earnest by the local chapters, and the new constitution was largely ignored. Although the immediate result of Sun's efforts was disappointing, he was not discouraged, realizing that this was only a beginning, and as such, he was indeed quite contented with his penetration of the Chih-kung T'ang. As shown by the support he later received from the Chih-kung T'ang branches in America and Canada, this initial groundwork was important. Concluding his American tour, he sailed for Europe in late 1904, where he scored impressive successes among overseas Chinese students.

At the time Chinese students in Europe were no more than a few score and most of them were from the Hupeh province in central China. They were sent to Europe to study modern technology by the viceroy of Hupeh, Chang Chih-tung, who was to set up modern schools in his province to introduce new Western knowledge. Many of the students, upon their return from abroad, soon formed a radical core to agitate for drastic measures to save the country. After the abortive uprising by the royalists in Wuhan in 1900, the students became increasingly restive and the tempo of their activities quickened. According to one of the participants, in Wuch'ang, one of the three cities in Hupeh known as Wuhan, they frequently met at a place called Hua-yuan Shan (Garden Hill), and were soon known as the "Hua-yuan Shan clique."[47] Their strategy was to try to awaken the public by introducing radical

---

46 *Ibid.*, p. 153.

47 Chu Ho-chung, "O-chou T'ung-meng Hui chi-shih" (Origins of the T'ung-meng Hui in Europe). *Kuo-ming wen-hsien,* Vol. II, p. 253.

publications brought in from Japan on the one hand and to penetrate into the New Army to influence the new recruits on the other. The radical activities were tolerated to a great extent by Chang Chih-tung, and by his successor, Tuan Fang, a Manchu. The fact that the overt anti-Manchu agitations by the radical students were tolerated at the time was perplexing. One explanation offered by a contemporary was that after the coup of 1898 and the Boxer Rebellion of 1900, many less conservative local officials obviously saw reform as necessary and therefore were reluctant to suppress the radical movement in earnest.[48] They were lukewarm in checking the agitation only for the purpose of placating Peking. The fact that it was Tuan Fang who later moved to send many of the radicals abroad when the agitation became too intense to cover up seems to lend support to this reasoning. As many of the students sailed for Paris, Berlin, and Brussels, they sought, through the help of others, to establish contacts with Sun Yat-sen, about whom they had heard and whom they were anxious to meet.

In the winter of 1904, Sun arrived in London from the United States and as frequently was the case, he was so short of funds that he was unable to continue his planned trip to the European continent. The students at Paris, Brussels and Berlin were quick to lend a helping hand, and Sun soon arrived in Brussels to a welcoming group of over 20 persons, including one Chu Ho-chung, who rushed there from Berlin to meet him. In the week that followed, there were enthusiastic discussions between Sun and the students. Chu later recalled that they debated with Sun intermittently for three days and three nights. The gist of the debate, according to Chu, was that while Sun advocated the use of secret societies as the chief force of revolution, the students were in favor of the New Army and stressed the importance of intellectual leadership. With the support he received from the secret societies during the two previous attempts at revolt, and with the experience of reorganizing the Chih-kung T'ang in America, Sun strongly believed that the secret societies could and should be used for the revolutionary cause. The students, however, argued otherwise. Chu recalled that he said the following during the heat of the debate: "The illiterate and lowly members of the secret societies can hardly be expected to

---

48 *Ibid.*,

understand the noble ideals of revolution. How, then, can you rely on the secret societies as the mainstay of the revolution? Your previous setbacks can be directly attributed to your failure to win the support of more intellectuals." At this point, Chu said, Sun seemed deeply moved, and declared that from now on, the revolutionary cause would be pushed among Chinese students abroad and that the students must regard themselves as leaders, Chu said that upon hearing this, they were so excited that they replied with one voice: "This is what we expected you to say from the bottom of our hearts!"[49] The next day, at Sun' suggestion, they took an oath one after another, pledging themselves to the goals of the revolution. Sun personally wrote the oath as follows:

> I, ________, pledge myself, in sacred witness of the Heaven, to the goals of driving away the Tartars, restoring China, establishing a republic and equalizing land ownership. I will submit myself to the severest punishment if I ever waver in fulfilling this pledge.[50]

Over thirty students in turn took the oath and so the first revolutionary body was formed in Brussels. Despite its modest size, it signified the rallying of young Chinese intellectuals to the revolutionary cause and opened up a new and vitally significant area for Sun's revolutionary movement. For Sun, this not only represented a personal triumph, but also a turning point in his long and hard campaign.

Following his short stay in Brussels, Sun was invited to Berlin by the Chinese students there and soon the second Chinese revolutionary body on the European continent was established, with an initial membership of twenty persons. This was followed by a meeting in Paris, where a dozen more Chinese students became revolutionary followers.[51]

Significantly enough, although the students swore to join the revolution under Sun's leadership, in neither of the three cases was there any mention of the name of the revolutionary body to which they had joined. Contemporaries differed in their interpretations. Sun himself referred to the meetings in Brussels, Berlin and Paris as the first

---

49 *Ibid.,* p. 256.

50 *Ibid.,* pp. 256-57.

51 Sun Yat-sen, "Sun Wen hsueh-shuo," p. 35.

three meetings of the T'ung-meng Hui, while calling the large-scale meeting in Tokyo later in that year the fourth.[52] Wu Chih-hui argued that the name T'ung-meng Hui did not come into existence until after the Tokyo meeting, and therefore the organizations in Brussels, Berlin and Paris were actually branches of the Hsing-chung Hui.[53] Chu Ho-chung, who became a member in Berlin, later recalled that on the night when he took the oath in Berlin, there was no mention of the name of the organization.[54] Feng Tzu-yu, who played an important part in the Tokyo meeting at which the T'ung-meng Hui was formally organized, wrote that the three organizations were not known as T'ung-meng Hui branches until they received orders from the general headquarters in Tokyo in late 1905, and that at the time of their formation, they did not have a fixed name except that they were referred to as "revolutionary party."[55] The squabble over the name is of course meaningless. But Feng's argument is worth noting in that it tends to show the subtle change of Sun's revolutionary idea. Between the formation of the Hsing-chung Hui in 1894 and the rise of the revolutionary bodies in Europe, there was a lapse of over ten years. Through these years, Sun had mostly run an one-man show.[56] By 1905, as far as its narrow objectives and limited membership were concerned, the Hsing-chung Hui had largely out-lived its usefulness. As has been already mentioned above, the organizing of the students in Europe represented an important step forward in Sun's revolutionary movement in that he had broadened the basis of the revolution and invigorated it with the new blood of the young intellectual elite. To couple with the new image of his revolutionary movement, it is possible that he had by this time already thought of discarding the old name and adopting a new one. As he returned triumphantly to Tokyo from Europe in the summer of 1905, he received a hero's welcome from the Chinese students there. The stage was already set for the conglomeration of all radical forces to give birth to the T'ung-meng Hui.

---

52 *Ibid*,.

53 Wu Chih-hui, "Chung-shan hsien-sheng nien-hsi" (Chronology of Sun Yat-sen), *Chung-hua-min-kuo k'ai-kuo wu-shih-nien wen-hsien* (Materials on the Fifty Years of the Republic of China), ed. Committee on the Compilation of Materials on the Fifty Years of the Republic of China (Taipei: Cheng-chung Book Co., 1963), Ser. I, Vol. 9, p. 236, (hereafter *WSNWH*).

54 Chu Ho-chung, *op. cit.*, p. 259.

55 Feng Tzu-yu, *op. cit.*, p. 188.

56 Sun Yat-sen, "Sun Wen hsueh-shuo," p. 32.

Chapter II

THE ORGANIZATION OF THE T'UNG-MENG HUI

The formation of the T'ung-meng Hui in Tokyo in 1905 represented an important turning point in the revolutionary movement against the Manchu government. Its significance lay in the fact that for the first time various anti-Manchu forces effected a merger, putting themselves under the banner of this new organization. Before the formation of the T'ung-meng Hui, there were, as already mentioned in the preceding chapter, many radicals in Tokyo, grouped largely according to their native provinces. Three organizations stood out among others, namely, the Hsing-chung Hui, the Hua-hsing Hui, and the Kuang-fu Hui. One Chinese historian aptly described the formation of the T'ung-meng Hui as a merger of the Hsing-chung Hui of Kwangtung, the Hua-hsing Hui of Hunan, and the Kuang-fu Hui of Chekiang provinces.[1] The anti-Manchu strength was greatly increased as a result of the emergence of the T'ung-meng Hui. The new body proved superior to its formerly independent components in various ways: in organizational setup, in leadership, in resources and, most importantly, in offering a concrete program and a guiding ideology. For Sun Yat-sen, this was a personal triumph midway through his long and arduous career; he had by now passed the stage of associating himself chiefly with the lower secret society members and had entered upon the stage of winning the support of the intellectual class. Now, he no longer needed to couch his revolutionary ideas in ambiguous words for fear that the audience might regard him as too radical and dangerous; he could openly elaborate and articulate his ideas because he found more and more receptive audiences. Papers were published in Tokyo and elsewhere to

1 Hua Lin-i, *Chung-kuo Kuo-min-tang shih* (History of the Kuomintang of China) (Shanghai: Commerical Press, 1928), p. 4.

propagate the revolutionary cause. Fund-raising campaigns were conducted in more and more places as branches of the T'ung-meng Hui were set up. Revolts were staged one after another and the revolution was indeed snow-balling. In his autobiography, Sun proudly recalled that the T'ung-meng Hui had "gathered the best talents of the country." On the day of its formation in Tokyo, he said, "I became convinced that I could at last see the consummation of the revolution in my life."[2] We shall start by examining the organization of the T'ung-meng Hui in this chapter.

SUN'S ARRIVAL IN TOKYO

Before he set out in 1903 on his trip to the United States and later to Europe, Sun had left instructions with his followers in Tokyo to recruit new blood from among the students to prepare for the formation of a new revolutionary body.[3] When he was in Paris in early 1905, he told the students there, after they had taken the oath to become members of the yet unnamed revolutionary organization, that they should study hard in order to contribute to the national reconstruction after the republic was born, while the immediate task of carrying out the revolution would be done by the students in Japan.[4] He was now returning to Tokyo with the establishment of the new organization in mind.

News of Sun's arrival was apparently communicated to Tokyo before hand, for on the day of his arrival in Yokohama, he received a rousing welcome from over 100 persons, mostly students who had rushed there from Tokyo. The exact date of his arrival is unavailable, but it was apparently in the latter part of July, as the following will show.

At the time Tokyo was not only the center of Chinese students, but also the haven for Chinese radicals, who stayed there in exile for one reason or another, some because of their opposition to the Empress Dowager, others because of their open plot against the Manchus. The

2 Sun Yat-sen, "Sun Wen hsueh-shuo," p. 35.

3 Tsou Lu, *Chung-kuo Kuo-min-tang shih-kao* (Draft History of the Kuomintang of China) (Taipei: Commerical Press, 1965), p. 23.

4 Chu Ho-chung, "Ou-chou T'ung-meng Hui chi-shih," p. 117.

best known in the former category was Liang Ch'i-ch'ao, and in the latter category, Huang Hsing. Huang had arrived in Tokyo in the previous year, escaping there after an unsuccessful attempt at insurrection against the Manchus in his native province of Hunan in central China. As the leader of the Hua-hsing Hui, which was responsible for the Hunan plot, he still had a large following both in Tokyo and in Hunan. He and Sun might have heard of each other, but they had never met up to that time. Not long after Sun's arrival in Tokyo, through the introduction of a Japanese mutual friend, Miyazaki Torazo, Sun came to know Huang, who was later destined to become his chief military aide. The two revolutionary leaders apparently hit it off well and talks for cooperation among their followers were immediately under way. While Sun had long planned for a grand union of all revolutionary factions, Huang is said to have responded enthusiastically to his proposal by promising to bring in all members of his Hua-hsing Hui.[5] With preparations going ahead at a quick pace, the T'ung-meng Hui was soon formed in Tokyo.

Concerning the exact date of the formation of the T'ung-meng Hui, there have been different versions. One participant, T'ien T'ung, said the inauguration meeting took place on July 24, 1905, at the home of a Japanese, Uchida Ryohei. Uchida's home was also the headquarters of the Black Dragon Society, a Japanese secret society which was sympathetic to the Chinese revolutionists.[6] Another participant, Feng Tzu-yu, said the meeting took place some time in the latter part of July, but he could not recall the exact date.[7] Fortunately, there is still another source that can shed authoritative light on the issue, and that is Sung Chiao-jen's diary. Sung was a fellow Hunanese of Huang Hsing and a member of the Hua-hsing Hui, who took part in the Hunan plot in 1904 and later escaped to Japan, where he, together with others, published a magazine, *Erh-shih Shih-chi Chih Chih-na* (Twentieth Century China). He later played an important part in the T'ung-meng Hui and eventually became one of the most outstanding leaders of the revolution. After the birth of the republic, he was an influential figure

---

5 Feng Tzu-yu, "Chi Chung-kuo T'ung-meng Hui" (Reminiscences of the T'ung-meng Hui), *Ko-ming wen-hsien,* Vol. II, p. 147.

6 T'ien T'ung, "T'ung-meng Hui ch'eng-li chi" (The Formation of the T'ung-meng Hui), *Ko-ming wen-hsien,* Vol. II, p. 142.

7 Feng Tzu-yu, "Chi Chung-kuo T'ung-meng Hui," p. 147.

in the Parliament and was a potential candidate for prime minister during the early days of Yuan Shih-k'ai's Presidency. His strong advocation of a parliamentary system drew upon him the wrath of the ambitious Yuan, who had him assassinated in 1913. Sung's diary covered the period 1905-1907, and is the single most important original source on the early activities of the T'ung-meng Hui.

According to Sung, he first learned of Sun's imminent arrival in Japan from Miyazaki Torazo on July 19, when Miyazaki told him that Sun was "expected to reach Tokyo in a few days." The Japanese, an ardent admirer of Sun, offered to introduce Sung to the Chinese revolutionary leader.[8] In his diary entry of July 25, Sung recorded that Sun had already arrived in Tokyo, and that he was ready to meet him very soon.[9] It is apparent that the exact date of Sun's arrival in Japan must have been between July 19 and 25.

Sung's first meeting with Sun Yat-sen took place on July 28, at the office of his magazine. Also present were Miyazaki and Ch'en Hsing-t'ai, better known by his other name, Ch'en T'ien-hua. Sun began by asking about the "general situation of student activities in Tokyo and the number of comrades," and then he embarked on an "eloquent discourse of the revolutionary situation in general and the tactics in particular."[10] Sung continued in the entry for July 28:

> Sun argued convincingly that the most urgent task at present is the organization of comrades, and that China is faced with the imminent danger not of partition from without, but of dissension from within. He lamented the fact that many provinces tried to go their own way in opposing the Manchus without aiding each other or uniting their forces. Such chaotic situation would only weaken the nation and benefit the Great Powers which were intensifying their interference in the internal affairs of China. Repeatedly, he emphasized the importance of unity and leadership. Take the south China provinces of Kwangtung and Kwangsi for example, he said, the secret societies there are quite powerful and the Manchus have been unable to pacify them. If the secret society members can be put under the leadership of a hard core

8. Sung Chiao-jen, *O-chih li-shih* (My History) (Taipei: Book World Co., 1962), p. 65.
9. *Ibid.*, p. 67.
10. *Ibid.*, p. 69.

of some hundred able men, there can well be a successful uprising against the Manchus.[11]

Their first meeting lasted for several hours, with Sun doing most of the talking. Apparently captivated, Sung gladly accepted Sun's invitation to another meeting at the headquarters of the Black Dragon Society two days later. It was at this preparatory meeting, on July 30, according to Sung, that the groundwork for the formation of the T'ung-meng Hui was laid. Twenty days later, on August 20, the T'ung-meng Hui was formally inaugurated.

FORMATION OF THE T'UNG–MENG HUI

While preparations were under way for the formation of the T'ung-meng Hui, there was, however, some objection to the projected grand union despite the fact that Sun Yat-sen was at the time highly regarded by the various exiled groups in Tokyo. Provincial sentiment had been traditionally strong in China and the exigencies of exile life abroad tended to further foster provincialism. This was borne out by Sung's description of the Hunan group at a meeting to discuss the question of joining forces with Sun's followers. The gathering took place at Huang Hsing's residence on July 29, the day after Sung's first meeting with Sun. Knowing that Huang had already promised Sun to join forces, some members of the Hua-hsing Hui expressed reservations and Liu Lin-sheng sounded his outright objection to "joining Sun's society." The discussion apparently came to no conclusion and Huang was quoted as saying that "we should join Sun's society in name, but maintain our own identity in spirit."[12] Huang's ambiguity may be open to different interpretations, but what he said was certainly far from the rosy picture as painted by enthusiastic Kuomintang historians at a later date.[13]

Not only were there conflicting records about the date on which the preparatory meeting was held, there were conflicting records about the meeting place as well. While Feng Tzu-yu was not sure of the date

---

11 *Ibid.*

12 *Ibid,*

13 See *supra*, note 5.

but agreed with Sung Chiao-jen on the headquarters of the Black Dragon Society being the meeting place, T'ien T'ung differed with both of them on the location of the preparatory meeting. He said the preparatory meeting, not to be confused with the founding meeting later, was held at the home of Cheng Chia-sheng, not long after Sun had arrived in Tokyo, with eighty-nine persons in attendance. It was at that meeting, he maintained, that the name T'ung-meng Hui was decided upon after some discussion, and then the oath was finalized with those present taking the oath.[14] However, T'ien's version was based on his recollection some twenty years after the event, and he might have mistaken one of the less important gatherings for the preparatory meeting of the T'ung-meng Hui. As a matter of fact, there had been a number of gatherings at which Sun was present and personally administered the oath to new recruits prior to the formation of the T'ung-meng Hui. Teng Mu-han, who was among the first to meet Sun in Tokyo, testified in 1936 that he was inducted into the revolutionary party at one of the gatherings before the T'ung-meng Hui was formally organized.[15]

Sung Chiao-jen's diary not only recorded the date and locale of the meeting, it also included a brief account of the meeting in the entry of July 30:

> In the early afternoon [of July 30], I went to the headquarters of the Black Dragon Society. I arrived there when the meeting had already started. There were about seventy persons present, and Sun delivered the opening speech. The speech lasted for more than an hour in which Sun first explained the necessity of revolution, and went on to size up the revolutionary situation and then dwelled on the methods. After Sun finished his speech, Huang rose to say that the main purpose for the meeting was to form a new revolutionary body, in which all those present were invited to join by signing their names and taking an oath. All complied. After the oath-taking, Sun told all of us some secret signals. Then the meeting proceeded to elect a group to take up the drafting of regulations and platforms. Huang Hsing and a few others were elected.[16]

---

14 T'ien T'ung, *op. cit.*, p. 142.

15 Teng Mu-han, "Chung-kuo T'ung-meng Hui ch'eng-li shih-jih k'ao" (An Inquiry into the Inauguration of the T'ung-meng Hui), *Ko-ming wen-hsien,* Vol. II, p. 247.

16. Sung Chiao-jen, *op. cit.,* p. 70.

Also in the drafting group were Sung himself and Wang Ching-wei, then a political science student and a young revolutionary. Gifted in both oratory skill and writing ability, Wang was to become one of Sun Yat-sen's most trusted lieutenants and faithful disciples for many years to come. By an irony of history, he later became a traitor during the Sino-Japanese war and died in disgrace.

That the T'ung-meng Hui was then still a secret organization was clearly shown by the fact that secret signals were used by its members, as recorded in Sung's diary. Although the Japanese authorities generally adopted a rather tolerant attitude toward the Chinese revolutionists, on the other hand they certainly did not want to see the student activities go on completely unchecked, for Japan still maintained diplomatic relations with the imperial government in Peking. As a matter of fact, at the constant prodding of the Chinese Legation in Tokyo, the Japanese government later became increasingly stringent in curbing the Chinese revolutionists. The revolutionists, on their part, were just as careful about revealing their real identity. Even in Sung's diary, the word "T'ung-meng Hui" never appeared. Instead, it was always referred to as "a certain soceity." Names of important persons were likewise not recorded, but simply referred to as "Mr. so and so," obviously for security reasons.

The preparatory meeting is of great significance not only because it laid the groundwork for the establishment of the T'ung-meng Hui which soon followed, but also because of the representative character of the participants. Of the eighteen provinces of the then China, seventeen were represented. The only province which was not represented was the northwestern province of Kansu, which at the time had not sent any students as yet to Japan.[17] At the meeting, there was some discussion about the name of the new revolutionary body to be formed. One proposal wanted it to be called Tui-man T'ung-meng Hui (Alliance Society Against the Manchus), but Sun vetoed the idea. He said the purpose of the revolution was not merely to overthrow the Manchu Dynasty, but also to substitute a republican form of government for the monarchy. Therefore, even Manchus would be welcome to join the

---

17. Feng Tzu-yu, *Chung-hua-min-kuo k'ai-kuo-ch'ien ko-ming shih,* Vol. I, p. 195.

organization as long as they were for a republic. The name proposed by Sun, Chung-kuo Ko-ming T'ung-meng Hui (Revolutionary Alliance Society of China), was thus unanimously adopted. For reasons of prudence, the word "revolutionary" was usually dropped from the name, which was known for short as T'ung-meng Hui. At the end of the meeting, when Sun was shaking hands with his new followers, the ceiling at the rear of the room suddenly collapsed. On the spur of the moment, Sun is said to have remarked: "This is an omen of the downfall of the Manchu Dynasty." Thereupon all present joined him in cheers and the meeting ended on a happy note.[18]

As the drafting group was busy working on the regulations and organizational details of the T'ung-meng Hui, a large-scale welcome meeting was planned for Sun in Tokyo by the students, many of whom were apparently shifting their loyalty from the constitutional monarchy to Sun's republicanism. One of the principal organizers of this meeting was Sung Chiao-jen. The meeting was described as an unprecedented affair in terms of its size and the enthusiasm it generated, and the Japanese called it "the most enthusiastic meeting of Chinese students ever held in Japan."[19] One source said more than 1,300 persons attended the meeting and that when Sun was delivering his speech inside, an additional several hundred persons milled outside the packed auditorium where the meeting was held.[20]

According to Sung, the meeting was held on August 13, at a place he had helped to rent. The meeting lasted for some four hours, from two until six o'clock in the afternoon. His diary contained this description:

> At two o'clock, Sun Yat-sen arrived at the meeting hall and was given a standing ovation. I delivered the opening speech, and then invited Sun to address the meeting. When Sun was speaking, there were approximately some 600 to 700 persons in the room and latecomers were still filing in. As the crowds at the front door grew bigger and bigger and the entrance was blocked, the policemen ordered the door closed, leaving

---

18 *Ibid.*

19 Lyon Sharman, *Sun Yat-sen, His Life and Its Meaning* (New York: John Day, 1934), p. 97.

20 Tsou Lu, "Chung-kuo T'ung-meng Hui" (T'ung-meng Hui of China), *Hsin-hai ko-ming,* Vol. II, p. 4.

> the crowds outside. Failing to gain admittance, the crowds complained loudly. I climbed to the top of the door and explained the occasion to the policemen, who were good enough to open the door again to allow everybody in. Sun's speech lasted till four o'clock.[21]

The theme of Sun's speech at the welcome meeting was a call to save the country and to make it strong. The way to achieve these goals was by learning the best from the West. He said the reason why China was now backward compared with others was becuase China had too long been contented with its centuries-old civilization and had thus reached a stage of stagnation, while others were making progress by leaps and bounds. Urging the Chinese people to shake loose their old sense of pride and superiority, he stressed that it was not a shame to learn from others, pointing to the fact that Japan had learned from China and surpassed China; and that the United States had learned from Britain and surpassed Britain. With her great land mass and large population, China was adequately equipped to become the most powerful country on earth only if the people exerted themselves by learning the most advanced political system and scientific technology from the West. In an open challenge to the constitutional monarchists, he termed constitutional monarchy the second best system, adding that there was no reason why China should choose the second best instead of the best, meaning a republican form of government.[22]

This speech was a mild one compared with his other speeches, for in it Sun nowhere mentioned the word revolution, nor did he make any racist charges against the Manchu "aliens." Apparently mindful of the audience with different political leanings whom he was addressing, he tried to make the widest possible appeal by restricting himself to the theme of nationalism. Seven days after Sun addressed the enthusiastic student gathering, the T'ung-meng Hui was formally organized in Tokyo on August 20.

THE ORGANIZATION OF THE T'UNG-MENG HUI

The meeting on August 20 was generally regarded as the first plenary meeting of the T'ung-meng Hui because it was at this meeting

21 Sung Chiao-jen, *op. cit.*, p. 73.

22 *Kuo-fu ch'uan-shu,* pp. 363-65.

that the regulations were adopted, setting forth the organizational setup of the new revolutionary body. It was also at this meeting that officers were elected and a decision reached to publish an official organ.

The meeting was held in the house of a Japanese, Sakamoto Kinya. One source said over 300 persons were present.[23] According to Sung Chiao-jen, he arrived at the meeting place at one o'clock that afternoon, an hour ahead of schedule, and "there were already about one hundred persons there."[24] The meeting began at two o'clock. The first business was the reading of the regulation, totalling thirty articles, and this was done by Huang Hsing. "As Huang Hsing read, some members cut in at times to sound their objection to certain passages, and then deletions or insertions were made," so recorded Sung in his diary.[25] After completion of the reading of the regulation, there followed the election of officers of various departments, and Sun Yat-sen was unanimously elected chairman.

The basic organizational setup of the T'ung-meng Hui included a general headquarters, located in Tokyo, and eighteen "shadow branches," one for each of the seventeen provinces in China in addition to the city of Shanghai, with branch heads elected from among those in Tokyo. The general headquarters at first seemed to have been based on some idea of checks and balances, with three independent branches roughly resembling an executive, a legislature and a judiciary. The following chart shows the organizational setup of the T'ung-meng Hui at the time of its formation and the persons who headed the various branches and departments:[26]

---

23 Feng Tzu-yu, "Chi Chung-kuo T'ung-meng Hui" (Reminiscences of the T'ung-meng Hui), *Ko-ming wen-hsien,* Vol. II, p. 149.

24 Sung Chiao-jen, *op. cit.*, p. 75.

25 *Ibid.*

26. This chart is prepared on the basis of information contained in Feng Tzu-yu, "Chi Chung-kuo T'ung-meng Hui," and T'ien T'ung, "T'ung-meng Hui ch'eng-li chi" (The Founding of the T'ung-meng Hui), both in *Ko-ming wen-hsien,* Vol. II, p. 142-51.

- Tsung-li (Chairman) Sun Yat-sen
  - Executive
    - General Affairs: Huang Hsing
    - Secretariat: Ma Chun-wu, Ch'en T'ien-hua
    - Interior Affairs: Chu Ping-lin
    - External Affairs: Ch'eng Chia-sheng, Liao Chung-k'ai
    - Treasury: Hsieh Liang-mu
    - Management: Ku Ssu-shen
  - Judiciary
    - Chief Judge: Teng Chia-yen
    - Attorney General: Sung Chiao-jen
  - Legislature-Speaker: Wang Ching-wei, with eighteen members.
  - Branches
    - Hopeh: Chang Chi
    - Honan: Tu Ch'ien
    - Hupeh: Shih Kung-chiu
    - Hunan: Ch'iu Shih-k'uang
    - Kwangtung: Ho T'ien-han
    - Kwangsi: Liu Ch'u
    - Szechuan: Ting Hou-fu
    - Shensi: K'ang Pao-chung
    - Shansi: Wang Yin-fan
    - Kiangsu: Kao Chien-kung
    - Shantung: Hsu Ching-hsin
    - Anhwei: Wu Ch'un-yang
    - Shanghai: Ts'ai Yuan-p'ei
    - Kiangsi: Chung Chen-ch'uan
    - Fukien: Lin Shih-shuang
    - Kweichow: P'ing Kang
    - Yunnan: Lu Chih-i
    - Chekiang: Ch'iu Chin

In reality, however, the idea of checks and balances had hardly been put into practice. It was soon to become quite clear that the executive branch was by far the most powerful of the three, and the judicial branch fell into oblivion before it hardly got off ground. That the executive branch was much more powerful than the other two branches was shown not only by its size, but also by the fact that practically all important functions of the T'ung-meng Hui were performed by its departments. According to the regulations, all heads of departments were to be appointed by the chairman, and this made it beyond any doubts that the chairman was in possession of real power. Among the six departments, the general affairs department was the most important. The regulations stipulated that during the absence of the chairman, the head of the general affairs department was to act in his behalf. Illustrative of the importance of the general affairs department was the appointment as its first head of none other than Huang Hsing, who was regarded as the "co-founder of the Republic of China."[27] For all practical purposes, the department had become the executive office of the chairman. The secretariat ordinarily should perform most of the administrative duties, but actually this was not the case, for even membership rosters were kept at the general affairs department.[28]

The treasury department also performed only limited functions. In the main it was only responsible for collecting membership dues from those who were in Tokyo at the time, while fund-raising campaigns

---

27 Hsueh Chun-tu, *op. cit.*, p. vii.

28 A partial list of the members of the T'ung-meng Hui for the years 1905-1906 had first been in the safe-keeping of Liu K'wei-i, the last head of the general affairs department. When Liu left Tokyo for China after the revolution of 1911, he turned over the list, together with other secret documents, to Ho T'ien-chun, then the treasurer, for safe-keeping. Later when Ho also returned to China, he took the list with him and destroyed all other documents. In 1939, the list was turned over to the Kuomintang's Committee for the Compilation of Party History in wartime Chungking. The list recorded the names of 960 members, including most of those who joined the T'ung-meng Hui in Tokyo in 1905 and 1906, and also some who joined in Kuala Lumpur, Singapore, Hanoi, Hong Kong and European capitals during the same period. The list, hand-written in a 38-page notebook, contained such information as name, age, native place, address, date on which oath was taken, and names of witnesses at the oath-taking. It is reproduced in *Ko-ming wen-hsien,* Vol. II. pp. 158-217.

elsewhere generally were conducted by local branches independently. The foreign affairs department, the interior department, and the management department never seemed to have their duties spelled out in concrete terms. Because of the prominence of the general affairs department, they were insignificant from the very beginning. A year after the formation of the T'ung-meng Hui, the heads of the three departments successively returned to China for one reason or another, and the three departments became practically non-existent.[29]

The judiciary branch was apparently meant as a disciplinary body for the members, but it was an insignificant organ as far as its function was concerned. One year after the formation of the T'ung-meng Hui, this branch existed all but on paper only. As a matter of fact, it was officially dropped from the regulations as revised in 1906. Chang Chi, one of the "judges," later served as head of the general affairs department; and Sung Chiao-jen, the "attorney general," was later active in other areas, particularly in propaganda work.

The legislative branch likewise was weak from the very beginning despite the fact that there were, at the time of its formation, eighteen elected members and that the able and versatile Wang Ching-wei was the first "speaker." It disintegrated in less than one year chiefly because its members either returned to China or were shifted to other posts. For example, Wang Ching-wei had to devote a great part of his time to propaganda work. Hu Han-min, another important figure, soon was shifted to the secretariat post and was later sent to Singapore to head a branch office there. Feng Tzu-yu, too, later left for Hong Kong to organize a branch in the British colony to coordinate activities in the South China region.

The "branches" in all the provinces were misleading, because they were all formed in Tokyo, and only existed on paper at the time of their formation. Some later moved back to China, such as the one in Shanghai headed by Ts'ai Yuan-p'ei and the one in Chekiang headed by Ch'iu Chin. However, at the time of their formation in Tokyo, they were chiefly for the purpose of recruiting new members from among the students hailing from the various Chinese provinces.[30]

---

29 Feng Tzu-yu, "Chi Chung-kuo T'ung-meng Hui," pp. 149-50.

30 *Ibid.*, p. 150.

SUMMARY

From Sun Yat-sen's arrival to the formation of the T'ung-meng Hui in Tokyo, it had been barely a month's time. Judging from the pace at which the revolutionary activity was moving ahead, one is compelled to conclude that the formation of the T'ung-meng Hui was a personal triumph in which Sun could justly take pride. To be sure, the T'ung-meng Hui was far from perfect, as the above analysis has shown, but its very birth clearly showed the momentum of the revolution. Before Sun's arrival in Tokyo, exiled Chinese reformers and rebels there were virtually without a leader and in a state of anarchy. There were men who had incurred the wrath of the Manchu government through radical writings; there were plotters and insurrectionists; but there was not a single organization which could unify an appreciable number of the people with divergent origins and aspirations. Hu Han-min in his autobiography gave a very succinct account of the situation then. He came to Tokyo as a student in 1904 for the second time, and was enrolled in a junior college of law and political science. One of his best schoolmates and close friends was Wang Ching-wei. He recalled that at the time, anti-Manchu sentiment was strong among the students, but beyond emotional outbursts few seemed to have concrete ideas about how the Manchus could be overthrown and how reforms could be carried out once the Manchus were toppled. As a student of political science, he said he was deeply worried about the state of affairs. Speaking of the students, he said:

> The components of the Chinese students then in Tokyo were quite complex. Some came to Tokyo only as opportunists, eyeing for the best chance to go back to China as returned students so that they could win good positions in the officialdom. Some had noble ambitions. There were those who devoted their full energy to their school work, paying little attention to anything else. This type was found mostly among those who studied natural sciences. There were those who hardly went to school at all, but wandered around all the time, making friends and talking about the problems of the day and yet doing nothing. They were found mostly among those who studied social sciences. As far as their political ideas were concerned, some blindly believed that China should make Japan the model of the future and learn everything from her; others were not satisfied with Japan and wanted to adopt Western ways by learning the technology and political systems of Europe and America. Their ages varied greatly; many were in

their 40's or 50's, but the youngest were only six or seven. Their origins varied even more: some came from rich or noble families; others were sons of poor peasants. There were leaders of secret societies with a price on their heads; and there were those who had already in the officialdom and were seeking shortcut to fame and fortune. In terms of their political leanings, these diversified elements were roughly divided between revolutionists and constitutional monarchists, with the latter having the edge. There were also some who started out as revolutionists but shifted their favor towards constitutional monarchy by the time they completed their education. All in all, although the Chinese students in Japan were lively and full of vigor, on the other hand, one must admit that the 20,000-odd students were a crowd of most diversified people.[31]

It was within this "crowd of most diversified people" that Sun Yat-sen succeeded in establishing a revolutionary body in less than a month's time. In a very real sense, the T'ung-meng Hui provided the badly needed leadership for at least a considerable portion of the disorganized and restive students and other radicals. Structurally the T'ung-meng Hui was not as effective an organization as many would have liked it to be, and subsequent events would show that the center of the organization always shifted with Sun Yat-sen, wherever he travelled, despite the fact that the general headquarters remained in Tokyo. Moreover, not all who joined the T'ung-meng Hui were of one heart, as factionalism later developed among the leaders in Tokyo. But despite all this, the formation of the T'ung-meng Hui was an event of great importance, for from that time on the Chinese revolutionary movement had entered upon a new stage by greatly broadening its foundation. By this time the revolution was no longer a few individuals plotting against the established government but a big movement that began to snowball. Propaganda was vigorously pushed, branches established, and military campaigns launched one after another, on an increasingly larger scale. Why did the T'ung-meng Hui win the support of the intellectuals? What did it have to offer? As we have examined the physical aspects of the T'ung-meng Hui, we shall turn next to the ideological aspects by examining its revolutionary ideas and programs.

---

31 Hu Han-min, "Tzu-chuan" (Autobiography), *Ko-ming wen-hsien,* Vol. III, p. 385.

Chapter III

THE GOALS AND PROGRAMS OF THE T'UNG-MENG HUI

The formation of the T'ung-meng Hui not only signified the physical expansion of the revolutionary movement, it also meant a great step forward in the ideological field. Revolutionary goals were now stated in more unequivocal and more sophisticated terms, and new ingredients were added. Heretofore, Sun Yat-sen had not had many occasions to expound seriously his revolutionary ideas. After the formation of the T'ung-meng Hui, he found ample opportunities. In *Min Pao* (Citizen's Journal), the organ of the T'ung-meng Hui, he first enunciated his now famous Three People's Principles, namely, Nationalism, Democracy and People's Livelihood, which showed how his ideas had matured through the years.

For the first time, a detailed revolutionary blueprint, the program of the Military Government,[1] was formulated and promulgated within a year of the formation of the T'ung-meng Hui. The program was meant to be a blueprint for governing the areas to be liberated from under the Manchu rule. It consisted of a group of important documents, including a manifesto, regulations on the organization of the revolutionary army, and civil administration measures. This program perhaps more than anything else testified to the fact that the revolutionary movement by now no longer consisted of sporadic uprisings launched by young radicals in collaboration with the lowly secret society members; it had become an organized movement, with clearly spelled out aims and a program on how the aims were to be achieved. Moreover, because these documents

1 Full text of the program is to be found in Tsou Lu, *Chung-kuo Kuo-min-tang shih-kao,* pp. 43-71; and Feng Tzu-yu, *Chung-hua-min-kuo k'ai-kuo-ch' ien ko-ming shih,* Vol. I., pp. 213-44.

to a large extent represented the crystalization of Sun Yat-sen's revolutionary ideas, they offered a valuable source for one to examine the evolution of Sun's thinking.

By analyzing the revolutionary goals and programs, this chapter aims at putting the ideological aspect of the T'ung-meng Hui in perspective.

OATHS AND PROGRAM OF MILITARY GOVERNMENT

That the T'ung-meng Hui inherited from its predecessor, the Hsing-chung Hui, its basic revolutionary goals is beyond doubt. The question to be asked is whether, during the span of eleven years, from 1894 to 1905, between the formation of the two organizations, had there been any significant changes in the goals? To answer this question, the best way is to look at the wording of the oaths that had been in use during this period. Admittedly, oath-taking is a rather plebeian practice, but apparently Sun took it very seriously and insisted on it. This leads one to wonder whether it was not a clear indication of the influence of the secret societies on Sun.[2] Record shows that Sun had insisted on one going through this plebeian ritual before becoming a member of the revolutionary body, and he had on occasions gone into great length to explain the necessity of oath-taking.[3] Since Sun attached such great importance to oath-taking, the contents of the oath would naturally be worded with utmost care to insure that it would best express the revolutionary goals to which anyone taking it was pledging himself. It is therefore important that we trace the oaths used from time to time to see how they had evolved, and examine the significance of each of the changes.

To begin with, the oath that was used at the time the Hsing-chung Hui was inaugurated in Honolulu in 1894 was as follows:

> I, __________, native of __________ County, __________ Province, will devote myself to the task of driving out the Tartars, restoring China

---

2 Lyon Sharman, *Sun Yat-sen, His Life and Its Meaning* (New York: John Day, 1934), p. 97.

3 Chu Ho-chung, *op. cit.*, p. 256.

and establishing a federal government. I do swear under God that I will not change my mind.[4]

Stated in a compact way, this oath thus consists of three slogans: Drive out the Manchus! Restore China! Establish federal government!

This oath apparently was used until 1903, when the first known change was made. In that year, at the short-lived secret military school established in Tokyo by the revolutionisits, students were required to take an oath that consisted of four slogans instead of three. The added slogan was "Equalize Land Ownership!" [5] This revision was of great significance for it represented the introduction of a new and controversial element into the body of revolutionary ideas contained in the oath. In the following year, when Sun toured the American continent to reorganize the Chih-kung T'ang, he included the same four slogans in its constitution which he drafted. Article II of the constitution said: "The Chih-kung T'ang is dedicated to the goals of driving away the Tartars, restoring China, establishing a republic and equalizing land ownership."[6]

In early 1905, when Sun formed branches of his revolutionary organization in Paris, Brussels, and Berlin, taking in for the first time Chinese students there, an oath apparently containing the same four slogans was used. There were some students who regarded the oath-taking as unnecessary and others who considered it a practice of poor taste, but eventually all took the oath administered personally by Sun.[7] When the T'ung-meng Hui was formed in Tokyo in the autumn of 1905, the oath used was substantially identical with what had been in use since 1903, except that it was worded in a more elaborate way. It reads as follows:

> I, ___________, native of _________ County, __________ Province, do swear under Heaven that I will do my utmost to carry out the tasks of driving away the Tartars, recovering China, establishing a republic

---

4 Feng Tzu-yu, "Tsui-ch'u chih Hsing-chung Hui ho tsui-hou chih Hsing-chung Hui," (Hsing-chung Hui, Its First and Last Meetings), Wu Hsiang-hsiang, ed., *Chung-kuo chin-tai-shih lun-ts'ung,* Ser. I, Vol. 8, p. 22.

5 *Ibid.* p. 27.

6 See *Supra,* Chapter I, Note 46.

7 Chu Ho-chung, "Ou-chou T'ung-meng Hui chi-shih," p. 256.

and equalizing land ownership. I solemnly undertake to be faithful to these principles. If ever I betray my promise I am willing to submit to the severest penalties imaginable.[8]

The program of the Military Government was the only comprehensive program put out by the revolutionists. Prepared by Sun Yat-sen and his close associates, it made its first appearance in Tokyo in 1906. The program included the following documents: a manifesto of the Military Government; a set of rules defining the relationship between the Military Government and the local governments; regulations governing the organization and discipline of the revolutionary army and pay scales; regulations on civil administration in recovered areas and for the requisition of supplies; a declaration to foreign powers; and three statements, one intended for the general public, one calling on the Manchu army to defect, and one announcing the abolition of all taxes imposed by the Manchus. In late 1906, when Sun left Tokyo for Indo-China where he established a T'ung-meng Hui headquarters in Hanoi, a slightly modified program was issued by the Hanoi headquarters. This modified text, in mimeographed form, is now in the Kuomintang archives.[9]

The manifesto of the Military Government was undoubtedly the most important of all the documents in the group. For the first time it explained, in a capsule form, the meaning of the four slogans of the T'ung-meng Hui, showing that by now Sun's revolutionary ideas had taken a more definite form. It stressed that the revolution was a people's revolution, because not only was political reform sought in the

---

8 Direct translation from Chinese text found in Feng-Tzu-yu, "Chi Chung-kuo T'ung-meng Hui," *Ko-ming wen-hsien,* Vol. II, p. 148. An earlier English translation of this oath is found in T'ang Leang-li, *The Inner History of the Chinese Revolution* (New York, 1930), p. 49. At two points, however, T'ang's translation does not seem to conform strictly with the original. It omitted the words "recover China," and it freely translated the words "equalize land ownership" into "equitable redistribution of land." For purpose of comparison, T'ang's translation is quoted here in full: "I swear under Heaven that I will do my utmost to work for the overthrow of the Manchu Dynasty, the establishment of the republic and the solution of the agrarian question on the basis of the equitable redistribution of the land. I solemnly undertake to be faithful to these principles. If I betray my trust, I am willing to submit to the severest penalties imaginable."

9 Feng Tzu-yu, *Chung-hua-min-kuo k'ai-kuo-ch'ien ko-ming shih,* Vol. I, p. 218.

form of substituting a republic for the existing monarchy, but social reforms in terms of improving the welfare of the people as well. Three lofty ideals were put forth, namely, freedom, equality and fraternity. These lofty ideals, it asserted, were for the people, and were to be achieved by the people themselves, while the Military Government was there for the sole purpose of providing leadership. Thus, the revolution was as much the responsibilty of the Military Government as it was ultimately that of the people. The four slogans are elaborated in the manifesto as follows:

(1) Drive out the Tartars: The Manchus of today were originally the eastern barbarians beyond the Great Wall. They frequently caused border troubles during the Ming Dynasty; then when China was in a disturbed state they came inside Shanhaikuan, conquered China, and enslaved our Chinese people. Those who opposed them were killed by the hundreds of thousands, and our Chinese have been a people without a nation for two hundred and sixty years. The extreme cruelties and tyrannies of the Manchu government have now reached their limit. With the righteous army poised against them, we will overthrow that government, and restore our sovereign rights. Those Manchu and Chinese military men who have a change of heart and come over to us will be granted amnesty, while those who dare to resist will be slaughtered without mercy. Chinese who act as Chinese traitors in the cause of the Manchus will be treated in the same way.

(2) Restore China: China is the China of the Chinese. The government of China should be in the hands of the Chinese. After driving out the Tartars we must restore our national state. Those who dare to act like Shih Ching-t'ang or Wu San-kuei (both were traitors) will be attacked by the whole country.

(3) Establish the Republic: Our revolution is based on equality and aims to establish a republican government. All our people are equal and all enjoy political rights. The President will be publicly chosen by the people of the country. A Constitution of the Chinese Republic will be enacted, and every person must abide by it. Whoever dares to make himself a monarch shall be attacked by the whole country.

(4) Equalize land ownership: The good fortune of civilization is to be shared equally by all the people of the nation. We should improve

our social and economic organization, and assess the value of all the land in the country. Its present price shall be received by the owner, but all increases shall belong to the State, to be shared by all the people, in order to create a socialist state, where each family within the empire can be well supported, each person satisfied, and no one fail to secure employment. Those who dare to control the livelihood of the people through monopoly shall be ostracized.[10]

The manifesto then went on to detail the specific steps by which the revolution was to be achieved. For the first time, the now famous and controversial three-stage revolution theory of Dr. Sun was seen in writing, although in a rather brief way. The three stages are government by military law, government by provisional constitution and government under constitution, which we shall discuss later.

The declaration to foreign powers contained seven points intended to serve two main purposes, namely, to gain recognition by foreign governments and to assure the safety and property rights of foreigners in China. It declared that all treaties that China had concluded with foreign countries would remain in force and payments on all foreign debts would continue. On the other hand, it stressed that any assistance given the Manchu Court would be regarded as a hostile action. It expressed the Military Government's intention to maintain friendly relations with all nations in the interest of world peace.[11] The original text of the declaration, in English, was believed to be the work of Ike Kyokichi, a Japanese who took part in the Chinese revolution. Well-versed in English language, he for some time served as Sun's English secretary when the latter was in Indo-China in 1906.[12]

The declaration intended for the public in the liberated areas sought to assure the people of the good conduct of the revolutionary army and to urge them to carry on their daily life as usual.[13] The declaration on

---

10 English translation adapted from Ssu-yu Teng and John K. Fairbank, *China's Response to the West* (Cambridge: Harvard University Press, 1954), Atheneum, 1963, pp. 227-28. Another version of English translation, not as accurate, is to be found in Lyon Sharman, *op. cit.*, pp. 118-19.

11 Feng Tzu-yu, *Chung-hua-min-kuo k'ai-kuo-ch'ien ko-ming shih*, Vol. I, p. 234.

12 *Ibid.*, p. 309.

13 *Ibid.*, pp. 233-34.

the abolition of the taxes imposed by the Manchus listed "ten crimes" allegedly commited by the Manchus and, in a repetitious way, condemned the Manchus for oppressing the Chinese people.[14] The declaration calling on the Manchu army to defect was chiefly aimed at the vast majority of Chinese serving in the Manchu army. It urged the Chinese to stop killing their own people and to turn against their "alien" Manchu masters.[15] All three documents were characterized by a heavy anti-Manchu tone that bordered on racism.

In addition to the above, a few words should be said about the regulations governing the civil administration and the requisition of military supplies in the recovered areas. This set of regulations, different from other documents that constituted the program, contained the actual working directives. For civil administration in each recovered area, it provided that a civil affairs bureau should be set up to keep law and order, and to perform such emergency functions as civil defense, care for the homeless, and drafting of the able-bodied. In regard to military requisitions, the regulations provided for confiscation of all official Manchu property, compulsory purchasing of necessary supplies, and borrowing contributions from the rich. On the basis of the requisitions, military currency was to be issued against fifty per cent silver dollar reserve. The issuance of the currency was to be put under the close supervision of a civilian board of ten or more members, formed by those civilians who had contributed the most.[16]

NATIONALISM

As pointed out earlier, the formation of the T'ung-meng Hui saw Dr. Sun's ideas taking a more definite form. Despite the fact that Sun had been regarded by some as not a very systematic thinker, and the fact that his ideas and policies changed with the circumstances from time to time,[17] some basic, unchanging ideological guideposts can be detected in his thinking. To begin with, two important elements can be

---

14 *Ibid.*, pp. 240-44.

15 *Ibid.*, pp. 234-40.

16 *Ibid.*, pp. 224-32.

17 Shao Chuan Leng & Norman Palmer, *Sun Yat-sen and Communism* (New York: Praeger, 1960), p. 5.

seen in the secret oaths and in the manifesto of the Military Government, namely, nationalism and republicanism. These two ingredients in Dr. Sun's thinking had been consistently held by him as the cardinal objectives of the revolution. Indeed, these two ideas had become the forerunner of two of Dr. Sun's three famous principles. They provided the backbone of the Principle of *Min-tsu* (Nationalism) and the Principle of *Min-ch'uan* (Democracy), which together with the later-day added Principle of *Min-sheng* (People's Livelihood) constitute the Three People's Principles.

The kind of nationalism espoused by Dr. Sun was based on both anti-imperialist and anti-Manchu sentiments. These two sentiments were not unrelated in Dr. Sun's mind, and indeed his anti-Manchu attitude was apparently the result of his conviction about the inability of the Manchu government to cope with the onslaught of imperialism from the West. Imperialism made him aware that his country was in danger of being partitioned into colonies by the great powers, and therefore he took upon himself the task to save the country. He saw in Western technological advance and democratic institutions the best remedy for his country, and he tried to petition the Manchu Court for reform. This is well borne out by his early writings. Later, when he saw no prospect for peaceful reforms to be carried out by the conservative and inept Manchu government, he began to turn into a radical revolutionist plotting against the government. The fact that the Manchus were "aliens" added a nationalistic appeal to his revolution. As time went on, it was only natural that the anti-Manchu theme was emphasized more and more, not only because the incompetence of the Manchus had been proven, but because his ultimate goal was the establishment of a republic, which could be realized only after the Manchus were overthrown.

Although the secret oath of the Hsing-chung Hui in 1894 contained the slogan of "driving away the Tartars," anti-Manchu sentiment was not openly expressed at this time. Instead, the emphasis of the revolutionary propaganda was placed on the danger of foreign imperialism, which was portrayed as a serious threat to China's survival. The preamble of the Hsing-chung Hui's manifesto declared: "China is now circled by the great powers, who have all along had their eyes on the rich natural resources of our country. One after another, they have encroached upon us, taking away our land by pieces and by chunks. Our country is facing the imminent danger of being cut up."[18] Article I of the manifesto again stressed that the people's sufferings were aggravated because of "long foreign exploitation."[19] The following year, when the Hsing-chung Hui was enlarged in Hong Kong, a revised manifesto was issued, which again dwelt on the imminent danger to China of foreign partition. Deploring the deterioration of political situation in China, it asserted that the basic cause of China's weakness lay in the public ignorance of the danger of foreign domination. The manifesto declared: "There is a prevailing lack of realization of the simple fact that once China is partitioned, our posterity will forever be slaves of others." It went on to pose the following question: "Whose responsibility will it be if our 5,000 years of civilization goes into oblivion?"[20] Meanwhile, Sun organized the Agricultural Society in Canton, ostensibly to promote the study of agricultural techniques as a way of improving the country's economy. Actually, it was a front organization for his revolution. In a public statement recruiting new members for the Society, it was again pointed out that at a time when the nation was being exploited by foreign powers, all those who cared about the future of their country should do their part as responsible citizens.[21] Thus from these early pronouncements of Sun's, we can see that although his anti-Manchu sentiment was hidden from the surface, the anti-imperialist ingredient in the nationalism he espoused was unmistakable.

A few years later, having weathered what he himself described as the most difficult period in his revolutionary career, his verbal attack on the Manchus picked up with the pace of his activities. On his trip to Hawaii in 1903 and to the U.S. continent later on, he made several important statements. The first among them was a long rebuttal of the argument of the K'ang-Liang group, published in a Chinese newspaper in Hawaii. He denounced the royalists as unpatriotic because they advocated the preservation of an "alien government" and its enslave-

---

18 *Kuo-fu ch'uan-shu,* p. 351.

19 *Ibid.*

20 *Ibid.*

21 *Ibid.,* p. 357.

ment of the Chinese.[22] But in justifying his revolution, Sun's chief argument was still the failure of the Manchu government to cope with Western imperialism that threatened the very survival of China. He said: "The Manchu government has reached the end of the tether. It has lost all the strategic points in the country and even its own place of origin (Manchuria). The country is being cut up at the rate of losing a hundred square miles of land a day and several cities a month. The present trend will only end in the total loss of the country. The only hope of survival lies with the people. If the people can wake up to the reality and rise up in a general revolution to overthrow the rotten and dying Manchu government, China will be respected, not partitioned, by the powers."[23] In order to put an end to the practice of "ceding Shantung today and selling out Kwangtung and Kwangsi tomorrow,"[24] the Manchu government must be gotten rid of and China restored to Chinese, Sun said. Ridiculing the Manchus for adopting a pro-Russian policy, he chided them for their ignorance of the fact that it was the Russians who had seized their homeland, Manchuria.[25] Bringing home his argument, Sun pointed to the simple logic which he charged the royalists never seemed to understand: "Since the Manchu government has unabashedly assumed the role of the subservient running dog of the great powers, handing over to them whatever territories they may demand, the only logical way to save the country from partition is to replace the Manchu government."[26]

A few days later, Sun wrote an open letter to his fellow Cantonese, explaining the basic differences in the objectives of the royalists and the revolutionists, which many overseas Chinese in Hawaii had been led to believe were one and the same. It may be recalled that in 1899, when Liang Ch'i-ch'ao was talking about possible cooperation with Sun in Tokyo, he was ordered by his master K'ang Yu-wei to go to Hawaii to set up a Pao-huang Hui branch there. Sun in fact had introduced Liang to many of his friends there. In organizing the Pao-huang Hui branch, Liang had taken advantage of Sun's earlier work. To the rather

---

22 *Ko-ming wen-hsien,* Vol. III, p. 292.

23 *Ibid.,* p. 293.

24 *Ibid.*

25 *Ibid.,* p. 294.

26 *Ibid.,* p. 293.

unsophisticated overseas Chinese, he skillfully preached the "similarities" between "preserving the emperor" and revolution. Many overseas Chinese were convinced, and the majority of those who thus joined the Pao-huang Hui were previously members of Sun's Hsing-chung Hui. In that same year, in a letter to K'ang, Liang reported that "most active members of Pao-huang Hui here were all previously Sun's men." "The people here," he continued, "whether they are members of the Hsing-chung Hui or not, all know Sun." Even so, Liang reported proudly, "I was able to make seven out of every ten of them members of our society."[27]

The invasion of the domain of the Hsing-chung Hui by the Pao-huang Hui took place not only in Hawaii, but in Japan and other places as well.[28] After Sun's open break with Liang, the time for stating publicly the revolutionists' differences with the royalists had long been overdue. Sun's open letter was to serve this purpose. In it, Sun accused the royalists of pretending to be revolutionists while actually trying to "prolong the life of the Manchu Court at the expense of continued enslavement of the Han people." In angry words, he did not hesitate to distinguish between the Manchus as "nomadic barbarians of an inferior race" and the "great Han people with 4,000 years of civilization."[29] He openly called K'ang and Liang traitors because they had sold themselves out to the "aliens" by serving the "aliens" and oppressing their own race.[30] He appealed to his Cantonese brethren to remember the disgrace of the "loss" of the country 260 years ago and urged them to join the revolution to restore China to the "400 million Han people."[31] Later in that year, he traveled to the American continent, where he wrote an article "The True Solution to the Chinese Problem." In it, he expressed the same view, asserting that what was now commonly known as the "Chinese government" was actully the "Manchu government," since the Chinese had lost their own power.[32]

---

27 Ting Wen-chiang, *Liang Jen-kung hsien-sheng nien-p'u ch'ang-pien ch'u-kao* (Draft Full-length Biographical Chronology of Liang Ch'i-ch'ao) (Taipei, 1958), Vol. I, p. 124.

28 Feng Tzu-yu, *op. cit.*, pp. 41-42, 68.

29 *Ko-ming wen-hsien,* Vol. III, p. 299.

30 *Ibid.*

31 *Ibid.*, p. 300.

32 *Kuo-fu ch'uan-shu,* p. 369.

Comparing these statements with Sun's earlier writings, a significant shift can be detected. It is a shift in emphasis from anti-imperialism to anti-Manchus. While the anti-imperialist emphasis was by no means abandoned as the revolution progressed, the anti-Manchu theme was being increasingly stressed in the propaganda of the revolutionists, reaching almost racist proportions. A few more examples may be cited here for illustration. In a speech at the welcoming meeting for him in Tokyo in July, 1905, Sun spoke of the signs of a growing nationalistic feeling among the Chinese, and he exhorted all to work hard for the cause of nationalism until China became a first rate democratic republic.[33] If Sun did not make it clear what he meant here by "nationalistic feeling" and "nationalism," he left little doubt in another speech a year later. "Nationalism originates from the innate nature of man. It has been over 260 years since the Manchus took over our government, but we Hans, even small children, will readily recognize a Manchu and will not mistake him as a Han. This the basis of nationalism," Sun said.[34] "The essence of nationalism, as far as China is concerned at this time," he continued, "is that we should never allow another people to take over our government. We can claim that we have our own country only as long as we are in control of our government. If our government is in the hands of the people of another race, then we cannot claim that we still have our own country."[35] The same sentiment runs through the program of the Military Government of the T'ung-meng Hui, with the emphasis particularly on the sufferings inflicted by the Manchus. The repeatedly stressed theme was that the Manchus were originally alien "barbarians," and that the domination of 400 million Han people by some five million alien "barbarians" was intolerable. In a declaration by the T'ung-meng Hui soon after the successful Wuch'ang uprising in October, 1911, the anti-Manchu theme was pushed to the extreme. With the uprising a success after repeated setbacks, the morale of the revolutionists was at an all time high and the declaration was apparently intended to further arouse anti-Manchu sentiment so that the revolution might swiftly culminate in the overthrow of the Manchu government. The declaration in particular mentioned the heroic resistance against the Manchus waged at the end

---

33 *Ibid.*, p. 363.
34 *Ibid.*, p. 479.
35 *Ibid.*

of the Ming Dynasty by loyal Ming gernerals and the subsequent massacres committed by the Manchus.[36]

While the official T'ung-meng Hui documents and Sun's statements appear to stress the political objectives of anti-Manchu nationalism in terms of restoring the government into the hands of the Chinese, others had gone further than that in expressing their anti-Manchu sentiments. Their invectives were sometimes in the most insulting language possible. One example is Ch'en T'ien-hua, a royalist-turned revolutionist who in December, 1906 killed himself by jumping into the sea in protest against the Japanese government's restrictive policies toward the Chinese students. In a popular tract that he wrote, named *Ching-shih chung* (Warning Bell), he castigated the Manchus for their suspicion and oppression of the Han people on the one hand and for their "shameful subservience" to the foreign powers on the other. Writing in the plain vernacular style, he said that under the Manchus, China had actually already been partitioned by the powers for scores of years because they had practical control of China's revenues, railroads and mines and enjoyed other privileges. He denounced the Manchus for "willingly selling out China to the great powers and not returning it to the Han people."[37] In another tract, entitled *Meng-hui-t'ou* (Quick Awakening), he called himself an exile from a conquered nation, and prayed to Huang Ti, the legendary first emperor of China, for his heavenly power to awaken his countrymen so that they would all rise to drive out the alien Manchus.[38] In a letter he wrote before he committed suicide, he stressed that there was absolutely no possibility of Manchus and Hans cooperating for the good of the nation. In order to save China from demise, he said, the Manchu government must be overthrown.[39]

Chang Ping-lin's anti-Manchu utterances probably surpassed all in severity. In the preface to Tsou Yung's *Ko-ming chun,* Chang spoke of China as having been "swallowed up by the barbaric Tartars" for 260 years. He denounced men like Tseng Kuo-fan, Tso Tsung-t'ang and Li Hung-chang, all Chinese generals, for serving as tools of the Manchus in

---

36 *WSNWH,* Ser. I, No. 11, p. 280.

37 *Hsin-hai ko-ming,* Vol. II, pp. 112-43.

38 *Ibid.,* pp. 144-45.

39 *Min Pao* (Citizen's Journal), No. 2, p. 3

suppressing the patriotic and nationalist Taiping rebellion.[40] On the first anniversary of the publication of the *Ming Pao* in 1906, he read a commemorating message before a gathering of 6,000 persons in Tokyo. In the message, composed by himself, Chang solemnly appealed to all past emperors of China for their blessings in the revolutionary cause.[41] He omitted the emperors of the Yuan Dynasty because to him, the Mongols, who established that dynasty, were aliens like the Manchus, and therefore were unworthy to be mentioned with the Chinese emperors.

In view of the strongly anti-Manchu invectives, there have been criticisms that the revolutionists had resorted to racism in their propaganda.[42] However, in determining whether the charges are justified, caution should be exercised. To be sure, many of the invectives were heavily colored with racist overtones, but what should be pointed out is that as far as the revolution was concerned, the objective had never been a blind opposition to the Manchus on racial grounds. The revolution sought the removal of the Manchu regime for the fulfillment of a specific objective, namely, the establishment of a republican form of government. Hypothetically, if the Manchus had been agreeable to a republican form of government, anti-Manchu invectives naturally would not have reached such intensity and indeed there probably would not have been a revolution in the first place.

Moreover, it would be wrong to regard all anti-Manchu invectives as sheer propaganda, aimed only at toppling the Manchu government. Anti-Manchu sentiment was real, and had been so for a long time. To begin with, the traditional idea of Chinese being the masters of the country had a history dating back to the time even before Confucius. It is commonly known to Chinese historians that in writing the *Ch'un Ch'iu* (Spring and Autumn Annals), one of the earliest chronicles on Chinese history, Confucius had in mind as one of his main purposes to preserve the authentic history of the Chinese nation when various minority groups were vying for power in China at the time. Chang Ping-lin said his anti-Manchu nationalism was the direct result of

40 Feng Tzu-yu, *op. cit.*, p. 132.

41 *Ibid.*, p. 119.

42 Sharman, *op. cit.*, p. 116.

reading the *Ch'un Ch'iu*.[43] Hu Han-min, too, accused the Manchus in the early years of their rule of trying to distort Chinese history by identifying themselves as ethnically of the same origin as the Han people.[44] Is is no secret that throughout their rule, the Manchus, being a minority, had tried hard to control the Han people. Domestic opposition had always been the main fear of the Manchus, despite the fact that save for the Taiping Rebellion, they were able to prevent large-scale organized resistance. However, foreign imperialism provided the first chance for the revival and eruption of Chinese nationaliam. When the ineptness of the Manchu government was gradually exposed in the face of Western imperialism, the narrow Chinese nationalism was strengthened. Once openly advocated, nationalism with its magic pull soon reached near and far, penetrating the lowly secret societies as well as the intelligentsia. After the formation of the T'ung-meng Hui in Tokyo, many Chinese students there deserted the Pao-huang Hui to which they had originally belonged and joined the T'ung-meng Hui. In a letter to K'ang Yu-wei in November, 1906, Liang Ch'i-ch'ao reported to his master: "The revolutionists are quite strong in Tokyo. Among the 10,000 Chinese students in Japan, over one half followed the revolutionary cause."[45] From 1904 to 1906, those who deserted the Pao-huang Hui and joined the revolution numbered "several thousand," according to one contemporary.[46] Speaking of the triumph of the revolutionists over the royalists, another contemporary said the victory was largely attributable to the simple and clear-cut anti-Manchu cause of the revolutionists, which soon won wide acceptance almost like a religion.[47] Hu Han-min called the anti-Manchu propaganda a "fundamental success."[48]

There was evidence that at the time when many revolutionists were loudly expressing their strongly anti-Manchu views, Sun Yat-sen had already begun to caution his followers against confusing the objectives

43 Chang Ping-lin, *Tzu-ting nien-p'u* (Autobiographical Chronology), entry under the year 1880.

44 Hu Han-min, "Tzu Chuan" (Autobiography), *Ko-ming wen-hsien,* Vol. III, p. 375.

45 Ting Wen-chiang, *op. cit.,* Vol. I, p. 218.

46 *Min Pao,* No. 5, p. 140.

47 Letter from Yang Tu to Liang Ch'i-ch'ao, Ting Wen-chiang, *op. cit.,* Vol. I, p. 237.

48 Hu Han-min, "Tsu Chuan", p. 429.

of the national revolution with blind hatred of the Manchus, and he stressed that vengeance psychology was wrong and should be gotten rid of. In his speech on the first founding anniversary of the *Min Pao* in 1906, he said: "I have heard some people say that our national revolution is aimed at the extinction of the Manchus as a race. This is a grave mistake. Our revolution aims to recover our government from the Manchu control. We do not hate the Manchus on ethnic grounds. We only hate those Manchus who have brought about miseries to the Han people and we want only to drive those Manchus from their present position. When our revolution begins, we will not hurt any Manchus who do not stand in our way. We should never seek vengeance by wanton killing."[49] Earlier, Ts'ai Yuan-p'ei also stressed that the nature of the anti-Manchu movement should be political, not racial.[50] As a further proof of Sun Yat-sen's consistent idea about the political objective of the national revolution, it should be pointed out that once the national revolution succeeded, he immediately advocated the "grand union of five races." In one of his first proclamations as Provisional President of the Republic, he said: "One of the basic elements of a nation is people. Another is territory. Today we shall unite the lands of the Hans, the Manchus, the Muslims, the Mongols and the Tibetans as one country, and unite all five races as one people."[51]

Thus despite the harsh language used in the revolutionary propaganda and the passionate anti-Manchu sentiments that are evident in the writings of many contemporaries, one may safely conclude that as far as the revolution was concerned, anti-Manchu in the sense of racial antagonism was never an objective in itself. The revolutionists did preach the distinction between the Manchus and the Hans, or Chinese, but the motive undoubtedly was to discredit the Manchu government rather than to tell the people that the Manchus were "barbarians." The revolution had never parted from its political objective, namely, the establishment of a republic, which required as its pre-requisite the replacement of the Manchu monarchy. We shall now turn our attention to republicanism, the second persistent theme of the revolution.

---

49 *Kuo-fu ch'uan-shu,* p. 479.

50 Ts'ai Yuan–p'ei, "Ch'iu-man lun" (On Hating the Manchus), *Su Pao* (Kiangsu Journal), April 11, 12, 1903.

51. *Kuo-fu ch'uan-shu,* p. 396.

REPUBLICANISM

Like nationalism, republicanism, too, had early roots in Sun Yat-sen's mind. As we have pointed out earlier in this chapter, one of the three slogans of the Hsing-chung Hui was the establishment of a "federal government" in China. Just what Sun meant by establishing a federal government was not explained, but judging from Sun's early training and experience, it is obvious that he was inspired by the American system of government. In the first major revision of the oath of his revolutionary organization in 1903, the phrase "establishing a federal government" was replaced with a more precise phrase of "establishing a republic" as opposed to the existing monarchy. Since then, the word republic had been consistently used in oaths and statements. Inasmuch as the idea of a republic was alien to the long tradition of monarchy in China, there is little doubt that Sun had borrowed it from the West. As a matter of fact, Sun and his followers had on numerous occasions made it quite clear that this was the case. It is true that in later days, when Sun began to seriously expound the theory of republicanism and in particular to try to design a framework to put republicanism into practice, new ingredients, largely indigenous, were added, but that development did not change the fact that the original idea came from the West.

In his writings and talks, Sun repeatedly mentioned the progress of European and American countries and said that China should and must catch up with them by learning from them. "Although we cannot wholly copy Europe and America," he once said, "yet we can observe them and study their experience in democracy carefully. . . .Western nations have gained not a little experience in the past century, and this experience, along with their various new theories, should be used as data in our study."[52] In fact he went as far as to declare that China's tide of revolutionary ideas came from Europe and America, and that one of the reasons for his belief that China should adopt democracy and republicanism was to "follow the world current."[53] He often equated his Three Principles of the People with the revolutionary watchwords of the West. Speaking of the watchwords of the French

52 Sun Yat-sen, *San Min Chu I*, p. 293.

53 *Ibid.*, p. 181.

revolution, liberty equality and fraternity, he once said: "Liberty" in the French revolutionary watchword and 'People's Nationalism' in our watchword are similar. The People's Nationalism calls for freedom of our nation. 'Equality' is similar to our 'Principle of People's Rights', which is to destroy autocracy and make all men equal. . . . The idea in 'Fraternity' is similar to our 'Principle of People's Livelihood,' which plans for the happiness of our four hundred millions."[54] At another time, he compared his Three Principles with Lincoln's government of the people, by the people and for the people.[55]

At times, Sun seemed to be using the terms republicanism and democracy interchangeably as if they were one and the same. A close look at his writings would reveal that he did so intentionally, and with good reason. Essentially, he believed that while democracy should be the ultimate goal of the revolution, the best way of attaining it is under a republican form of government. Since he had much admiration for the British parliamentary democrary, the question may well be asked, why, then, should he insist on republicanism in China? This, in fact, is one of the central points in the debate between the revolutionaries and the royalists. While a more detailed analysis will be made in the next chapter, suffice it to say here that Sun believed that republicanism was the most advanced system in the West, and that in learning from the West, China should learn the best. He made this point very clear in a speech before a welcome meeting in Tokyo in 1905.[56] In his rebuttal of the royalists views earlier in Honolulu, he had stressed that since monarchical tyranny was in effect in China, democracy was possible only through a change of the monarchical system.[57] Expanding on this line of argument, he later listed three reasons why republicanism was necessary in China, and why it could be achieved only through revolution. First, he quoted from Confucius and Mencius asserting that the great Chinese sages had since very old days taught the importance of the people, whose will the emperor must abide by. This,

---

54. *Ibid.*, p. 214.

55. Sun Yat-sen, *Fundamentals of National Reconstruction* (Chungking, 1945), p. 21.

56. *Kuo-fu ch'uan-shu,* pp. 363-65.

57. Sun Yat-sen, "Po Pao-huang Pao Shu" (A Rebuttal of the Royalist Paper), *Ko-ming wen-hsien,* Vol. III, p. 296.

he contended, showed that China had democratic ideas even in ancient times. Second, he said, since the Manchus had clung to power and refused democratic reform, it was idle to expect them to practice genuine democracy even under an assumed constitutional monarchy. The third reason was probably the most cogent. As long as the powers of the nation were vested in a single emperor, ambitious persons would all want to be emperor, and the result would be bloody fighting. In order to put an end to such a state of affairs, it would be best to adopt a republican form of government and to allow the people to exercise the real power through a democratic constitutional design.[58] This design was to be based on his theory of a "five-power constitution," which he first enunciated in 1906, in a speech at a meeting commemorating the first founding anniversary of the *Min Pao.*

Here again, the influence of the West on Sun's ideas was evident. He adopted the Western system of the separation of three independent branches of government and added two others, both traditionally Chinese, to make up his theory of a "five-power constitution." To the three branches of government in the West, namely, the executive, the legislative and the judicial, he added the examination and the supervision. This innovation was chiefly based on his criticism of the existing Western system, which he believed still left much to be desired. In a speech, he said: "In America, where public servants are either elected or appointed, there is no established system setting up qualifications of public servants. Thus people gifted in oratorical skills often get elected while the less talkative, though perhaps more able and better learned men, go down in defeat at the polls. . . . Recently a civil examination system was introduced in America, but it applies only to junior officials. Moreover, it is administered by the executive branch of government and is therefore not independent. In the future Constitution of the Republic of China, an independent agency should be provided for and charged with the responsibility of recruiting and screening candidates for public offices, free from interference by any other branch of government."[59] In regard to the power of supervision, he criticized the American practice of vesting this power in the

---

58 *Kuo-fu ch'uan-shu,* p. 1004.

59 *Ibid.,* p. 482.

legislature, thus resulting in possible "Congressional dictatorship."[60] He felt that a supervisory body should also be independent and free from control by other branches of government. With five independent branches, he believed the government could function more effectively in responding to the needs of the people. On the side of the people, he stressed the means by which the people could control the government, namely, by the four rights of election, recall, initiative and referendum.[61]

The five-power constitution thus provided the basis for the organizational setup of Dr. Sun's ideal government. How was this ideal government to be brought about and how were the people to learn the function of such a government which was a novelty to them? Here comes into the picture another of Dr. Sun's famous and controversial designs, namely, the three-stage revolution theory.

POLITICAL TUTELAGE

As has been pointed out earlier, the three stages in Sun's revolutionary theory were the stage of military government, the stage of provisional local self-government under the military rule, and the stage of constitutional democracy. To quote from a Western interpreter of Dr. Sun's theory, the three stages can be best explained as "(1) the acquisition of political power by the teachers of the new ideology, (2) the teaching of the new ideology and (3) the practice of government by people in accordance with the new ideology."[62] According to the program of the Military Government, during the first stage, in order to maintain law and order, martial law would be in effect in each liberated area and local administration would be under the direct control of the Military Government. For each county, the period of military rule was set for a maximum of three years. When the three-year period expired in a given county, or if order had been firmly established before the time limit, the country would be ready to enter the second stage, whereupon martial law would be lifted and the Military Government

60 *Ibid.*

61 *Ibid.*, p. 238; Sun Yat-sen, *San Min Chu I*, p. 275.

62 Paul M. A. Linebarger, *The Political Doctrines of Sun Yat-sen* (Baltimore: Johns Hopkins University Press, 1937), p. 207.

would grant the power of local self-government to the people of the county. Local assembly and officials would be elected through popular elections and a Provisional Constitution would be promulgated specifying the rights and obligations of the people and the relationship between the Military Government and the people. The maximum length of this transitional rule was to be six years. After this, a national assembly was to be called to write a constitution and in accordance with it, to inaugurate a civilian national government, formally taking over all powers from the Military Government. The President and the parliamentarians were to be elected and constitutional rule would begin.[63]

The stage on which controversy centered, however, was the second stage. The idea behind it, as the T'ung-meng Hui manifesto made clear, was that between the completion of the military stage of the revolution and the beginning of constitutional democracy, there was to be a transitional period in which to prepare the people for the exercise of their full democratic rights. However, actual development did not turn out that way. After the birth of the republic, China was very much in chaos. After the early experiment in republicanism was thwarted by the ambitious Yuan Shih-k'ai, Sun's idea about the second stage of revolution underwent a marked change – from provisional local self-government under the guidance of military rule to the now well-known "political tutelage" under the Kuomintang.

In the Constitution of the Chung-hua Ko-ming Tang (China Revolutionary Party), organized by Sun in 1914 to oppose Yuan, the idea of political tutelage under one-party government was explicitly included. Drafted by Sun himself, the Constitution said that "all military and civil affairs of the country will be the responsibility of the members of our Party" during the revolutionary period "between the first action of the revolutionary army and the promulgation of the Constitution."[64] In particular, Sun pointed out that once the Manchu government was overthrown, many party members became complacent and relaxed in their efforts, erroneously believing that the revolution

---

63 Teng and Fairbank, *op. cit.*, p. 228.

64 Chang Ch'i-yun, *Tang-shih kai-yao*, p. 165.

had already been accomplished and that the Three People's Principles would no longer be necessary. This, he asserted, was chiefly responsible for the disintegration of the party and for the revolution to stop short of bringing about genuine constitutional democracy in China. In order to revitalize the party so as to carry out the unfinished task of the revolution, strict discipline would be put into force and the principle of "party leadership" over the national government was to be strictly observed before the promulgation of the Constitution.[65] Later in Dr. Sun's *Outline of National Reconstruction,* the principle of one-party leadership was again stressed as essential to the training of the people for democracy. A detailed program of political tutelage was worked out.[66] In theory and in practice, the political tutelage idea has drawn frequent criticisms most notably because it has been compared to the Bolshevik proletarian dictatorship.[67]

In assessing the idea of political tutelage, certain criteria should be established to facilitate a sensible evaluation. It appears that two questions may be asked, and the answers to them may serve to put the issue in perspective. The first question is why did Sun think a transitional period necessary in China? Secondly, was there any guarantee against the Military Government, which was supposed to "tutor" the people, from becoming a dictatorship by not yielding the power to the people? To answer both questions, the best way is to let the record to speak for itself. Speaking of the necessity of having a transitional period between the end of military action and the beginning of constitutional government in which to prepare the people for democracy, Sun once said: "Our Chinese people have long been under the rule of monarchy. The slave psychology is deeply rooted in the people's minds, which cannot be eradicated without passing through a period of preparatory training."[68] He described the relationship between the people and the party as that of a child to the parent during the tutelage period. Since the revolutionary party bore the infant, he said, it was "obliged to nurse it like a mother and train it,

---

65 *Ibid.*

66 *Kuo-fu ch'uan-shu,* pp. 156-57.

67 Shao-chuan Leng and Norman Palmer, *op. cit.,* p. 50.

68 Sun Yat-sen, *Memoirs of a Chinese Revolutionary* (London: Hutchinson and Co., 1927), p. 146.

and only by training the people could it carry out its parental duty. And for this, the period of preparatory training was necessary, so that the child could be given experience and training up to its years of discretion, up to that moment when it could take over power itself."[69] Because of the long centuries of absolute rule under a monarchy, the people had become so apathetic about politics to the point of almost complete ignorance. They could hardly be expected to be able to exercise the tremendous powers of the nation thrusted upon them all of a sudden. It was therefore extremely dangerous to entrust the heretofore apathetic and inexperienced people with the burden of running the nation in a democratic way once the monarchy was overthrown.

In jumping from the stage of military government directly to the stage of constitutional democracy, without passing through a transitional stage to train the people, there were at least three dangers, one following another, Sun said. In the first place, before the remnants of the old order were all cleared up and people were given necessary orientation in the objectives which the revolution had sought, a new order could not be very effectively established. Secondly, even if a constitutional democracy was established on the surface, it would prove to be no more than a cover up for despotism to go on under its name. Thirdly, when the time arrived, even the name of democracy would be put aside.[70] This was precisely the case of the brief unsuccessful experiment with republicanism following the 1911 revolution, when impatient revolutionists overruled Sun and hastily introduced full parliamentary democracy. The parliament had never had any semblance of its counterparts in the West, and in the end Yuan Shih-k'ai simply dissolved it when he considered the time ripe for him to restore the monarchy and to install himself on the throne. Sun believed that this was primarily the result of the lack of political sophistication on the part of the people on the one hand, and the impact of the age-old monarchical rule on the other. Without a transitional period to allow the nation to become used to the new system, the ambitious and the opportunistic were apt to take advantage of the bewilderment created

---

69 *Ibid.*, p. 137.

70 *Kuo-fu ch'uan-shu*, p. 1045.

by the sudden change to advance their selfish interests. Sun was so convinced of the necessity of a period to prepare the people for democracy that when Frank J. Goodnow, Yuan Shih-k'ai's American adviser, advocated Yuan's monarchy, Sun even conceded Goodnow's good intentions because, he thought, Goodnow realized the political ineptness of the Chinese masses after long centuries of monarchical rule.[71] While this should in no way be construed as Sun's approval of Yuan's monarchy, it does show how strongly Sun felt about the need of a period of adjustment before democracy could be practiced in China.

As to the second question, the record shows that from the very beginning, Sun had been aware of the pitfalls of the Military Government turning dictatorial and that to guard against it, he had conceived a built-in guarantee in his design. To begin with, in the manifesto of the T'ung-meng Hui, provisions were made for the promulgation of a provisional constitution, detailing the relationship between the Military Government and the local governments in terms of their respective spheres of authority and responsibilities. In other words, although the Military Government still ruled the nation after the conclusion of the hostilities of the revolution, it would no longer rule with unlimited authority; its authority would only be based on a binding agreement with the local governments. The people would be guided to participate actively in local governments in order to learn to be responsible citizens in a democratic country. The idea of a written agreement between the Military Government and local governments was significant, because it clearly showed that Sun had no intention of allowing the Military Government to continue to possess unlimited power beyond the military stage of the revolution, and that the role of the Military Government was to help, rather than hinder, the development of local self-government for the eventual realization of universal constitutionalism.

In addition to the idea of a provisional constitution, there was a further check on the Military Government, as contained in the T'ung-meng Hui manifesto. That was the limit of the transitional period

---

71 Ts'ui Shu-ch'in, *San-min Chu-i hsin-lun* (A New Study of the Three Principles of the People) (Taipei, 1955), pp. 122-23.

to six years. Although the time limit was not mentioned in the constitution of the Chung-hua Ko-ming Tang and the *Outline for National Reconstruction,* because the prolonged period of warlordism had made it impossible to conclude the transitional period in time, the ultimate objective of constitutional democracy was still consistently upheld. Moreover, the program for political tutelage in the *Outline for National Reconstruction* was an elaborate design. It provided for detailed steps by which local self-government was to be carried out first in each county, and then in each province when all counties within its jurisdiction had achieved self-government. When self-government had been achieved in over one half of the provinces in the country, a national assembly should be convened to write a Constitution, according to which, a civilian government should be established to take over from the Military Government.

That the three-stage revolution did not work out the way it was supposed to is an acknowledged fact and a regrettable one at that. But to attribute subsequent developments in China to the unsoundness of the three-stage revolutionary theory, and particularly to the second stage of political tutelage, would be an unjustifiable over-simplification of the facts. The course of development in China after 1911 was very complicated, with numerous factors at work at one time or another. While these factors are beyond the scope of the present study, suffice it to say that the three-stage revolution idea was conceived in the light of a realistic appraisal of the situation in China, and that it was aimed at highly idealistic ends. In short, it sought to respond to the needs of the times. As we can see from the foregoing, the repeated emphasis was on the lack of a political sense on the part of the people and therefore on the necessity of training them in the exercise of their rights before full democracy could become a reality. On the need of education, even Sun's critics agreed with him. Lyon Sharman, for example, does not criticize the idea of political tutelage as such; rather, he questions the qualifications of the "tutors" in these words:

> It is too readily taken for granted that the educated classes are already prepared for democracy and qualified to tutor the masses ...... It is the educated leaders of the people who have so far been tested in democratic functioning; it is by them that all experiments have been made; it is not the masses but the educated leaders who have over and over failed[72]....

72 Sharman, *op. cit.*, pp. 371-72.

What Sharman has stressed here is essentially what Dr. Sun had foreseen and sought to prevent, namely, the danger of dictatorship growing out of political tutelage. This concerns the second question which we tried to analyze above. From the record we found that as originally conceived, political tutelage was never meant to enhance military or one-party dictatorship. On the contrary, it sought to avoid that danger with built-in checks. It may be further pointed out that at all times the ultimate goal of the revolution had been stated in unequivocal terms, namely, to bring about genuine democratic republicanism. The one-party rule during the tutelage period was not an end in itself; it was rather a design by which it was hoped to reach the higher goal of republicanism. It is in this respect that the political tutelage of the Kuomintang differed basically with the proletarian dictatorship of the Bolsheviks despite the outward resemblance. If the nearly two decades of chaos following the 1911 revolution represented the failure of the experiment of republicanism in China, the failure cannot be attributed to Dr. Sun's ideas. For the unfortunate situation during that period had hardly provided the chance to put Dr. Sun's ideas to a real test.

PRINCIPLE OF PEOPLE'S LIVELIHOOD

Having examined the first two elements of the body of ideology that the T'ung-meng Hui stood for, we shall now move to a third theme, an economic one, which together with nationalism and republicanism constituted the forerunner of Dr. Sun's Three People's Principles. This is commonly known as the Principle of People's Livelihood.

During the period under review, Dr. Sun's idea about what has since been known as the Principle of People's Livelihood was far from being complete. Essentially, it appeared to be dealing only with the problem of urban land during this period. Sun had, since very early days, paid attention to economic development. Of the four recommendations he made to Li Hung-chang, three concerned national economy. But at that early stage, he had not begun to see serious economic and social problems that required drastic, revolutionary measures to cope with. His chief concern then, like those of most other reformers, was how to modernize China to make it strong. A major change in his revolutionary ideas took place after he was kidnapped in London in 1896. For some time after his release he stayed in England, observing and studying Western systems. In the summer of 1897, he sailed for Japan by way of Canada, at a time when America was in the midst of the pre-progressive era of protest and revolt. It was during this period that his observations convinced him that although Europe and America enjoyed democracy and material well-being, they were still beset by economic and social problems inherent in the capitalist system. Speaking of his experiences during this period, he said later:

> During these two years, I learned much from what I saw and heard. I began to realize that although their countries are strong and they enjoy democracy, the European people have not reached the stage of maximum happiness because there are many economic problems left unsolved. This is why there are socialist movements in Europe. In order to solve the problems in China once and for all, I therefore began to advocate the Principle of People's Livelihood alongside the Principles of Nationalism and Democracy. This is how my Three People's Principles was completed.[73]

However, despite Sun's claim of having conceived of his third principle at such an early date, it was rather simple in contents and narrow in scope, and it remained so through the 1911 revolution.

Explaining the purpose of his Principle of People's Livelihood in a message to the first issue of the *Min Pao* in 1905, Sun said it was aimed at carrying out a social revolution, which was yet to be carried out by the most advanced countries in Europe and America. According to him, nationalism first appeared in the West following the collapse of the Roman Empire, when many nations became independent. At the end of 18th century and the beginning of the 19th century, democracy was on the rise when constitutional movements succeeded in many countries. With the scientific advancement and the increase in wealth as a result of the opening up of national resources, economic problems soon arose on the heels of political problems and the twentieth century was bound to be an era for solving the problems relating to people's livelihood. Although the Western countries had long succeeded in political

---

73 *Kuo-fu ch'uan-shu,* p. 33.

revolution, he said, their social problems were aggravating. "Though the Western countries are powerful, their people are really in distress. Judging from the frequency of general strikes and the growth of anarchism and socialism, a social revolution is not far off," he said.[74] He believed that in China, the situation was different. Economically under-developed, China had not yet reached the stage where she would face the inherent problems of capitalism, and it is therefore important that preventive measures should be taken before hand to avoid the problems. The Principle of People's Livelihood, he said, was designed to perform that task. By adding this principle to the Principles of Nationalism and Democracy, the Chinese revolution would in one stroke succeed in both political and social revolution, thus surpassing even the most advanced Western countries. The idea of avoiding the pitfalls of capitalism was a persistent factor in Dr. Sun's mind. In 1912, right after the founding of the republic, he said: "Today there are no wealthier countries than Britain and America; there is no more enlightened country than France . . . . but the gap betwixt the poor and the wealthy in these countries is too great. And so it comes to pass that the thought of revolution still rankles in the minds of many."[75]

The first appearance of the phrase "equalizing land ownership" was in 1903, when it was included in the oath used at the secret military school set up by Sun in Tokyo. Since then, it had been consistently used. It was mentioned in the Constitution of Chih-kung T'ang in America, which Sun helped to reorganize in 1904; and it was one of the four slogans of the T'ung-meng Hui at its founding in Tokyo in 1905. To begin with, the meaning of "equalizing land ownership" calls for clarification. While Sun spoke of equalization of land ownership, another term was used in *Min Pao* to describe the land policy of the revolutionary party. The term used was *t'u-ti kuo-yu,* which, literally translated, means "nationalization of land" or "state ownership of land." It was listed as one of the six objectives of *Min Pao* in its third issue. In that issue, however, *t'u-ti kuo-yu* was translated, rather ambiguously, as "equal enjoyment of land for all."[76] The use of

---

74 *Ibid.,* p. 392.

75 Sun Yat-sen, "China's Next Step," *The Independent* (New York), July 13, 1912, p. 1315.

76 *Min Pao,* No. 3, p.11.

different terms and different versions of translation added to the ambiguity that had already existed. Further complicating the issue, some revolutionists seem to have actually advocated nationalization of land. Hu Han-min said that after the revolution, people "will not have ownership of land."[77] Feng Tzu-yu also once emphasized that private ownership of land should not be allowed.[78] To clarify the issue, two questions must be asked. Did Sun at that time advocate outright nationalization of land? Or, if not, did he advocate a redistribution of land? From Sun's writings, one can find that the answers to both the above questions are in the negative, for as we shall see, Sun at that time was chiefly concerned with the unearned increments of land which he believed should not be enjoyed by the landlords alone, but by the nation as a whole. Accordingly, he advocated a policy, largely based on Henry George's single tax theory, which he thought would transfer most of the unearned increments of land to the hands of the government for public welfare purposes.

A recurrent theme in numerous of Sun's speeches and writings during this period was that the increase in the value of land was the result of social progress, and therefore it should be enjoyed by the society as a whole, not by the landlords alone. The method he proposed to achieve this end, in a nutshell, was to fix the price of all land at a certain level, with the subsequent increments going to the government for public welfare. This, as we can see, is primarily in line with David Ricardo's differential rent theory, the unearned increment theory of John Stuart Mill, and particularly of Henry George. As a matter of fact, Sun made it no secret that he borrowed heavily from Henry George, whose eloquent portrayal of social injustice in modern society as a result of land monopoly deeply impressed him.[79] His admiration for George's single tax theory was so expressed in an interview with American journalists in 1912: "The teachings of your single-taxer, Henry George, will be the basis of our program of reform. The land tax as the only means of supporting the government is an infinitely just, reasonable, and equitably distributed tax, and on it we will found our

---

77 *Ibid.*, p. 13.

78 *Ibid.*, No. 4, p. 114.

79 Sun Yat-sen, *Memoir of a Chinese Revolutionary*, pp. 36-37.

new system."[80] Actually, Sun did not go as far as to urge the confiscation of all unearned increments of land, as George's theory would require. Nor did he insist on making land tax the sole source of revenue of the state. In another speech in 1912, he made it plain that the kind of land tax he would advocate would not even be based on a progressive rate, but on a flat rate of one or two per cent.[81]

Sun's analysis of the problems in the West under the capitalist system, superficial as it was, clearly showed that he was influenced by socialist thinking. Despite his later severe criticism of Marxism, he was at this time favorably disposed to socialism and his prophecy about the coming of social revolution in the West was not too different from that of Marx. But as his ideas continued to evolve, he increasingly departed from Marx and his criticism of Marx grew in intensity. He flatly rejected the Marxian theories of historical materialism, class struggle and surplus value, and pointed out the inaccuracies of Marx's predictions. Moreover, he stressed that his solution for economic problems was totally different from that of Marx. In this respect, the influence of another Westerner was evident. The man was Maurice William, an American medical doctor, who later became a member of the Kuomintang. Referring to the social revolution theory in William's book *The Social Interpretation of History,* Sun later said:

> He (William) sets forth the view that the materialistic conception of history is wrong; that the social problem, not material forces, is the center which determines the course of history, and that subsistence is the heart of the social problem. . .the problem of livelihood is the problem of subsistence. The new theory of this American scholar tallies exactly with the third principle of our party. William's theory means that livelihood is the central force in social progress, and that social progress is the central force in history; hence the struggle for a living and not material forces determines history.[82]

Borrowing from others to formulate his own ideas, Sun was heavily influenced by socialism in his thinking. That is understandable, in view

---

80 *The Public* (Chicago), April 12, 1912, p. 349, quoted in Leng and Plamer, *op. cit.*, p. 25.

81 *Kuo-fu ch'uan-shu*, pp. 489-90.

82 Sun Yat-sen, *San Min Chu I*, p. 383.

of the socialist agitations during this period. Aside from widely contacting socialists of different shades, Sun was said to have met Lenin and other Russian revolutionary exiles while in Europe.[83] Socialist influence continued to bear upon him after his arrival in Tokyo in 1905, and his convictions about "equalizing land ownership" were bolstered by his Japanese friends, particularly Miyazaki Tamizo. Brother of one of Sun's closest associates, Miyazaki Torazo, Tamizo had concentrated his efforts on working out a solution to agrarian inequalities ever since the early Meiji days when his family had suffered many hardships. His final solution was along the lines of Henry George's single tax plan. In 1906, he published an influential little book on his theory. Miyazaki Tamizo had wide contacts among the Japanese socialists and his book apparently fortified Sun convictions.[84]

That Sun's land policy was influenced by socialism is beyond doubt; but it cannot be regarded as radically socialist because it did not call for outright nationalization of land. What Sun sought was essentially a taxation system to check monopoly of land, and furthermore a channeling of unearned increments to the government to be enjoyed by all. This mildly socialist policy, however, was not easily accepted by others. Indeed no sooner had it been declared as one of the chief objectives of the T'ung-meng Hui, than a great debate ensued between the revolutionists and the royalists on its theoretical soundness and practical feasibility. Even within the ranks of the revolutionary party, Sun often had to go to great lengths to convince his followers. Following the 1911 revolution, one of the most frequent criticisms made of Sun was that his ideas were too advanced to be realized in China, and were therefore impractical. Like his program of three-stage revolution, his land policy was largely ignored during the chaotic years after the 1911 revolution.

The above presentation has shown that the T'ung-meng Hui as a revolutionary organization had certain clearly stated goals and for the realization of the goals, it had developed a body of working programs.

---

83 Robert Payne and Stephen Chen, *Sun Yat-sen: A Portrait* (New York: John Day, 1946), p. 48.

84 Marius Jansen, *The Japanese and Sun Yat-sen* (Cambridge: Harvard University Press, 1954), pp. 118-19.

The ideas behind the programs were chiefly those of Sun's, and we have explored to some extent the evolution of Sun's ideas and the various factors which helped shape the course of the evolution. We have found that the T'ung-meng Hui was dedicated to the high ideals of republicanism and democracy. Despite the disappointing failure of the experiment of republicanism after the revolution of 1911, there seems to be no justifiable reason to doubt the goodwill of Dr. Sun or to lightly dismiss the feasibility of his untested program. Republicanism and a mild socialism unquestionably are the two main themes in his ideas. It is on these two issues that the revolutionists and the royalists launched their celebrated great debate. In order to see how these two themes were explored and articulated, we shall turn to the great debate in the next chapter.

Chapter IV

DEBATE BETWEEN ROYALISTS AND REVOLUTIONISTS

The debate between the royalists and the revolutionists actually began as early as 1900, after Liang Ch'i-ch'ao had established a Pao-huang Hui branch in Honolulu and returned to Tokyo. Since then, he and his master, K'ang Yu-wei, had steadily written in defense of constitutional monarchy. In numerous articles in the *Hsin-min Ts'ung Pao,* they dwelt on the merits of a constitutional monarchy and on how such a system was suited to China. A revolution in China, in their opinion, would accomplish nothing, but would only lead to chaos by breaking up the existing order. Instead of strengthening China, a revolution would only further weaken China and the only ones to benefit would be the great powers, who were seeking to cut up China. To make the Chinese people accept the Manchu rule, they spared no effort in stressing that the Hans and the Manchus were of the same ancestry and that they should, and could, live together harmoniously. It was not a disgrace, they argued, for the Hans to accept Manchu rule. The revolutionists, of course, argued otherwise. Deeply committed to republicanism, they believed that the monarchical government, be it controlled by the Manchus or the Hans, must be done away with first. They held republicanism as the most advanced form of government; they believed that a constitutional monarchy, under which the very target of the revolution--the Manchu government--would be preserved, would not be able to solve the problems in China, nor would it be able to prevent the emperor from becoming despotic.

After the formation of the T'ung-meng Hui, its organ, the *Min Pao,* soon began publication and immediately it took up the task of launching a series of spirited debates with the *Hsin-min Ts'ung Pao,* organ of the royalists. The theme of the debate went beyond constitutional monarchy versus republicanism. When the platform of the T'ung-meng Hui became known, the socialist features of the economic program of the revolutionists soon became another target of attack by the royalists. The attack was countered by vigorous defense in the *Min Pao.* These debates were no mere rhetoric; the advocates on each side, probably the best talents the nation could offer at the time, were sincerely arguing about the future of the nation. In ably articulating the issues, they made little effort to hide a deep sense of personal conviction in what they believed in. From a broader view, the issue of constitutional monarchy versus republicanism can perhaps be viewed as primarily a contention between Western democratic currents and traditional Chinese philosophy of benevolent monarchy; and the fight over "equalizing land ownership" may be viewed as the first test of acceptability of socialism by Chinese intellectuals of the traditional school. Both issues seem to remain unsettled even to this day. Could constitutional monarchy have been a better system for China? How did the royalists argue their case? In rejecting the revolutionists' land policy as being socialistic, what did the royalists advocate? How socialistic, after all was the revolutionists' land policy? And in particular, should the Chinese Communists have been allowed to lay claim to Sun's economic thinking as being identical to theirs? These are vital questions. This chapter will be devoted to an exploration of these questions by examining the sources.

MIN PAO VS. HSIN-MIN TS'UNG PAO

At the time when preparations were under way for the formation of the T'ung-meng Hui in Tokyo in 1905, Sun Yat-sen suggested the publication of a journal as the official organ of the T'ung-meng Hui to propagate the revolutionary cause.[1] His suggestion was warmly received by others. At the founding meeting of the T'ung-meng Hui on August 20, 1905, Huang Hsing formally proposed that the *Erh-shih Shih-chi chih Chih-na* (Twentieth Century China), a magazine published by the students from Hunan province, should from now on become the official organ of the T'ung-meng Hui. Speaking for his group, Huang said since

1 Hu Han-min, "Tzu Chuan," p. 388.

over half of the members of the magazine had now joined the T'ung-meng Hui, it was their decision to suspend the publication of the magazine and turn it over to the T'ung-meng Hui. His proposal was enthusiastically applauded by those attending the meeting.[2]

The *Erh-shih Shih-chi chih Chih-na* began publication in Tokyo in early 1905. The prime mover behind it was Sung Chiao-jen, who was both editor and fund-raiser of the magazine. Supported only by contributions from some students out of their allowances, the magazine in its short life span suffered from serious financial difficulties and several times it nearly closed down, as Sung had vividly recorded in his diary. On August 27, 1905, the magazine was seized by the Tokyo police, because its second issue contained an article entitled "Japanese Politicians' Designs in China," which the Japanese Ministry of Interior found insulting.[3] The Japanese seized the undistributed copies of the magazine and several times summoned Sung for questioning about the revolutionary activities of the Chinese students. The Japanese also asked for the original manuscript of the magazine article, but Sung replied that it had been sent back to China. After some further questioning, the case was dropped.[4] The ban actually had little effect on the magazine anyway, for decision had already been reached earlier to discontinue it and Sung was already busy making arrangements for turning it over to the T'ung-meng Hui.

The organ of the T'ung-meng Hui made its debut on Nov. 26, 1905. The name *Min Pao* (Citizen's Journal) was adopted at the suggestion of Hu Han-min.[5] Chang Chi, a ranking member of the T'ung-meng Hui, was named publisher and editor of the *Min Pao* because of his command of the Japanese language, which was a must for outside contacts; but Hu Han-min was the actual editor.[6]

The *Hsin-min Ts'ung Pao* (New Citizen's Journal), organ of the royalists, was not totally unfavorable to the revolutionists during the

---

2 Sung Chiao-jen, *op. cit.*, p. 75.

3 *Ibid.*, pp. 77-78.

4 *Ibid.*

5 Hu Han-min, *op. cit.*, p. 388.

6 *Ibid.*

first few years of its publication. As pointed out earlier, Liang Ch'i-ch'ao, editor of the *Hsin-min Ts'ung Pao,* was at one time contemplating joining forces with Sun Yat-sen. Championing the cause of the emperor, the *Hsin-min Ts'ung Pao* at first openly called for the overthrow of the Empress Dowager. Liang's assertion that in China reconstruction was possible only after destruction--meaning the overthrow of the Empress Dowager – was, the revolutionists agreed, substantially helpful to the revolutionary cause.[7] However, after Liang's return to Tokyo from Hawaii in 1900, he began systematically extolling the virtues of constitutional monarchy and opposing revolution. Meanwhile, his master, K'ang Yu-wei, also wrote in the *Hsin-min Ts'ung Pao,* attacking revolution.

Even before the publication of the *Min Pao,* the revolutionists had already taken up their fight with the royalists. Ch'en Shao-pai was sent to Hong Kong by Sun Yat-sen as early as 1899 to start the *Chung-kuo Jih Pao* (China Daily) there in order to propagate the revolutionary cause. In 1905, Ch'en was joined by Feng Tzu-yu, who later took over the *Chung-kuo Jih Pao* and headed it for many years. In Shanghai, the *Su Pao* (Kiangsu Journal), under the editorship of Chang Ping-lin and others, had already begun to wage a relentless battle against the royalists before it was closed down by the Manchus in 1904. In Hawaii, the *Lung-chi Pao* (Prosperous Journal) was reorganized by Sun Yat-sen into the *Min-sheng Jih Pao* (People's Livelihood Daily) in 1904 to rival the royalist organ, the *Hsin Chung-kuo Pao* (New China Daily) there. In Singapore, the revolutionists started the *Chung-hsing Pao* (Restoration Daily) in 1907 to oppose the royalist-backed *Nan-yang Tsung-hui Pao* (South Sea General Daily). Papers were published in other cities, such as San Francisco and Vancouver, where the royalists also had their papers.[8] A war of words was on between the revolutionists and the royalists in many places, but the principal battle was fought in Tokyo, between the *Min Pao* and the *Hsin-min Ts'ung Pao.* In the *Min Pao,* many important articles were penned by Hu

---

7 Feng Tzu-yu, *Chung-kuo ko-ming yun-tung erh-shih-liu nien tsu-chih shih,* p. 61.

8 Feng Tzu-yu, *Chung-hua min-kuo k'ai-kuo-ch'ien ko-ming shih,* Vol. I, pp. 52-53.

Han-min and Wang Ching-wei. According to Hu, Sun Yat-sen often dictated his ideas to them and asked them to do the actual writing.[9]

CONSTITUTIONAL MONARCHY VS. REPUBLICANISM

In 1902, K'ang Yu-wei, after an extended tour of Europe and America, wrote *K'ang-nan-hai tsui-chin cheng-chien shu* (Recent Political Views of K'ang Yu-wei), in which he severely lashed out at the revolutionists and strongly advocated a constitutional monarchy. Meanwhile, his ideas were published in capsule form in an article in the *Hsin-min Ts'ung Pao.* In essence, he made two points. First, the division between the Hans and the Manchus was unnecessary; and second, political freedom of the Chinese people could be achieved without resort to revolution, which meant bloodshed. Among other things, K'ang asked the following questions: Were the Hans opposed to the Manchus simply because they were Manchus as such, or because they ran a bad government? Was it necessary for China to get rid of the Manchus in order to build a new country, or should the nation embrace all ethnic groups on a harmonious basis, including the Manchus, the Hans, the Miaos, the Moslems as well as the Tibetans?[10] K'ang's views were immediately challenged by Chang Ping-lin, who was then in Shanghai, associated with the *Su Pao.* Chang wrote a spirited treatise, which was published as a pamphlet in Shanghai and was soon widely acclaimed in intellectual circles.[11] In reply to K'ang's arguments, Chang made the following points: (1) The nature of the Manchu rule was basically tyrannical and discriminatory. Under such rule, neither political freedom nor genuine monarchical reform was possible. (2) Throughout Chinese history, the practice had always been for an alien ethnic group to be absorbed into the Han race. Since the Manchus had stubbornly clung to their discriminatory practices and oppressed the Hans, assimilation was out of question. (3) It was impossible to expect the Manchu government to undermine its own rule by voluntarily surrendering its power to the people. Under such circumstances, a

---

9. Hu Han-min, *op. cit.*, p. 388.

10 K'ang Yu-wei "Pien Ko-ming Shu" (The Case Against Revolution), *Hsin-min Ts'ung Pao,* No. 16, pp. 59-61.

11. Feng Tzu-yu, *Chung-hua-min-kuo k'ai-kuo-ch'ien ko-ming shih,* Vol. I, p. 134.

revolution carried out by the people would prove to be an easier way of achieving constitutional democracy. (4) To say that the people were too conservative to support a revolution was unsound reasoning, for the people would find constitutional monarchy just as novel as a republican form of government. Since the first task was the enlightening of the public, the task could best be accomplished through a revolution that was aimed at securing the world's most advanced political system. (5) Under the discriminatory rule of the Manchus, the Chinese national conscience had been suppressed so long that the continued enfeebling of the Chinese nation was inevitable. The end result might well be that the Chinese nation would one day become the slaves not of the Manchus, but of the Western powers.[12]

Meanwhile in 1903-1904, Sun Yat-sen published two important essays defending his revolutionary cause. The first was entitled "The Preservation and Partition of China," published in the *Chiang-su Yueh Pao* (Kiangsu Monthly), a magazine put out in Tokyo by Chinese students from the Kiangsu province. The other one, entitled "The True Solution of the Chinese Question," which he wrote while he was in the United States in 1904, was intended primarily for Americans. In the first essay, he contended, in a nationalistic vein typical of his writings, that it was the Manchu government that could not be preserved and that it was the Chinese nation that could not be partitioned. He listed three reasons why the Manchu court could not last long: failure to reform itself, foreign imperialism, and lack of support of the people.[13] On the other hand, he stressed that the Chinese people, long accustomed to be a unified country, would violently resist partition by the Western powers to the bitter end.[14] In the second essay, Sun proposed that the "true solution" to the China problem was to do away with the Manchu government and to establish a democratic Chinese republic, which would cease to be a bone of contention among the great powers, thus eliminating a potential source of trouble on the world scene.[15] Chang Ping-lin and Sun thus set the general pattern and directions for the ensuing debate with the royalists.

---

12. Chang Ping-lin, *Chang-shih ts'ung-shu* (Collected Works of Chang Ping-lin) (Taipei, 1958), Vol. II, pp. 29-44.
13 *Kuo-fu ch'uan-shu,* p. 367.
14 *Ibid.,* p. 368.
15 *Ibid.,* pp. 369-70.

In a long article serialized in the first two issues of the *Min Pao,* Wang Ching-wei, expanding on the general arguments of Sun and Chang, made one of the most detailed expositions of the political aims of the revolution. He stressed the importance of distinguishing the Hans from the Manchus, and declared that the purpose of the revolution was not only to get rid of the inept government, but also to end the domination of the Chinese by an alien minority. He had this comment on constitutional monarchy under the Manchus:

> Constitutional monarchy is vigorously preached by many intellectuals and it appears to be the hope of many common people. Let us first hypothetically think about a perfect constitution. Under this constitution, first, the Hans and the Manchus would be equal citizens, enjoying the same rights and fulfilling the same obligations. Secondly, they would forget the past grudges they had held against each other and would from now on live harmoniously forever. This, I submit, is only wishful thinking. I am fully convinced that should such a constitution become a reality, it would only mean the perpetuation of the rule of the Manchus as conquerors and the Hans under them as the conquered. A simple metaphor will help explain this: If a bandit, after forcibly taking over a household and making himself its head, starts to make some benevolent gestures to his captives, would he be able to convince them that he is the real master of the household? Would the genuine master of the household be contented and willingly submit to his authority, or would he continue as ever to regard the bandit as an arch-enemy? The answer is crystal clear. I fail to understand why those who so enthusiastically advocate constitutional monarchy fail to realize this simple truth.[16]

Wang went on to declare that a constitution was not to be a mere decree of the crown, but should be an expression of the wishes of the people, aimed at extending the rights of the people and curtailing the absolute authority of the government. "How, then, can we expect the Manchu government to work out a constitution to tie its own hands?" he asked.[17] In many contemporary constitutional monarchies, he continued, although the constitution was outwardly decreed by the crown, the people invariably had the real control. "But in China, the situation is different. Because of the fact that the Manchus are aliens,

16 Wang Ching-wei "Min-tsu ti kuo-min" (Nationalistic Citizens), *Min Pao* (Citizen's Journal), No. 1, pp. 24-25.

17 *Ibid.*, p. 25.

they resort to the trappings of constitutional monarchy only to placate our people in order to solidify their rule. We should remember that when Greece was under the rule of Turkey, and Belgium under the rule of the Netherlands, the Greeks and the Belgians asked not for a constitution, but for independence."[18]

Thus in the view of Wang Ching-wei, the chief reason why there were people who welcomed constitutional monarchy in China was because of their failure to see the difference between democracy and nationalism. He reasoned:

> While democracy aims at polictical ends, nationalism in present day China must be based on racial grounds. If our present tyrannical government were run by people of our own race, then the problem of nationalism would not arise, and all we should seek would be democracy. Since our government today is in the hands of an alien race, we must apply nationalism first to drive away the aliens, or all the talk about democracy would be meaningless. It therefore pains me to see some of our ignorant people show their enthusiasm upon hearing the proposal of constitutional monarchy under the Manchus. I can't help but deeply hate the K'ang-Liang group for spreading their falsehood to mislead the public.[19]

On the royalist side, Liang Ch'i-ch'ao was closely following the arguments of his master, K'ang Yu-wei. In a long article in the *Hsin-min Ts'ung Pao,* entitled "The Soul of China," Liang went to great length to expand on his master's ideas. In the first place, he argued, the Hans were not well enough prepared to establish a new form of government, because they had little experience in democracy throughout their history. Second, he rejected the revolutionists' advocation of opposing the Manchus on racial grounds. What was objectionable was the government, not the Manchu people, and thus whether that government was run by either the Manchus or the Hans was immaterial. Third, justifying the Manchu rule, he castigated the revolutionists for holding narrow racist views. There was no reason why China could not be, as it had already been, built on a multi-racial basis, he argued.[20]

---

18 *Ibid.*

19 *Ibid.*

20 Liang Ch'i-ch'ao, "Chung-kuo hun" (The Soul of China), *Hsin-min Ts'ung Pao* (New Citizen's Journal), Nos. 38, 39.

In pointed reply, Wang Ching-wei in his article in the *Min Pao* admitted that China lacked a democratic tradition similar to those of many Western countries, but since men progressed with each passing day, there was no reason to assume that China should cling to its past and refuse new ideas. Second, he made it clear that the anti-Manchu policy was based on nationalism and opposition to the tyrannical government was for democracy. While a difference must be made between the racial and political objectives, the revolution was aimed at both objectives. In the third place, Wang denied the charges of racism, but contended that assimilation must take the form of other ethnic groups joining the Hans, as had been the case throughout Chinese history prior to the Manchu Dynasty.[21]

Wang Ching-wei's argument that the Manchus could not afford a system of genuine constitutional monarchy was supported by many others who wrote along the same lines in the *Min Pao.* Chu Chih-hsin declared bluntly that for the Manchus to practice constitutionalism would be tantamount to committing political suicide.[22] He conceded that there existed intense racial antagonism between the majority Hans and the minority Manchus, but this antagonism would only grow, not abate, under an assumed system of constitutional monarchy, which would be simply a guise under which to perpetuate the minority rule. He further argued that only under democracy as promised by the revolutionary party could there be hope of gradual disappearance of the racial barrier.[23] Chu was joined by Wang Tung, who insisted that genuine constitutionalism was possible only after a successful revolution against the oppressive rule of the Manchus.[24]

Around the turn of the century, Japan was often looked upon with admiration by Chinese radicals, revolutionists and reformers alike. The successful experience of Japan's modernization was often

---

21 Wang Ching-wei, *op. cit.*, pp. 29-30.

22 Chih Sheng (pseud. of Chu Chih-hsin), "Lun Man-chou sui yu li-hsien erh pu-neng" (On the Futility of Constitutionalism Under the Manchus), *Min Pao,* No. 1, pp. 33-34.

23 *Ibid.*, pp. 37-38.

24 Chi Sheng (pseud. of Wang Tung), "Lun Chih-na li-hsien pi hsien-i ko-ming" (Revolution Must Precede Constitution in China), *Min Pao,* No. 2, p. 41.

held as an example for China to follow. However, to the royalists, Japan's success had an added meaning in that the success was achieved under a constitutional monarchy. The revolutionists were quick to prevent the royalists from drawing an analogy between what they were advocating for China and what had taken place in Japan. Typical arguments advanced by the revolutionists in this regard were expressed in the following passage:

> The success of the Meiji Restoration in Japan can be attributed to the return of power to the crown and the overthrow of the shogunate. In China, our own royal house in fact had been overthrown by the Manchus over 200 years ago and the present government is just like the Tokugawa Shogunate in Japan. Without toppling the shogunate, Japan would never be what it is today; without doing away with the Manchus, China will never be restored to the Hans. This is why we are opposed to following Japan's example of constitutional monarchy. This is why we advocate republicanism in China. We must realize the different situation in China and not copy Japan blindly. For China, there is no better way out besides republicanism.[25]

While it appeared that the revolutionists in stressing the differences between the Hans and the Manchus were adopting a racist line, it was the Manchus, however, who had actually followed a highly discriminatory policy on racial grounds from the beginning of their rule in China. Intermarriage was banned until the last years of the dynasty; Manchu attire was universally enforced; the officialdom and the military were largely in the hands of the Manchus; and differential treatment was accorded the Manchus and the Hans in regard to private properties, to name the grievances of the Hans in just a few areas. In the second of his serialized articles in the *Min Pao,* Wang Ching-wei pointed out that although the Manchus were only one-eighth of the Hans in number, they occupied two-thirds of the official positions in the country.[26]

In the third issue of the *Min Pao,* apparently acting on Sun Yat-sen's instructions, Hu Han-min made a belated attempt to explain

---

25 Szu Huang (pseud. of Ch'en T'ien-hua) "Lun Chung-kuo i kai-ch'uang min-chu cheng-t'i"(On the Appropriateness of Adopting Republican Form of Government in China), *Min Pao,* No. 1, p. 49.

26 Wang Ching-wei, *op. cit.,* No. 2, p. 9.

the six principles espoused by the revolutionary organ. In a long article, he summed up the essence of each of the six principles. The first three, he said, represented the revolutionary party's domestic objectives. They were the overthrow of the inferior government, the establishment of a republic, and the nationalization of land. The last three principles, namely, the preservation of world peace, cooperation between nationals of China and Japan and international cooperation in the economic development of China, were primarily the guideposts of the revolutionary party's foreign policy. On the first principle, his arguments did not go beyond those already made by others as described above, except that he particularly emphasized the fact that assimilation of the Manchus into the Hans was impossible under the existing circumstances. The Manchus in fact not only steadily refused to assimilate, but had on the other hand tried to force the Hans, as an overwhelming majority, to assimilate into the Manchus.[27]

Thus in the first three issues of the *Min Pao,* the revolutionists had largely stated their position. Although their arguments were not very orderly, and at times appeared repetitious and lacking in focus, several general guidelines, however, could be discerned and the general direction of their arguments was clear. To put it in a simple way, they were unequivocably for republicanism and regarded a revolution to overthrow the existing government as necessary for the achievement of that goal. Having made their firm commitment to republicanism known, they sought to back up this basic stand with arguments from many angles. On the other side, the royalists had never accepted republicanism in either a theoretical or practical sense. They rejected republicanism categorically and in its place, advocated a constitutional monarchy. Before a constitutional monarchy could be established, an "enlightened dictatorship," in Liang Ch'i-ch'ao's words, was to be set up as the first step in that direction. Thus it was on the basic issue of republicanism that both sides launched their celebrated war of words. As in any debate, the flying of words back and forth often degenerated into boring polemics and even outright personal attack, but the central theme over which the fight was carried out was never for a moment lost in the seemingly endless struggle. As the debate proceeded, the

27 Hu Han-min, "*Min Pao* chih liu-ta chu-i" (Six Major Principles of *Min Pao),* No. 3, pp. 8-9.

revolutionists felt it necessary to once again clearly state the issue and they did so by publishing a twelve-item "outline of debate" in a supplement to No. 3 of the *Min Pao.* The outline, although apparently partisan in tone, is still worth quoting in full:

1. *Min Pao* for republicanism; *Hsin-min Ts'ung Pao* for dictatorship.

2. *Min Pao* for constitutional democracy; *Hsin-min Ts'ung Pao* for an "enlightened dictatorship."

3. *Min Pao* believes the present government is bad and therefore advocates its overthrow through revolution; *Hsin-min Ts'ung Pao* believes the people are bad and therefore expresses the hope for a dictatoral government.

4. *Min Pao* aims at constitutional democracy, and preaches revolution and education as the means of attaining the goal; *Hsin-min Ts'ung Pao* merely hopes for a dictatorial government and doesn't say how it can be established.

5. *Min Pao* advocates political revolution and racial revolution simultaneously; *Hsin-min Ts'ung Pao* advocates enlightened dictatorship and political reform.

6. In *Min Pao's* opinion, the revolution is a political revolution from the standpoint of overthrowing the monarchical rule, and a racial revolution from the standpoint of driving out the Manchus; *Hsin-min Ts'ung Pao* believes the two revolutions cannot be carried out simultaneously.

7. *Min Pao* believes that in China today, political revolution can only be achieved through the use of force; *Hsin-min Ts'ung Pao* believes it can be effected through petition.

8. *Min Pao* believes that in carrying out the revolution, force must be emphasized; *Hsin-min Ts'ung Pao* believes that coercion is to be applied only when petition has been turned down.

9. *Hsin-min Ts'ung Pao* believes that the way of applying

coercion is through refusal to pay taxes and assassination; *Min Pao* believes that refusal to pay taxes and assassination are only part of the measures of revolution, and there are other measures.

10. *Hsin-min Ts'ung Pao* opposes revolution but promotes nihilism; *Min Pao* believes all nihilists are revolutionary, and their purpose is not merely to commit assassination.

11. *Min Pao* believes the purpose of revolution is to bring about a republic; *Hsin-min Ts'ung Pao* believes that revolution will result in tyranny.

12. Mindful of social problems, *Min Pao* advocates socialism to solve them; *Hsin-min Ts'ung Pao* believes socialism is nothing but a means of arousing degenerates and other undesirables of society.[28]

As we can see from this outline, most of the points on the side of the revolutionists were a summary of the arguments which we have already described above. On the other hand, what the *Min Pao* alleged as the attitude of the *Hsin-min Ts'ung Pao* was chiefly taken from a long article by Liang Ch'i-ch'ao, entitled "On Enlightened Dictatorship," which was serialized in the *Hsin-min Ts'ung Pao* in its first ten issues of 1906. This ten-chapter, book-length article was the most complete and systematic exposition of the stand of the royalists. It is important that we examine this article carefully in order to find out how the royalists, through their spokesman, argued their case. The article was a well-organized one, with a clearly stated theme and an unmistakable purpose. The author first sought to define what he called "enlightened dictatorship," then went on to describe under what condition this form of government would be suitable, citing many past examples both in China and in the West, and concluded that an "enlightened dictatorship" would be best suited in China under the existing circumstances.

In a typical social Darwinian way of interpreting the evolution of the human race – natural selection and survival of the fittest – Liang first pointed out force as the most elementary factor in survival, asserting that this was true of individuals, and of society as well as of a

---

28 Direct translation from *Min Pao,* No. 3, supplement.

state. In the case of the state, therefore, he inferred, absolute power for the ruler was necessary, and if the power was used for good and benevolent purposes, the regime would be an "enlightened dictatorship."[29] To Liang, what was important was not what kind of political system, i.e., form of government, a country adopted, but whether that government was "enlightened" or not.[30] He gave his criteria for an enlightened government: Under that government, a person should be allowed freedom to such a degree that it would not interfere with the freedom of the others;[31] and the government should always put people's welfare above everything else.[32] To illustrate his point, he said Louis XIV showed himself to be a dictator by declaring "I am the State," while King Frederick showed himself to be an "enlightened dictator" by saying "the King is the chief public servant of the State."[33] As far as calling for reforms to make the country strong is concerned, it appeared that the royalists and the revolutionists agreed on this goal. But the difference between them lay in their totally different approaches to the goal, a difference so serious as to be beyond reconciliation. While the revolutionists saw in democracy the best hope for the country's future and looked upon America's republican form of government as a model, the royalists chose to look for evidence from other sources to support their arguments. Liang made it no secret that he cared very little about what he understood as Western democracy and he mentioned the British and American systems only very briefly, calling them "exceptions." In a sweeping way, he criticized Montesquieu's theory of three branches of government as theoretically unsound and practically never realized because it "violates the indivisibility of sovereignty."[33] On the other hand, he dealt in great detail with France, Germany, Russia and Japan, all of which, according to him, practiced "enlightened dictatorship" in varying degrees and all were now strong countries.[34] Liang's prescription for China's future thus went like this: (1) China should never look for a republican

---

29 Yin Ping (pseud. of Liang Ch'i-ch'ao), "K'ai-ming chuan-chih lun" (On Enlightened Dictatorship), *Hsin-min Ts'ung Pao,* No. 73, p. 11.

30 *Ibid.*, p. 14.

31 *Ibid.*, p. 11.

32 *Ibid.*, p. 13.

33 *Ibid.*, No. 75, p. 31.

34 *Ibid.*, No. 74, pp. 11-13.

constitution: (2) China today was not even ready to become a constitutional monarchy; and (3) China today should adopt a system of "enlightened dictatorship" as a transitional step before progressing to constitutional monarchy.[35]

Having just criticized Western democracy, Liang, however, went on to contradict himself. He soon turned to say that democracy was not really bad but rather it was far too advanced to be capable of realization not only in China, but in many advanced countries as well. Thus he declared: "A parliamentary system is good and all admire it. But even Japan and Germany do not practice it because they know their people are not up to it yet."[36] He said that the American colonies had constitutions even before their independence, and France had undergone six changes of government in seventy years and it was not clear now if the French were ready for a republic. "How long," he asked, "would it then take to make the Chinese ready for a republic?"[37]

Liang did not stop at rejecting Western democracy as a viable system for China, he went a step further. He declared that China was not even ready for what he defined as a system of constitutional monarchy, i.e., absolute power for the emperor and a parliament as an advisory body. In the last installment of his long treatise, he said not only were the Chinese not properly prepared for a constitution, but many basic requirements prior to the promulgation of a constitution were yet to be met. Among other things he listed the following: Absence of a nationality law, education not popularized, tax rates not unified, voting districts not set up, census not taken, judiciary system not well established, poor transportation facilities, etc.[38] All these, and many others, could not possibly be done in ten or even fifteen years, he asserted. "How can the revolutionists claim they can build a beautiful and perfect republic within a few years of a revolution that would see much bloodshed and unprecedented destruction?" he asked.[39] Even those for a constitutional monarchy were wrong in

35 *Ibid.*, No. 75, pp. 10-11.

36 *Ibid.*, p. 33.

37 *Ibid.*, pp. 24-25.

38 *Ibid.*, No. 77, pp. 7-9.

39 *Ibid.*, p. 9.

believing that a piece of paper decreed by the emperor would take care of all the problems, he added.[40] Liang's theme was by now clear beyond any doubt: Not only was republicanism unsuitable to China; even constitutional monarchy was too advanced a system for China under the existing circumstances. China, he believed, should adopt a system of "enlightened dictatorship" to prepare itself for the day when it would be ready to become a constitutional monarchy.

It would be difficult for one to follow Liang's argument through logically in view of his seemingly contradictory comments on Western democracy. In one breath, he criticized Western democracy as theoretically unsound but also called it too advanced a political system. The only explanation one can possibly offer, it appears, is Liang's eagerness to show that democracy was not for China. In addition, in view of Liang's sweeping criticism of Western democracy and his strong advocation of what he called an "enlightened dictatorship" in China, one may well question if he, living more than half a century before our time, really understood the essence of democracy at all. If one keeps in mind the fact that Liang's real objective was to prove that an enlightened dictatorship was best for China, one can perhaps better appreciate the lack of consistency in his argument as a result of his eagerness to justify his own stand.

The position of the royalists can be summed up thus: At the outset, they had basic distrust in what they understood as the Western democracy represented by either British parliamentary system or American federal republicanism. Moreover, they believed the Chinese people were not up to the level where they could practice democracy anyway. On the positive side, the royalists prescribed what they believed to be the best-suited system for China, namely, an "enlightened dictatorship" leading eventually to constitutional monarchy.

In their rebuttal, the revolutionists concentrated their fire on Liang's proposal of an enlightened dictatorship and on his assertion that the Chinese people were not up to the standard of practicing democracy. On the first point, Wang Ching-wei wrote that under the

---

40 *Ibid.*

so-called system of enlightened dictatorship, everything would depend on the ruler being an "enlightened" man and yet there was practically no way of assuring that such would be the case. "In a democracy, laws can prevent a ruler from abusing his power; under a dictatorship, there is no legitimate way of checking misrule, and merely hoping the ruler to be virtuous serves little purpose," Wang declared.[41] Recognizing the importance of the personality factor in politics, Wang insisted that laws were just as important, if not more so. "Liang's enlightened dictatorship apparently puts too much reliance on man and too little on law," he said.[42] And above all, an enlightened ruler "cannot be expected of the present government."[43] On the second point, Wang rejected Liang's contention that since the growth of democracy in the West dated back over 1,000 years, it was impossible for China to catch up in ten or twenty years. "If Liang's words are to be taken seriously, are we going to go through the various stages of European development before we can learn democracy? There is no reason why we can't imitate and learn fast," he retorted in a way that was typical of many of Sun Yat-sen's statements.[44] Besides, he continued, Chinese tradition was not completely void of democratic thought, citing the fact that feudalism was broken down in China as early as over 2,000 years ago. "The difference between China and the West in this regard is not a matter of substance, but a matter of degree, and this makes it easy for China to catch up," Wang asserted.[45] He further pointed out that while Western democracy stressed the importance of people, China, too, had a well-known tradition that "the mandate of heaven reflects the will of the people," and the difference here again was only a matter of degree.[46] "What we should do now is to foster the learning of the West and to develop what we have in our own cultural heritage in order to speed up the realization of democracy in China, not to retard the progress by idly

---

41 Wang Ching-wei, "Po *Hsin-min Ts'ung Pao* tsui-chin chih fei ko-ming lun" (A Rebuttal of the Recent Non-revolution Advocacy in the *Hsin-min Ts'ung Pao), Min Pao*, No. 4, p. 25.

42 *Ibid.*, p. 27.

43 *Ibid.*, p. 28.

44 *Ibid.*, p. 29.

45 *Ibid.*, p. 30.

46 *Ibid.*, p. 31.

wishing that an 'enlightened dictatorship' would be established by the Manchus," he concluded.[47]

Charges and counter-charges similar to those already cited, often repetitious and tedious, continued in the *Min Pao* and the *Hsin-min Ts'ung Pao* in the ensuing issues, but as far as the main theme of republicanism versus constitutional monarchy is concerned, there was little that had not been said.

The revolutionists' commitment to a republic was just as firm as that of the royalists to a constitutional monarchy. And the difference between the two was further widened by the fact that the monarchy to which the royalists were committed were Manchu. This fact made an already irreconcilable difference even more irreconcilable and strengthened the revolutionists' hatred of the royalists. The revolutionists advocated a republic for several reasons, as we have, through the words of the contemporaries, discussed above. First and foremost, they believed the republican form of government to be the most advanced in the West and that in learning from the West, there was no reason why China should not look for the best. Second, the revolutionists did not totally discount constitutional monarchy as a viable form of government, but they were adamant in insisting that it would not suit the situation in China, chiefly because China had had a system of absolute monarchy for so long, and anyone on the throne would likely continue to abuse the unlimited power. Besides, ambitious persons would continue to aspire to the throne and this would be a potential source of continued civil war. The sure way of preventing this naturally would be to do away with the monarchical system of government once and for all. Third, they insisted, a constitutional monarchy would not be possible in the true sense of the term under the Manchus, in view of the racial difficulties between the Manchus and the Hans. For their own survival and in order to ensure their continued rule of the vast nation as a minority ruler, the Manchus must continue to rely on discriminatory and repressive measures, which were diametrically opposed to what would be the situation under a genuine constitutional monarchy. Thus aside from their opposition to a constitutional monarchy as a matter of principle, the revolutionists were even more vehement in their

---

47 *Ibid.*, pp. 32-33.

opposition to a particular constitutional monarchy under the Manchus, because in their view, it was a theoretical and practical impossibility. Should one come into existence, it must be a disguised one.

On the other side, the royalists totally rejected democracy at the outset. Even though they advocated a constitutional monarchy, they made it quite clear what they sought ultimately was a constitutional monarchy patterned not after that of Britain, but that of Japan, under which the emperor would have undisputed authority. To the royalists, it mattered little whether or not a government was "of the people" and "by the people," as long as it was "for the people," to borrow Lincoln's famous phrases. They would be contented with an "enlightened dictatorship," dedicated to the welfare of the people. On these premises, they naturally opposed everything which the revolutionists advocated. Indeed after the diametrically opposed positions of the royalists and the revolutionists had been stated, the ensuing charges and counter-charges practically lost their meaning. It soon became clear that what was at issue here was not just a matter of substance but even more a matter of conviction. As is often in the case involving one's conviction, debate proves of little consequence in resolving differences, but would on the contrary only aggravate the antagonism between the parties. If a value judgement can be made of their respective positions, it can be said that while the royalists were primarily backward in their outlook, the revolutionists with all their good intentions were too far ahead of their time. In this regard, a student with some measure of familiarity with the American Revolution is apt to think of Randolph Adams' famed study of political philosophy of the American Revolution, in which he concluded that the ideals espoused by many revolutionary forerunners were too much ahead of their time.[48] An analogy may well be drawn here between the positions of the revolutionary forerunners of China and America.

DEBATE ON SOCIALISM

The second important subject of debate between the royalists and the revolutionists was Sun Yat-sen's controversial Principle of People's

48 Cf. Randolph G. Adams, *Political Ideas of the American Revolution* (New York: Barnes & Noble, 1958).

Livelihood. According to Sun, while the first two principles of his doctrine, Nationalism and Democracy, were designed to achieve a political revolution, the Principle of People's Livelihood was designed to achieve a "social revolution." As we pointed out in the previous chapter that during the period under review, Sun's ideas about this principle were far from being fully developed. In fact, his ideas continued to evolve well after the establishment of the republic. At this early stage, the Principle of People's Livelihood was expressed almost exclusively in Sun's proposed program of "equalization of land ownership." Even this program was at this time only conceived in rather vague terms, and none of its details were worked out. However, it is clear that in conceiving of this program, Sun had drawn primarily on socialist ideas. The royalists, on their part, were opposed both to the program and to a "social revolution," which in their opinion would do more harm than good to China. Although the debate was carried out on the issue of "equalization of land ownership," the implication went far beyond the immediate issue, for the debate in a real sense represented the first Chinese intellectual response to the novel idea of socialism which, like democracy, is primarily Western in origin. An examination of the debate will therefore help us understand to what extent socialism had exerted an influence in China during this period.

In their arguments on the necessity of a "social revolution" in China, the revolutionists followed the socialist line closely. They accepted the description of social injustice by the socialists that allegedly existed in many Western countries and were determined to prevent it from taking place in China. They were deeply concerned about the concentration of wealth in the Western capitalist countries. In typical socialist fashion, they regarded the concentration of wealth as the primary source of social injustice and other evils. Although China's economy was still in the pre-industrial stage and the fabulous rich had not yet appeared, they believed that preventive measures must be adopted so that China would not follow the same path of the Western capitalist countries. Since the people in the Western capitalist countries were already in distress and their governments were groping for ways to right the aggravating injustice, they said, China was indeed fortunate enough that it had not yet reached that stage and therefore was in a position to avoid it. If nothing was done, they believed, what had happened in the West would in time happen in China. It was therefore essential that along with the political revolution, a "social revolution" should be carried out simultaneously to forestall future economic and social problems. The program of the social revolution was Dr. Sun's "equalization of land ownership." The revolutionists believed that in pre-industrial China, the chief source of wealth was land. If this source of wealth could be regulated, future economic monopoly would not occur and the resulting social injustice would thus be forestalled. To put it in another way, the revolutionists believed that in seeking a solution to the economic problem in China, the first attention should be paid to the problem of distribution, and their program of "equalization of land ownership" was clearly aimed at solving the distribution problem.

Explaining the social ills of the West in typical socialist fashion and suggesting the proper policy for China, Feng Tzu-yu made one of the most detailed expositions of the revolutionary party's economic policy. His essay, first published in the *Chung-kuo Jih Pao* and later reprinted in the *Min Pao* in 1906, was said to have been written on the instructions of Sun Yat-sen.[49] Speaking of socialism as the tide of the day, Feng said:

> Technological improvement, increasing rent and decreasing wages gave rise to socialist parties in Europe, which are now very powerful, particularly in Germany. Socialists hold the majority in Germany's lower house, and all domestic policies in Germany are based on socialism. The growth rate of Germany's economy surpasses that of America and Britain. In France, the speaker of the lower house is a socialist. In Britain, Labor votes recently registered a sharp increase. In Russia, its revolution rocked the whole world. In many cases, the domestic policies of the socialists can be of help to our reform. . . In America, a Labor Party is growing in power, and socialism is overwhelming the new continent. In Japan, state socialism has been adopted. With socialism on the rise both in the West and in the East, how can China not be affected?[50]

---

49. Hu Han-min, "Tzu Chuan," p. 389.

50. Feng Tzu-yu, "Min-sheng chu-i yu Chung-kuo cheng-chih ko-ming chih ch'ien-t'u" (The Principle of People's Livelihood and the Future of China's Political Revolution), *Min Pao,* No. 4, pp. 98-99.

Continuing, Feng said that in the West, the disappearance of the tyranny of absolute monarchs was only followed by the rise of an even worse tyranny of plutocrats, under which monopoly was rampant and the masses of people fared more miserably than in previous days. He described the situation in England thus:

> According to the *London Times*, over 1,000,000 persons in London live on government relief. In another report, the *Times* said the rich built beautiful quarters for their dogs while the poor are left uncared for. If the gap between the rich and the poor is as wide as this in a country hailed as the mother of democracy, we can well imagine the situation in other countries.[51]

The comments on America almost resemble those we see in the Communist press nowadays:

> Standard Oil is the largest company in America. It has its own railroads, employs several million workers and has branches all over the world. It can, by a single move, affect the domestic business and international market. Its influence on the American government and Congress is very strong indeed. If the present trends continue, the President of America will soon be practically controlled by a few capitalists. Because they employ workers by the millions, they can easily use these voters to vote for their favorite candidates. In the end the President and members of Congress will be mere puppets of the few capitalists. The republican democracy in America is the fruit of much bloodshed, but it now is a tyranny by a few monopoly capitalists. This is hardly what George Washington, Benjamin Franklin, Abraham Lincoln and other great Americans had expected of their country. From the situation in America, one can easily understand that socialism is urgently needed.[52]

Having made all the prejudiced statements above, Feng, however, showed considerable restraint when he came to the central point of his article, namely, what system China should adopt. He declared that "extreme socialism is not suitable for China," and that "state socialism is the most desirable system," because it had been practiced in both Germany and Japan with good results.[53] Apparently following Sun's line, he said that in China the solution of the land problem was the most important task and the specific measure to be taken should be a

---

51 *Ibid.*, p. 100.

52 *Ibid.*, P. 101.

53 *Ibid.*, p. 109.

single tax system that would realize the goal of "equal enjoyment of land for all."[54]

While the revolutionists went to great lengths to show their concern over social injustice and to suggest a preventive policy in China, the royalists, on the other hand, were not impressed by their arguments. They criticized the revolutionists for misinterpreting the causes of social injustice, for misjudging the situation in China, and for suggesting a harmful policy. They believed that the most urgent economic problem in China was how to increase capital for industrial development, not the leveling of the already meagre wealth as the revolutionists had suggested. The Chinese economic problem had to do with poverty, not inequity, they asserted. What China needed was encouragement and protection for private enterprises in order to strengthen the economy, not a socialistic land policy that would enfeeble the already weak economy, they argued. Again it is advisable that we quote some contemporary sources to see how the royalists argued their case.

To begin with, the royalists were in substantial agreement with the revolutionists on the existence of social injustice in the Western countries. Liang Ch'i-ch'ao, too, was critical of the concentration of wealth in the West since industrial revolution, the laissez-faire economic doctrine, and the exploitation of the workers by the capitalists.[55] But the agreement ended there, for Liang believed that what had happened in the West would not necessarily happen in China, because of different historical and social backgrounds. In China, there was no great concentration of wealth as there was in many countries in the West. There existed no privileged aristocratic class in China, feudalism having broken down more than 2,000 years ago. In the absence of primogeniture, land holding, the chief source of wealth in agricultural China, had been fragmented through the centuries, he said. Given the different historical background and in view of the fact that China did not have monopolistic big business now, "there is no reason to assume that the difficulties of the West today are what we shall inevitably encounter

---

54. *Ibid.*, P. 118.

55 Liang Ch'i-ch'ao, "Cha-ta mou-pao" (Random Replies to a Certain Journal), *Hsin-min Ts'ung Pao,* No. 86, p. 9.

tomorrow," he asserted.[56] While the West was suffering from social injustice, its remedy should emphasize distribution; China was suffering from poverty, its remedy therefore should emphasize production. He rejected the land policy of the revolutionists, calling it an improvization based on ideas borrowed from Western utopian thinkers. What the revolutionists advocated, he said, was a system designed to "rob the rich of their possessions for distribution among the poor."[57] Just like Hung Hsiu-ch'uan, leader of the Taiping Rebellion, who alienated the intellectuals with his "religious revolution," the revolutionists would alienate the upper social stratum with their program of "social revolution," Liang said. "Their supporters will be primarily the poor and the illiterate, and even derelicts, gangsters and beggars, who would all go to share the wealth of the rich," Liang charged, adding: "I shudder to think what sort of government these people would be able to form!"[58]

Furthermore, Liang believed that the revolutionists were wrong in assuming that the concentration of wealth in the West, which had bred social injustice, was the result of concentration of land. This, he argued, was not the case. "Land concentration had taken place in the West long before the Industrial Revolution, but socialism did not appear until after the Industrial Revolution," he said.[59] In his opinion, capital, not land, was the most important factor. Liang admitted that unrestrained development of capitalism in the West had resulted in the present injustice, but if capitalism was to grow in China in the absence of an already established aristocratic class and under measured regulation, the same result would not occur.

As the difference between the revolutionists and the royalists appeared so wide and fundamental, it would be wrong, however, to come to the conclusion that Sun was a socialist and Liang was laissez-faire in his economic thinking. Although Sun did emphasize the problem of distribution and Liang did emphasize the problem of production, it must be noted that Sun had never expressed full

---

56 *Ibid.*, p. 16.

57 *Ibid.*, p. 20.

58 *Ibid.*, p. 21.

59 *Ibid.*, p. 22.

acceptance of socialism and Liang had never repudiated socialism in toto. Writing in Sun's behalf, both Feng Tzu-yu and Hu Han-min explicitly rejected "extreme socialism" as early as 1906.[60] The revolutionists had all along insisted that their land policy was a measure of state socialism, which they believed was suitable for China. In advocating private enterprises in China, Liang, too, relied more on what he believed to be their suitability in China rather than on the theory of laissez-faire economy. Moverover, considering the kind of constitutional monarchy championed by the royalists and the "enlightened dictatorship" advocated by Liang in particular, one will find it very unlikely that the royalists, while politically conservative, could possibly be economically so liberal as to advocate capitalism in China.

As to socialism, Liang on one occasion declared that he regarded socialism as a "noble and pure doctrine" and that he had high respect for it.[61] In fact, Liang said he was in favor of adopting some features of state socialism both during the period of "enlightened dictatorship" and after the promulgation of the constitution. He opposed the land policy of the revolutionists not because it was socialistic as such, but because he regarded it as too extreme a measure and furthermore because it was, in his opinion, unsuitable in China.[62] State socialism indeed provided a bridge between the royalists and the revolutionists. It may be concluded that while the political philosophies of the revolutionists and royalists are diametrically opposed, their difference in the field of economy is not irreconcilable. Even at this early stage, the difference appeared to be more a matter of degree than substance. There was a gap separating the royalists from the revolutionists as far as their economic thinking was concerned, but over that gap was a bridge provided by their agreement on the feasibility of some features of state socialism in China.

SUMMARY

The *Min Pao* was closed down by the Japanese government in November, 1908, after its twenty-fourth issue. The Japanese took the

60 *Min Pao,* No. 3, p. 11; No. 4, p. 109.

61 *Hsin-min Ts'ung Pao,* No. 79, p. 65.

62 *Ibid.*

action apparently at the urging of the Chinese government. A year later, Wang Ching-wei managed to secretly publish two more issues in Japan, Nos. 25 and 26, giving a Paris address. However, because of obvious difficulties, Wang was unable to continue his secret operation and the revolutionary organ thus ended its two-and-a-half year life. Earlier, the Japanese had politely but firmly asked Sun Yat-sen to leave Japan and Sun had sailed for Indo-China in March, 1907. In a letter to K'ang Yu-wei toward the end of 1908, Liang proudly wrote that with their leader banished and their organ banned, the revolutionists were "totally suppressed."[63] Actually, Liang's *Hsin-min Ts'ung Pao* had been closed down by the Japanese a year before the *Min Pao.* The successive disappearance of the two organs all but ended the war of words between the revolutionists and the royalists, although the issues over which the war had been waged were by no means resolved. It is true that the parties to the debate used many terms translated from Western languages in an ambiguous way which often caused confusion as to their exact meanings. It is also true that the debate at times sank to a low level, aimed chiefly at personal attacks. But the debate, as documented in the two journals, more than anything else served to put in sharp focus the issues over which the revolutionists and the royalists were divided.

In the political field, from Liang's criticism of Western parliamentary system, and from his advocation of an "enlightened dictatorship" as the first step toward a constitutional monarchy, one may conclude that as far as his political ideas were concerned, Liang was far from being a modern man. His understanding of democracy, to say the least, was partial and he primarily belonged to the generation that was too deeply steeped in the system of absolute monarchy to accept any novel idea. His confidence in an absolute monarchy was evident in his writings. Liang relied chiefly on Japanese sources and their translation in Chinese for his knowledge of Western democracy and for his criticism of it. He did not seem to bother with the fact that in Western countries, democracy was won only through long and arduous struggles. He rather naively believed that constitutionalism somehow could be equated to a system of benevolent absolutism in a monarchy.

---

63 Ting Wen-chiang, *op. cit.,* Vol. I, p. 245.

On the other hand, the revolutionists from the beginning of the debate actually had spoken a different language. They advocated constitutionalism in the Western sense of the word. Having spent the better part of his life abroad, it was natural that Sun Yat-sen was familiar with the actual workings of Western democracy. His observation was augmented by a knowledge gained through tireless readings of Western books. Although most articles in the *Min Pao* were penned by others, the important ones were done on his instruction, as Hu Han-min testified. Wang Ching-wei, too, mentioned several times that he was writing to expound Sun's ideas.[64] Considering the existing situation in China, they concluded that in order to make democracy possible in China, either under republican or monarchical form of government, a revolution to overthrow the Manchu government was necessary. Since the heavy price of a revolution was to be paid anyway, a republican form of government–the most advanced–should be adopted after the revolution.

A word should be said at this point about the relevance of the royalist position to the situation today. There are those who believe that the Chinese people tolerate some degree of totalitarianism and that Mao Tse-tung is but the latest in a cycle of innovators in the long Chinese history.[65] The implication is that history proves that the totalitarian Communist regime on mainland China today can be accepted by the Chinese people. Such argument is not well-founded. True the royalists did argue in favor of an "enlightened" absolute monarchy, but they did so only because they were backward-looking and did not understand democracy in its true sense. Later events such as Yuan Shih-k'ai's effort to install himself as emperor, which cost him his life, and the abortive attempt to reinstate the deposed Manchu Emperor P'u Yi, were examples showing that the Chinese people, despite their long monarchical tradition, were quick to reject both dictatorship and monarchy. The emergence of a totalitarian Communist regime on the Chinese mainland is a tragic event, but to try to provide that regime with historical sanction is unjustified.

---

64 *Min Pao*, No. 3, pp. 11, 14. Wang twice said his articles in the first two issues of *Min Pao* were "expressing Mr. Sun's views."

65 John K., Fairbank, *United States and China* (Cambridge: Harvard University Press, 1962), pp. 3-4 and 278.

In the economic field, we have discussed the difference between the revolutionists and the royalists in regard to socialism and the fact that both sides were in favor of state socialism. The latter is an important point because the revolutionists had consistently spoken in favor of state socialism. When Sun Yat-sen's economic program was spelled out in greater detail much later, it showed itself to be clearly a mixed economy, blending state and private enterprises. What Sun had advocated was neither utopia nor what has come to be known as "scientific" socialism. Despite the Chinese Communists' efforts to claim heir to Sun Yat-sen's economic thinking, the truth cannot be distorted. As a recent study has pointed out: "Communism is not the logical end result of the kind of revolution that Dr. Sun Yat-sen was championing for his country. Sun Yat-senism did not become fused into Communism, nor does the Communist victory represent the inevitable outcome of the revolution to which Dr. Sun devoted his life."[66]

66 Leng and Palmer, *op. cit.*, p. 180.

Chapter V
ESTABLISHMENT OF BRANCHES

The importance of the overseas activities of the Chinese revolutionists cannot be over-emphasized. It is all too obvious that both the T'ung-meng Hui and its predecessor, the Hsing-chung Hui, were established abroad and that Sun Yat-sen spent most of his revolutionary years on foreign soil. In addition, the first and most consistent supporters of the revolution were numerous overseas Chinese in Southeast Asia, the Americas, and other places. The overseas Chinese helped the revolutionary cause in many ways, but the most important contribution they made was undoubtedly in providing funds. In one way or another, the overseas Chinese did much to finance Sun Yat-sen's revolutionary movement, from the birth of the embryonic organization in Honolulu in 1894, through numerous military campaigns, to the establishment of the republic in 1912. It is indeed not an overstatement to say that without the overseas Chinese, the revolution would not have been possible in the first place. Sun Yat-sen, who knew this better than anybody else, often expressed his debt to the overseas Chinese by calling them the "mother of the revolution." In working among the overseas Chinese the revolutionists knew perfectly well that the first task was to build effective organizations and to establish liaison centers. This job they did with considerable success. With their branch offices and contact points established, either openly or secretly, in almost any place where there was a concentration of Chinese, the revolutionists were able to propagate their cause, to recruit new members, and most important of all, to enlist financial support. In establishing branches abroad and in their work among the overseas Chinese, the revolutionists were quick to adapt their techniques to local conditions. In some cases, they approached prominent local merchants and made use of their influence in local Chinese communities; in other cases, able cadres were dispatched to different localities to head the local branches; in still other cases, alliances were made with local secret societies to win them over to the revolutionary cause. In many areas, where the local governments were not at all favorable to the revolutionists, branches were outwardly known as clubs, libraries or bookstores, where revolutionary propaganda literature was supplied free. This was particularly true in Southeast Asia, which was then largely under British and Dutch colonial rule. Invariably at each strategic point, a newspaper was published by the revolutionists to serve as their organ, and a bookstore or club became the secret liaison center for the revolutionists. Considering the difficult circumstances under which the revolutionists labored at the time, one must admit that they did remarkably well in pushing the revolutionary movement among the overseas Chinese. To be sure, the revolutionists were constantly faced with difficulties, particularly in their fund-raising drives, but on balance, their success was admirable. This chapter will trace the expansion of branches at home as well as abroad, with particular attention paid to the fund-raising campaigns.

BRANCHES ABROAD AND AT HOME

A quick look at the situation immediately preceding the formation of the T'ung-meng Hui is in order. In Hong Kong, Ch'en Shao-pai, one of Sun Yat-sen's closest associates, was publishing the revolutionary organ *Chung-kuo Jih Pao.* However, the Hsing-chung Hui branch there, which Ch'en headed, was practically idle after two earlier uprisings, one in Canton in 1895 and the other in Huichow in 1900. The *Chung-kuo Jih Pao* was often in financial straits and several times it came close to folding up its printing press. For several years after 1900, Hong Kong had not been in the news as far as the revolution was concerned. It was not until after the formation of the T'ung-meng Hui in Tokyo in 1905 that Hong Kong again became a center both for liaison and for plotting revolts.

In America, although Sun Yat-sen had joined the Chih-kung T'ang and revised its constitution to include revolutionary planks as early as 1904 while he was in San Francisco, there was no evidence that he had succeeded in getting a large following from the overseas Chinese who, as pointed out earlier, were more interested in their own business and were only lukewarm toward Sun's revolutionary cause. There were

Hsing-chung Hui branches in Honolulu and San Francisco, but again their chief activities were limited to publishing newspapers. Besides, these newspapers had to fight the royalist influence and they generally suffered from the lack of able and full-time staff.

In the British and Dutch colonies in Southeast Asia, where Sun was banned for five years after the Huichow revolt in 1900, there had never been any Hsing-chung Hui branches, although Sun did have some contact with a few comrades and community leaders in Singapore. This handful of revolutionists and their supporters, too, were chiefly engaged in propaganda work, publishing papers, distributing revolutionary literature, and sponsoring occasional public speeches and rallies. Elsewhere in Southeast Asia, there was little organized effort among the overseas Chinese communities. The only places in the world where Sun was able to establish new organizations prior to the T'ung-meng Hui were several European capitals, which Sun visited early in 1905 and successfully persuaded the Chinese students there to organize several revolutionary groups. Sun Yat-sen of course fully realized the importance of overseas Chinese as an inexhaustible source of funds, supporters, and new recruits. Southeast Asia, with well over ninety per cent of overseas Chinese living there, naturally was uppermost on Sun's mind. In addition, Sun and many of the revolutionists were from South China, and therefore were frequently kin to the overseas Chinese, who were overwhelmingly of South China origin.

After the formation of the T'ung-meng Hui, the revolutionists quickly took steps to expand their organization through various ways. To facilitate the review of the growth of the T'ung-meng Hui both at home and abroad, a geographical breakdown, aided by a chronological order, seems to be appropriate.

Hong Kong – Because of its location as a gateway to mainland China and because previous revolts were planned here, Hong Kong was given immediate attention. Not long after the inauguration of the T'ung-meng Hui, Feng Tzu-yu and Li Tzu-chung were sent to Hong Kong from Tokyo with instructions to form branches in Hong Kong and Macao as well as in Canton across the borders. The appointment, issued by Sun Yat-sen on September 8, 1905, reads as follows:

> Sun Wen, Chairman of the Revolutionary T'ung-meng Hui of China, hereby entrusts Members Feng Tzu-yu and Li Tzu-chung with the mission of contacting comrades in Hong Kong, Macao, and Canton. Messrs. Feng and Li are patriotic and honest and are worthy of the duty entrusted to them by the T'ung-meng Hui. Messrs. Feng and Li are hereby given the power to accept and approve membership applications from those who wish to join the T'ung-meng Hui.[1]

After their arrival in Hong Kong later that year, Feng and Li worked with Ch'en Shao-pai to establish a T'ung-meng Hui branch there. To show that the new organization was different from its predecessor, all those who previously belonged to the Hsing-chung Hui were required to sign a pledge anew in order to qualify for membership in the T'ung-meng Hui. Ch'en Shao-pai was elected chairman and Feng, secretary.[2] Meanwhile, Feng, who previously was Tokyo correspondent for the *Chung-kuo Jih Pao,* now took over as editor and Li became a gymnastic teacher at a Hong Kong Chinese school.[3] The next year, Feng was elected chairman of the Hong Kong branch. From 1906 to 1907, the T'ung-meng Hui, through the Hong Kong branch, penetrated deep into three provinces, Kwangtung, Kwangsi and Fukien, all in south China. Agents were sent out from Hong Kong to many places to set up secret contact points and to recruit new members. Largely through personal acquaintances, these agents strove to establish ties with people of all levels. Secret agents were recruited in over a dozen major cities of the three provinces. Some of these people were store owners, others were school teachers. But the most important were those connected with the New Army and the secret societies. The secret societies in Ch'aochow and Huichow, and the New Army in Fangch'eng, infiltrated by the revolutionists to varying degrees, all figured in later revolts. From 1907 to 1908, it was claimed, over 200 hard core members were added to the Hong Kong branch.[4] In 1907, no less than four small-scale uprisings were attempted in eastern Kwangtung, with secret society

---

1 Feng Tzu-yu, *Chung-hua-min-kuo k'ai-kuo-ch'ien ko-ming shih,* Vol. I, p. 197 & illust. 6.

2 *Ibid.,* p. 176.

3 *Ibid.,* p. 197.

4 *Ibid.,* p. 179.

members as the main force. These uprisings failed one after another, and the Hong Kong branch was involved in uprisings in many ways.

Hong Kong was an important place either for buying arms or transhipping arms to and from other places, such as Japan. In 1909, a secret branch was established in Canton, capital of Kwantung, and it was said that in that year, over 2,000 persons joined the T'ung-meng Hui in Hong Kong and Canton. However, the figure is deceptive for most of them were soldiers in the New Army. They were said to have been won over to the revolutionary cause, thanks to the work of a junior officer in the New Army, Ni Ying-tien, who was a revolutionist. There was no record of just exactly how many of them had actually joined the revolutionary party, for none of them ever signed a pledge.[5] However, there is no doubt about the sentiment of many of those in the New Army who were stationed in Canton, for in January of the following year, they staged a revolt under the leadership of Ni and others. Apparently because of the increasing tempo of activities in South China, a new South China chapter of the T'ung-meng Hui, in addition to the Hong Kong branch, was established in late 1909 with Hu Han-min as head and Wang Ching-wei as secretary.[6] There was a division of labor between the two seemingly overlapping organizations, with the Hong Kong branch concentrating on party expansion and the South China chapter having overall charge over military affairs.[7] The revolt of the New Army in Canton in 1910 and the uprising of April 27, 1911, for example, were both plotted by the South China chapter, with the Hong Kong branch playing a supporting role.

The Americas – During his lifetime, Dr. Sun Yat-sen visited the American continent four times, staying for varying lengths. The first visit took place in 1896. He arrived in San Francisco in June, and during the ensuing three months, he crossed the American continent to New York, stopping at many cities en route to preach revolution among the overseas Chinese. That trip was far from fruitful, for he found the overseas Chinese in America "very conservative" and in each of the cities he visited, only "a few or a dozen showed any interest in what I

5 *Ibid.*, p. 181.

6 *Ibid.*, p. 182.

7 Feng Tzu-yu, "Chi Chung-kuo T'ung-meng Hui," p. 152.

preached."[8] He admitted that this trip "helped very little" the future revolution.[9] The second visit took place in 1904, when he spent the good part of the year again in a cross-continent tour in an effort to establish contact with the Chih-kung T'ang. This effort was not very successful either, as noted earlier. However, he did lay the groundwork for closer relations with the secret society of overseas Chinese in America, and in particular he succeeded in converting the *Ta-t'ung Jih Pao* (Great Commonwealth Daily), organ of the Chih-kung T'ang in San Francisco, to the revolutionary cause.[10] His third visit, in1909-1910, was important. It was during this five-month visit that he succeeded in establishing T'ung-meng Hui branches in a number of cities in the United States. Dr. Sun's last visit to the American continent was in 1911, when he also visited Canada. The chief purpose of this trip was fund-raising. It was in Denver, Colorado, that he learned of the successful uprising in Wuch'ang on October 10, which eventually led to the downfall of the Manchu Dyansty.

In his work among the overseas Chinese in America, Sun, aside from appealing to kinship among his Cantonese brethren, paid particular attention to the Chih-kung T'ang. He joined the Chih-kung T'ang as a member in January, 1904 while in Hawaii. In March, he arrived in San Francisco, where the Chih-kung T'ang had its general headquarters. On his arrival, he was held by the immigration authorities for illegal entry. It was the Chih-king T'ang president, Huang San-teh, who, together with some of Sun's Christian friends, helped to secure his release.[11] In the ensuing month, Sun toured the continent to preach revolution among the overseas Chinese, accompanied by Huang. Although the immediate result of his campaign was not satisfactory, Sun kept up his contact with the Chih-kung T'ang leaders. He fully realized that the Chih-kung T'ang, with branches in many cities, was potentially more important as a source of support than any local clan or fraternity organizations. Despite the fact that the Chih-kung T'ang was rather

---

8 *Kuo-fu ch'uan-shu,* p. 33.

9 *Ibid.*

10 Shao-nien Chung-kuo Ch'en-pao wu-shih chou-nien chi-nien chuan-k'an (Fiftieth Anniversary Special Commemorating Collection of the *Young China Morning Paper)* (San Francisco; *Young China Morning Paper,* 1960), p. 40.

11 *Ibid.,* p. 39.

inactive, there was at the time no other organization which could claim membership all over America. Sun's continued efforts to woo the Chih-kung T'ang culminated in a successful fund-raising campaign jointly conducted by the Chih-kung T'ang and the T'ung-meng Hui on the eve of the 1911 revolution.

Sun's first fund-raising drive in the American continent was conducted in 1904 while in San Francisco. Believing that Christians were more enlightened and more susceptible to new ideas, he preached among his Christian friends in San Francisco, hoping to establish a Hsing-chung Hui branch there. One day at a meeting held at a local Presbyterian church, following a captivating speech, Sun urged those in the audience to help the revolutionary cause by purchasing his "revolutionary army bonds." At a face value of ten dollars, each bond would be refunded with 100 dollars after the revolution. He added that those buying the bonds would automatically become members of the Hsing-chung Hui. However, the second part of his statement drew a negative response from those attending the meeting. The overseas Chinese had a practical consideration: they had relatives in China and they did not want them to get in trouble. They were willing to help with funds, but they were reluctant to become known as members of Sun's revolutionary organization. Sun was quick to realize their position. He thereupon declared: The purpose of the meeting was raising funds, and whether or not anyone cared to become a member of the revolutionary society was a matter of one's own choice. On his part, Sun added, he would be only too glad to respect the free will of each of them. To further ease their fears, Sun assured them that since the bond would not carry the name of the owner, anyone buying one would be protected from having his true identity revealed. His assurances paid off, for many in the audience rose to buy his bonds afterwards. In all, Sun was said to have sold over $4,000 worth of his "revolutionary army bonds" on that occasion.[12] This money made possible his cross-continent tour in the ensuing months in the company of Huang San-teh, president of the Chih-kung T'ang.

Sun's effort in winning over the *Ta-t'ung Jih Pao* is a good case of the revolutionist-royalist struggle abroad. The paper, although a

---

12 *Ibid.*, p. 75.

Chih-kung T'ang organ, was quite independent in its editorial policy. It was largely left in the hands of its editor, one Ou Chu-chia, who was a royalist by persuasion. At the time that Sun arrived in San Francisco in 1904, Ou started to attack Sun in his paper, and said among other things that the Chih-kung T'ang members should not be fooled by the revolutionists. Sun was by now already a sworn member of the Chih-kung T'ang and he was on good terms with its president Huang San-teh. Not bothering to distinguish between the revolutionists and the royalists, Huang, in a brotherly spirit typical of the secret societies, urged Ou to stop his attack and join forces with Sun. This Ou found difficult to oblige, because he was a faithful disciple of K'ang Yu-wei. Huang was quite annoyed and eventually decided to expel Ou from his organization. Sun lost no time stepping in to take over the paper. He first recommended Feng Tzu-yu as the paper's Tokyo correspondent and then placed a revolutionist, Liu Ch'eng-yu, in the post vacated by Ou. Liu sailed from Tokyo and entered the United States as a student.[13] On his arrival in San Francisco in late 1904, Liu became editor of the *Ta-t'ung Jih Pao.* For the first time, a revolutionary organ appeared in the American continent.

Branches of the T'ung-meng Hui were not established in the American continent until 1909, when Sun made his third visit there. From Europe, where he had travelled in France and England in a fruitless effort to get financial help, he sailed across the Atlantic and arrived in New York in Novermber, 1909. He was met by many of his Chih-kung T'ang friends. A few days later, a East America branch of the T'ung-meng Hui was formed in New York.[14] Travelling westward from New York, he successively established a Central America branch in Chicago and a West America branch in San Francisco. Even before the establishment of this branch, some revolutionists in San Francisco had already organized a society, known as the Shao-nien Hsueh She (Youth Study Club), and they were already in correspondence with the T'ung-meng Hui office in Hong Kong. As a matter of fact, they had received a communication from Hu Han-min, then head of the T'ung-meng Hui's South China chapter, giving cognizance to their

---

13 Feng Tzu-yu, *Chung-hua-min-kuo k'ai-kuo-ch'ien ko-ming shih,* Vol. I, p. 149.

14 *Shao-nien Chung-kuo Ch'en-pao wu-shih chou-nien chi-nien chuan-k'an,* p. 44.

organization and appointing Li Shih-nan as their head.[15] The West America branch later took in all the members of the Youth Study Club. Not long after its inauguration, the West America branch became the T'ung-meng Hui's general office in America. More branches, directly subordinate to it, were established in other cities. While the exact number of T'ung-meng Hui members in America at any given time is unavailable, it was said that before Sun left San Francisco for Hawaii in March 1910, "several hundred" new members were added to various branches.[16] Meanwhile, Feng Tzu-yu was sent to Canada to join the *Ta-han Jih Pao* (Great Han Daily) in Vancouver in 1910 and to set up a T'ung-meng Hui branch there. He, too, collaborated closely with the Chih-kung T'ang. So successful was his work that the Chih-kung T'ang sold its estate in Vancouver to support the April 28 uprising in Canton in 1911.[17]

In January, 1911, Sun arrived in New York from Europe for his fourth, and last visit. Like his trips before, his mission was to raise funds. This time he scored an impressive success with the Chih-kung T'ang. Arriving in San Francisco in June, he made the office of the *Young China Morning Paper* his temporary headquarters and immediately set in motion his fund-raising drive. An agency was established to issue the Gold Bonds of the Republic of China, with denominations of 10, 100, 1,000 dollars. However, he soon found out that it was difficult forthe T'ung-meng Hui to push the drive without the full cooperation of the Chih-kung T'ang. He sought out Huang San-teh and other leaders of the Chih-kung T'ang and proposed a fusion of the two organizations. His proposal was accepted in principle, and the formula finally worked out for the merger called for the unconditional admission of all T'ung-meng Hui members to the Chih-kung T'ang. This was a success for Sun, considering the usual reluctance of the secret society to accept a large number of outsiders without even going through the rituals and other routine formalities. To effect the decision, the T'ung-meng Hui branch and the Chih-kung T'ang each issued a statement, respectively

---

15 *Ibid.*, p. 76.

16 *Ibid.*

17 *Chung-kuo Kuo-min-tang ch'i-shih-nien ta-shih nien-piao* (Chronology of the kuomintang During the Past Seventy Years) (Taipei: Committee for the Compilation of Party History, 1964), p. 18.

informing their comrades and "brothers" of the move. With his followers now officially on brotherhood terms with the Chih-kung T'ang members, Sun realized that the time was ripe for an organized fund-raising drive under the auspices of the Chih-kung T'ang. A special fund-raising agency was soon established to conduct a nation-wide campaign.

Southeast Asia.--After the failure of the Huichow uprising in 1900, several revolutionists fled to Singapore and Yu Lieh, one of Sun's earliest associates, was among them. It may be recalled that Yu and Sun, together with two others, were known as "four great rebels" at the time when Sun was still a medical student in Hong Kong. After his arrival in Singapore, Yu, while practicing medicine, organized a society known as the Chung-ho T'ang to propagate the anti-Manchu revolution. His propaganda work seemed to be as successful as his medical practice, for within a few years, Chung-ho T'ang branches were established in Penang, Kuala Lumpur and other places, and many local secret society members became his followers.[18] Meanwhile, Yu became acquainted with several rich Singapore Chinese merchants, including Ch'en Ch'u-nan, who operated several lumber mills and canneries; and Chang Yung-fu, who was in the garment business. Both Ch'en and Chang were considered quite progressive compared with other businessmen at the time, for they read such publications as *Hsin-min Ts'ung Pao,* and they were deeply interested in the affairs of the mother country. At the height of the *Su Pao* case in 1903, for example, they sent a message to the British consul in Shanghai, urging the protection of Chang Ping-lin and Tsou Yung as political criminals.[19] This was regarded as the first explicit support for the revolutionary cause by the Chinese residents in Nan-yang, or South Sea, a geographical term which the Chinese then used to denote the area of today's Malaysia, Indonesia, the Philippines and Oceania. Later, they were said to have reprinted 5,000 copies of Tsou Yung's *Ko-ming chun* and smuggled them back to their native province of Kwangtung for free distribution.[20] As a further step in

---

18 Feng Tzu-yu, *Chung-hua-min-kuo k'ai-kuo-ch'ien ko-ming shih,* Vol. II, p. 105.

19 *Ibid.,* p. 106.

20 *Ibid.*

promoting the revolutionary cause, Ch'en and Chang put up a sum to publish a newspaper, *T'u-nan Jih Pao* (Develop South Daily), which made its debut in early 1904. Within a year of its publication, the paper was said to have increased its circulation from some 30 copies to over 2,000 copies.[21] Yu Lieh helped by sending for some of his friends in Hong Kong to come to staff the newspaper.

Having read a copy of the *T'u-nan Jih Pao* while in the United States and through his correspondence with Yu Lieh, Sun was heartened to learn of the budding revolutionary movement in Nan-yang, the region that covers present Southeast Asia. He was anxious to meet his new supporters. On his way from Europe to Japan in the summer of 1905, he wrote to Yu Lieh, expressing his wish to meet his new comrades in Singapore when his ship stopped off there. On the day the ship arrived, however, Sun found himself barred from landing because the five-year ban on him had not expired. Yu, together with Ch'en Ch'u-nan and Chang Yung-fu, boarded the ship to meet Sun. After the meeting, Sun continued his voyage to Tokyo, meanwhile keeping up correspondence with Ch'en. En route to Saigon, he wrote to Ch'en, expressing great pleasure at making his acquaintance and telling Ch'en that he was going to Tokyo to found a large organization for "early action." He spoke of many "enthusiastic comrades" he met in Saigon, and said that he expected to return to Nan-yang in two or three months to help with the revolutionary work there.[22] Having found the T'ung-meng Hui in Tokyo in August that year, he left Tokyo for Saigon en route to Europe in the winter on a fund-raising trip, and returned to the East in early spring the next year. He arrived in Singapore in April, 1906, this time with the founding of a branch there in mind. He landed without trouble as the five-year ban had already expired. A Singapore branch was soon set up as the revolutionary center for the Nan-yang area, embracing the British and the Dutch colonies. Ch'en Ch'u-nan was elected head of the branch and Chang Yung-fu his deputy.[23] The Singapore branch of the T'ung-meng Hui started off with twelve members, but the membership eventually grew to over 500 persons. A

---

21 *Ibid.*, p. 107.

22 *Ibid.*, p. 115.

23 *Chung-kuo Kuo-min-tang ch'i-shih-nien ta-shih nien-piao*, p. 12.

partial list compiled by Feng Tzu-yu contains the names of 248 members.[24] In organizing the Singapore branch, Sun adroitly appealed to the provincialism prevailing among the overseas Chinese. An appendix to the constitution of the Singapore branch specified that members were to be divided into four groups according to their native places, namely, those from Fukien province, Ch'aochow, Canton, and those speaking Hakka dialect. Each group was to elect a representative to keep contact with the T'ung-meng Hui branch office and from every ten members in the group, one person was to be elected to be responsible for keeping the members in touch with the others. This design was said to have been drafted by Hu Han-min and adopted at the founding meeting of the Singapore branch in late 1906.[25]

Meanwhile the *T'u-nan Jih Pao,* the revolutionary organ, which had been financed almost single-handedly by Ch'en since inception, was suffering from financial difficulties. To alleviate the plight, funds from other businessmen had to be sought. Eventually several others joined in supporting the paper, and with the coming of the new sponsors, the paper was reorganized to be known as the *Nan-yang Tsung-hui Pao* (South Sea General Daily). The new members on the board of directors, however, were less enthusiastic about revolution. As a matter of fact, they soon interfered with the paper's editorial policy by putting several persons with known royalist leanings on the editorial staff. A cleavage developed within the paper, which subsequently led to an open split between the opposing factions. Ch'en and his followers withdrew from the paper, whereupon the paper came completely under the control of the royalists. The revolutionists, however, did not give up. Ch'en and a number of others started another paper in 1907, known as the *Chung-hsing Pao* (Restoration Daily), which at one time or another boasted of such figures as Hu Han-min, Wang Ching-wei, T'ao Ch'eng-chang and others on its editorial staff. With the ban of the *Min Pao* and the *Hsin-min Ts'ung Pao* in Tokyo, the *Chung-hsing Pao* for some time engaged the *Nan-yang Tsung-hui Pao* in a continued revolutionists versus royalists debate. The debate apparently stimulated

---

24 Feng Tzu-yu, *Chung-hua-min-kuo k'ai-kuo-ch'ien ko-ming shih,* Vol. II, pp. 112-14.

25 *Ko-ming wen-hsien,* Vol. II, pp. 245-46.

the interest of the Nan-yang Chinese, for by 1909, the circulation of the *Chung-hsing Pao* went up to over 4,000.[26]

After the Singapore branch was established, agents were sent out on trips to various cities where Chinese congregated to make contact with local Chinese community leaders in an effort to establish more branches or set up liaison centers. Several branches were successively established, among which were the one at Kuala Lumpur and another at Penang, both set up in August, 1906.[27] Both Kuala Lumpur and Penang had large number of Chinese residents, and in both cases, prominent local Chinese businessmen became branch heads. Liaison centers were subsequently set up in over 100 towns throughout the British and Dutch colonies in the Nan-yang area.[28] These centers could be a bookstore, a library, an overseas Chinese school, an ordinary store, or just an individual. The most noteworthy technique the revolutionists employed in extending their influence in the Nan-yang area was the opening of a rather peculiar kind of store, known as the "shu pao she," or "book and magazine store," throughout the British and Dutch colonies. Invariably these stores were run by local Chinese, selling books, journals and newspapers but also distributing revolutionary propaganda. In most areas, where transportation was poor and people were rather uncommunicative, these stores naturally became information centers, playing the vital role of disseminating information and bringing the toiling Chinese residents into contact with the outside world. In the British colonies, over 100 such stores were either set up by or connected with the revolutionists on the eve of the 1911 revolution.[29] In the Dutch colonies, many such stores were affiliated with local Chinese schools. These schools were often short of competent teachers and the revolutionists spared no effort in helping them out. On many occasions, they helped to recruit people with known revolutionary leanings from China as well as from among Chinese students in Japan to serve as teachers in these schools. Through

---

26 Feng Tzu-yu, *Chung-hua-min-kuo k'ai-kuo-ch'ien ko-ming shih,* Vol. II, p. 122.

27 *Chung-kuo Kuo-min-tang ch'i-shih-nien ta-shih nien-piao,* pp.12-13.

28 *Hsin-hai ko-ming,* Vol. II, p. 53.

29 Feng Tzu-yu, *Chung-hua-min-kuo k'ai-kuo-ch'ien ko-ming shih,* Vol. II, pp. 134-137.

their students, these teachers were able to bring revolutionary ideas to the parents. In addition, their bookstores were exerting an educating influence on the general public.

After the establishment of the Singapore branch in early 1906, Sun returned to Tokyo. A year later, when he was expelled from Japan, he sailed for Indo-China and arrived in Hanoi in March, 1907. Sun's first contact with Chinese in Indo-China dated back as early as 1902, when he was invited by the French governor there to attend the Hanoi trade fair. While there, he associated himself with several rich merchants who were sympathetic with his revolutionary cause, and with the local Cantonese clan organizations. After the T'ung-meng Hui was organized in Tokyo, three branches were soon set up in Hanoi, Saigon and Haiphong respectively by local Chinese residents.[30] After his arrival in Hanoi in 1907, however, Sun not only established a headquarters, but also made a great effort to associate the revolutionary cause with local secret societies. Through his efforts, he was able to give at least assemblance of unity to the twenty-eight different societies among the Chinese in Indo-China. These societies, or tongs, as they were called, although of the same origin, had been feuding among themselves. Sun tried to smooth over their differences and in the meantime to remind them of their original anti-Manchu purposes, as he did to the Chih-kung T'ang in the United States. However, the more significant activity carried out by Sun while in Indo-China was not in his work among the secret societies, but in the military field. The one year period after Sun's arrival in Hanoi saw a series of daring military actions by the revolutionists, using Indo-China as a base from which to launch military campaigns. So alarmed were the French authorities that despite their early sympathy with Sun, they complied with the request of the Manchu government to expel him from Indo-China in March, 1908. All told, during the period from April 1907 to March, 1908, no less than six of what Dr. Sun later described as the ten abortive uprisings were launched in south China, and four of them were staged from Indo-China across the south China border. Overseas Chinese in Indo-China helped generously in these campaigns. Many not only exhausted their fortunes, but were ordered to leave the country after

---

30 *Hsin-hai ko-ming,* Vol. II, p. 67.

1908.[31] Expelled from Indo-China, Sun went to Singapore and for a while devoted himself to party-building and fund-raising.

Before 1908, in the Nan-yang area, as we have already noted, there were T'ung-meng Hui branches in many cities and a network of liaison centers scattered throughout the British and Dutch colonies. But the branch offices were generally independent of each other and there was relatively little direct connection between them as far as their activities were concerned. This was even more so between the liaison centers and other individuals. Above all, there was no single office to oversee and coordinate the activities in the whole area. Sun knew full well that in party-building, organization was important and he immediately took action to strengthen the organization after his arrival in Singapore. A Nan-yang regional office was established in Singapore in the autumn of 1908 to take charge of the party affairs in the whole area, and Hu Han-min, who followed Sun from Hanoi to Singapore after the failure of another military campaign a few months later, was put in charge of the new office. Among the important steps taken by the Nan-yang office to strengthen the organization were the promulgation of a uniform constitution for all local branches in the area and the setting up of a ground rule for periodical correspondence between them. The constitution, containing sixteen articles, was patterned after the constitution of the T'ung-meng Hui at Tokyo, but in a simplified form. It was distributed among all existing branches for implementation and was to be followed for the establishment of new branches. The most significant innovation in this constitution was Article XIII, which provided for the organization of all members according to that of the revolutionary army in order to ensure close contact among them. It called for a squad as the basic unit, consisting of eight persons. Three squads were to form a platoon, four platoons a company and four companies a battalion, totalling 405 persons.[32] A notice accompanying the constitution particularly emphasized the importance of this organizational setup in enhancing close relationship among the members, providing efficient communication and strengthening the organization. "Whenever the branch office issues an order," the notice stated,

---

31 *Ibid.*

32 *WSNWH*, Ser. I, No. 11, p. 504.

"the order will go to the company commanders and through the channel down to the squad leaders. In this way, each person only has to inform four others. When the order reaches the squad level, each squad leader will have no difficulty in transmitting it to the seven members of his squad. In collecting membership dues, the reverse order will be followed. The organization will therefore remain effective even if the membership in a certain place increases to several thousand."[33]

In addition to promulgating the constitution, Sun also distributed a personal letter to all local organizations, including local branches and liaison centers, containing the ground rules for correspondence between them. First, a list of all local organizations was attached to the letter, and each organization was required to communicate with all the others at least once every other month. Second, each organization was required to report any change of address to the Nan-yang regional office. Third, in case of the establishment of a new organization, the Nan-yang regional office would notify all the others of the news, and all were asked to send congratulatory messages to the new organization and keep up periodical correspondence with it.[34]

Aside from party-building, the revolutionists were engaged in constant fund-raising campaigns and propaganda activities. One example of the revolutionists' propaganda work was the organization of a "speech tour" in Singapore in the summer of 1911. According to Chou Hsien-jui, organizer of the tour, forty-two persons took part in the tour. They took to the streets of Singapore to make sidewalk speeches to the crowds on the nights of Tuesdays, Wednesdays, Thursdays, Fridays and Sundays.[35] In less than two months, according to a record kept by Chou and later deposited with the Kuomintang's Committee for Compilation of Party History, over 200 speeches were made before street crowds ranging from 300 to 600 persons.[36]

After the establishment of the Nan-yang office, Sun stayed in Singapore for some time and the *Chung-hsing Pao* became the

---

33 *Ibid.*, pp. 504-505.

34 *Ibid.*

35 *Ibid.*, p. 555.

36 *Ibid.*, pp. 555-59.

headquarters of the revolutionists. Because of supporting the *Chung-hsing Pao* and shouldering the main financial burden of several uprisings, the merchants in Singapore, despite their enthusiasm, began to feel the strain. After the series of uprisings in 1907-1908, Sun again was an unwelcome person to the local authorities wherever he went. While in Singapore, he had an added woe, which was created by some 600 revolutionaries, who were deported to Singapore by the French authorities after they had been defeated in one of the campaigns and retreated into Indo-China. They were mostly undisciplined secret society members who immediately started to create disturbances after landing in Singapore. With the help of Ch'en Ch'u-nan and others, Sun managed to resettle them on mines and in factories as workers, but some of them often came to the *Chung-hsing Pao* and even to Sun's residence asking for money. Eventually, many got into trouble with the local police and over twenty of them were once arrested on charges of looting. Sun was blamed for all the troubles and he was increasingly harassed by the local authorities.[37] In May, 1909, he moved the Nan-yang office to Penang and set off on another trip to Europe.[38]

Elsewhere in Southeast Asia, the revolutionists were also expanding their influence. In Burma, where the royalists had been entrenched, the revolutionists, through propagating anti-Manchu nationalism, were able to win over a number of overseas Chinese, including Chuang Yin-an, a rich merchant. Meanwhile, Chuang's newspaper, *Yang-kuang Jih Pao* (Rangoon Daily), was converted into a revolutionary organ. In December, 1908, Sun sent up a number of revolutionists to Rangoon to help establish a T'ung-meng Hui branch there and Chuang was elected chairman.[39] Later, after the closing of the *Yang-kuang Jih Pao*, a new revolutionary organ, the *Kuang-hua Jih Pao* (Restore China Daily), was published. Branches were subsequently established in other cities of Burma, but to avoid the watchful eye of the local authorities, they were ostensibly known as either libraries or bookstores.[40] According to the

---

37 Feng Tzu-yu, *Chung-hua-min-kuo k'ai-kuo-ch'ien ko-ming shih*, Vol. II, pp. 140, 212.

38 *WSNWH*, Ser. I, No. 11, p. 510.

39 *Ibid.*, p. 513.

40 *Ibid.*, p. 514.

membership records kept by one party official, from March, 1908 to the end of 1911, there were 2,343 membership cards issued in Burma.[41]

In Siam, now known as Thailand, a branch was established in 1908 with the help of Sun Yat-sen and others, who went there from Singapore. A revolutionary organ, the *Hua-hsien Jih Pao* (China-Siam Daily) was published. However, the Siamese government was quite stringent in its attitude toward the Chinese revolutionists. On the day that Sun arrived in Bangkok with Hu Han-min and others, the local Chinese community held a welcome meeting in his honor and several hundred persons were present. The Siamese government was alarmed. Sun was ordered to leave the country within a week and he was not allowed to "talk about politics" during his stay in Bangkok.[42] Sun left after ten days, leaving behind several of his men to help the *Hua-hsien Jih Pao.*[43]

Australia and New Zealand apparently suffered from the remoteness of their location. The Nan-yang headquaters never sent any agents there and consequently there was no branch established in Australia. However, the Chih-kung T'ang was quite powerful among the overseas Chinese in Australia and its organ, the *Min-kuo Pao* (Republic Daily), was favorable to the revolutionary cause. The revolutionist's contact with the local Chinese was chiefly through the Chih-kung T'ang. For the Canton uprising of April 28, 1911, The Chih-kung T'ang contributed a modest sum raised in Melbourne and Sidney.[44] In Wellington, New Zealand, a small group of merchants was in contact with the *Chung-kuo Jih Pao* in Hong Kong. In 1908, Feng Tzu-yu, who was editor of the *Chung-kuo Jih Pao* and head of the T'ung-meng Hui's Hong Kong branch, admitted the group to membership through correspondence and authorized the establishment of a branch in Wellington.[45] In the Philippines, there had been no organization until the spring of 1911, when an agent arrived there from Hong Kong to

41 *Ibid.*, p. 683.

42 *Ibid.*, p. 674.

43 *Ibid.*

44 *Ibid.*, p. 756.

45 Feng Tzu-yu, *Chung-kuo ko-ming yun-tung erh-shih-liu nien tsu-chih shih,* p. 169.

establish a branch in Manila. The rather late development of revolutionary activity in the Philippines was attributable to the restrictive immigration policy of the local authorities, which deterred the early arrival of T'ung-meng Hui agents to organize there local Chinese who were sympathetic to the revolutionary cause.[46]

Mainland China.–On mainland China, the situation was quite different as far as the organizational expansion of the T'ung-meng Hui was concerned. Although "shadow branches" were set up in Tokyo at the time of the inauguration of the T'ung-meng Hui, actually few branches were immediately established in China, apparently because of the watchful policies of the government in Peking and the local authorities. Revolutionary activities had to take various forms under different circumstances. In many cases, T'ung-meng Hui members, who returned from Japan to work in China, found it necessary to ally themselves with other radical groups or secret societies. Many organizations started out with no direct relations with the T'ung-meng Hui, although they might share the same goal. In other cases, activities were carried out by people who confessed that they had been inspired by the revolutionists and who later established direct contact with the T'ung-meng Hui. In any event, the T'ung-meng Hui proved to be all-inclusive in nature in that it was eager to cooperate with, and if possible, recruit whatever groups that could be broadly regarded as revolutionary. We shall again review the development of the party on mainland China on a geographical basis.

In south China, we have previously mentioned the inroads made in the Kwangtung province by the T'ung-meng Hui branch in Hong Kong. Another development worth mentioning was the flourishing of theatrical activities, which in some measure contributed to the popularization of the revolutionary cause. In the 1900's, many theatrical groups, both professional and amateur, sprang up in Kwangtung. The repertoires of their troupes included shows either depicting popular episodes of heroism, loyalty and fidelity in Chinese history or satirizing the Manchus. While newspapers and other publications were effective propaganda for the educated, the theater appealed to the unsophisticated and illiterate masses. The revolutionists apparently realized this and

46 *WSNWH,* Ser. I, No. 11, p. 752.

were trying to make use of the theater. In 1904, for example, a drama school was set up in Canton to train a group of boys and girls. Li Chi-t'ang, who financed an abortive revolt against the Manchus by the secret society members in 1900, provided financial support for the school while Ch'en Shao-pai, the veteran member of the Hsing-chung Hui and Sun Yat-sen's schoolmate, wrote most of the plays for the group. After a year's training, the group toured many villages in Kwangtung to perform before the peasants.[47] Another troupe, with the help of Ch'en Shao-pai, went to Nan-yang in 1906 on a performance tour, and it was warmly received by overseas Chinese wherever it went. In Singapore, members of the troupe met Sun Yat-sen, and they all joined the T'ung-meng Hui.[48] In December, 1905, Huang Hsing returned to Hong Kong from Tokyo. He went on to Kweilin, the capital city of Kwangsi province, where he helped organize some eighty men in the local garrison force into a secret T'ung-meng Hui branch. However, this branch was largely inactive and following the transfer of a junior officer, who was the leader of the group, it became all but non-existent.[49]

In Foochow, captial of Fukien province, a group of radicals set up their own organization at the time the T'ung-meng Hui was inaugurated in Tokyo in 1905. Known as the Han-tsu Tu-li Hui (Han Independence Society), its members included students, young army officers and secret society members. It soon established contact with the T'ung–meng Hui branch in Hong Kong by sending several men there to meet with Huang Hsing and Feng Tzu-yu. It eventually came into contact with the T'ung-meng Hui general headquarters in Tokyo and in the summer of 1906, it was converted to a T'ung-meng Hui branch when an agent arrived in Foochow from Tokyo with the necessary secret papers.[50] Its active participation in revolutionary activities was shown by the fact that over forty of its members took part in the abortive uprising in Canton on April 27, 1911.[51] A similar situation existed in

---

47 *Ibid.,* Ser. I, No. 12, p. 56.

48 *Ibid.,* p. 59.

49 Feng Tzu-yu, *Chung-kuo ko-ming yun-tung erh-shih-liu nien tsu-chih shih,* pp. 108-109.

50 *WSNWH,* Ser. I, No. 12, pp. 72-81.

51 Feng Tzu-yu, *Chung-kuo ko-ming yun-tung erh-shih-liu nien tsu-chih shih,* p. 124.

Kweichow, another province in south China. In 1907, a radical organization known as the Tzu-chih Hsueh She (Self-government Society) was established in Kweiyang, the capital city. The society, which was dedicated to democracy through the promotion of self-government, according to its charter,[52] was active in Kweichow throughout the period of constitutional movement under the Manchus and right into the Republic days. Through the connections of Kweichow students in Tokyo, among them P'ing Kang, who was head of the "shadow branch" for Kweichow in Tokyo, the T'ung-meng Hui established close ties with the society and admitted many of its members.[53] In Yunnan province, there was also radical groups formed by students in Kunming, the capital city. After the return of some T'ung-meng Hui members from Tokyo in 1906, the anti-Manchu agitation was stepped up. The activities generally followed the same pattern as elsewhere: forming secret groups, disseminating revolutionary literature, infiltrating the New Army, and associating with the secret societies.

In central China, there were T'ung-meng Hui branches established at different times in the Yangtze valley provinces, but these branches were not the only revolutionary organizations. There were other organizations seemingly unconnected with the T'ung-meng Hui; and there were individuals who were not members of the T'ung-meng Hui but who played an important role. In the former category, a case in point is the Kuang-fu Hui of Chekiang, which will be dealt with later.[54] In the latter category, the revolt of a number of junior officers and men in the New Army in Wuhan in October, 1911, which sparked the revolution, is a good example. Throughout the period under review, the revolutionary activities in the Yangtze valley centered on the infiltration of the New Army and the rallying of the secret societies.

To begin with, a T'ung-meng Hui branch was established in Shanghai in the spring of 1906, with Kao Chien-kung, who returned from Tokyo, as head. This branch was to be the revolutionary center for both the

---

52. *WSNWH*, Ser. I, No. 12, p. 95.

53. *Ibid.*, p. 102.

54. See *infra*, Chapter VI.

city of Shanghai and the province of Kiangsu, for which a separate branch had been originally planned in Tokyo but later abandoned. Disguised as a school, the Shanghai branch, however, hardly lived up to the original expectations. Aside from distributing revolutionary literature, the branch was largely inactive. Within one year, the school was closed down. For the next three years, in the words of one contemporary, the revolutionists made little headway in Shanghai and in the Yangtze valley.[55] In the province of Anhwei, the revolutionists succeeded in some measure in infiltrating the New Army. Wu Yang-ku, who joined the T'ung-meng Hui in Tokyo and became head of the Anhwei branch, returned to his native province in 1906 as a junior officer in the Anhwei New Army. Through his secret work, he is said to have won several hundred followers before he was ousted from the army a year later.[56] In Kiangsi province, the T'ung-meng Hui members collaborated with the secret societies to launch a poorly organized revolt in late 1906, only to be put down by the overwhelming Manchu troops.[57]

It was in the central China province of Hupeh that the revolutionists scored their most impressive success in winning over the New Army. The New Army units in the three cities of Wuch'ang, Hankow and Hanyang (known combinedly as Wuhan) were so thoroughly infiltrated by the revolutionists that they eventually staged a successful revolt in October, 1911. That uprising was triggered by two revolutionary organizations, one a front of the T'ung-meng Hui, the other consisting of a group of junior officers and enlisted men in the New Army. Not long before the uprising, the two organizations were merged. To begin with, a secret revolutionary organization had been formed by a group of soldiers in the Army Engineering Battalion in Wuch'ang a year before the T'ung-meng Hui came into being in Tokyo. Calling their organization K'o-hsueh Pu-hsi So (Science Study Club), these soldiers distributed revolutionary literature to their fellow soldiers and made frequent speeches criticizing government policies. When Huang Hsing was in Wuhan in 1904, on his way to his home province

55 *WSNWH*, Ser. 1, No. 12, p. 152.

56 *Ibid.*, p. 188.

57 Feng Tzu-yu, *Chung-kuo ko-ming yun-tung erh-shih-liu-nien tsu-chih shih*, p. 125.

of Hunan to launch a revolt, he received an enthusiastic welcome from the Wuhan group and was assured of help when his revolt took place.[58] However, when Huang Hsing's plot was foiled by the Manchu authorities, the secret meeting place of the Wuhan group was also raided by troops and police. Secret documents were seized, many members were arrested and the Wuhan group suffered total collapse.

In 1906, another secret organization, known as the Jih-chih Hui (Daily Learning Society), which was associated with the American Church Mission in Wuch'ang, was established. In much the same way as the K'o-hsueh Pu-hsi So, it secretly spread revolutionary ideas among the soldiers and students. However, Liu Ching-an, leader of the organization, was later arrested by the Manchus and the Jih-chih Hui was banned. The American Church Mission tried in vain through diplomatic channels to secure the release of Liu, who died in prison three months before the Wuch'ang uprising of October, 1911.[59] Although the two secret organizations were successively dissolved by the Manchu authorities, radical elements in the New Army continued their agitation, setting up organizations under various assumed names. In early 1911, their organization, after several changes of name, became known as the Wen-hsueh She (Literary Society). The Wen-hsueh She penetrated virtually all units of the New Army in Wuhan and it was directly responsible for sparking the October, 1911 uprising.

Meanwhile, several T'ung-meng Hui members formed the Kung-chin Hui (Common Advance Society) in Tokyo in 1907 as a front organization of the T'ung-meng Hui and later returned to Hupeh also to work in the New Army. With the same anti-Manchu objective and working among the same people, close cooperation between the two groups became a foregone conclusion and an alliance was eventually made. According to the Kung-chin Hui side of the story, the alliance was made at a meeting in Wuch'ang on September 24, 1911.[60] According to the Wen-hsueh She record, the alliance was effected on the day of the Dragon Boat Festival-fifth day of the fifth moon (June

---

58 *WSNWH*, Ser. I, No. 12, p. 199.

59 *Ibid.*, pp. 208-28.

60 *Ibid.*, p. 240.

1, 1911)-at the Wen-hsueh She headquarters.[61] Despite the different versions, the fact is that the two did unite and collaborate in plotting for the coming uprising.

After the establishment of the republic, the Wen-hsueh She was dissolved and all of its members joined Sun Yat-sen's party, then already known as the Kuomintang.[62] Despite the fact that the Wen-hsueh She had a history dating back before the founding of the T'ung-meng Hui and the fact that in allying with the Kung-chin Hui it retained its own identity, there is no denying that the Wen-hsueh She derived much of its revolutionary impetus from the T'ung-meng Hui, of which Sun Yat-sen was the official leader. Most of the propaganda material which the Wen-hsueh She distributed was supplied by T'ung-meng Hui members. The revolutionary movement, begun by Sun Yat-sen as a lone campaign, was spreading to various parts of the country with people of vastly different backgrounds campaigning under different organizations. In this heterogeneous movement the T'ung–meng Hui served as its fountainhead.

The Wen-hsueh She was one of the numerous groups in the nation-wide revolutionary upsurge, an upsurge that owed much to the ceaseless campaigning of the T'ung-meng Hui. It is only natural that the Wen-hsueh She members would look to the T'ung-meng Hui for guidance and assistance, and in fact they did just that. When the plot for the Wuch'ang uprising was being actively planned in the summer of 1911, two Wen-hsueh She representatives were sent to Shanghai to ask Huang Hsing and Sung Chiao-jen to come to Wuhan to help in the plot, and another representative went to Hong Kong to seek financial help from the T'ung-meng Hui south China branch.[63] Huang Hsing did not arrive in Wuhan until late October, two weeks after the first shots of the uprising were fired. The revolutionary mutineers were by now already in an awkward position, barely able to hold on to the city of Hangyang while Hankow and Wuch'ang were retaken by overwhelming Manchu forces. Huang's arrival was a big boost to the morale of the

---

61 *Ibid.*, p. 257.

62 *Min-chu Pao* (Democratic Daily), October 7 and 8, 1911.

63 *WSNWH*, Ser. I, No. 12, p. 279.

revolutionary troops. As an evidence of the weight of the T'ung-meng Hui and particularly of the personal popularity of Huang, he was immediately made commander-in-chief of the revolutionary forces in Wuhan.[64]

In north China, the situation was quite different. Apparently because of the distance, the revolutionists were not able to extend much of their influence to the north. Adding to the difficulty was the fact that the Manchu government was in Peking, and therefore security measures in north China were more stringent than in other areas of the country. Generally there was little organized movement of any significance before the Wuch'ang uprising. The earliest radical organization was the K'ang-O T'ieh-hsueh Hui (Resist-Russia Iron and Blood Society), set up in Manchuria before the Russo-Japanese war primarily as a patriotic organization against the Russians. Its leader, Ting K'ai-chang, later joined the T'ung-meng Hui, in 1906,[65] but his group carried out little activity before the Wuch'ang uprising. Another organization, equally ineffective, was the Kung-ho Hui (Republic Society), organized by Hu O-kung in Paoting, Hopeh province, in 1910.[66] It was not until the Wuch'ang revolution that Wang Ching-wei, released from prison where he had served because of his attempt to assassinate the Prince Regent in 1910, set up a T'ung-meng Hui branch in Tientsin.[67] However, before the Tientsin branch had time to begin its planned assassination campaign, the republic was born.

From the foregoing, several patterns in the expansion of the T'ung-meng Hui can be discerned in different places. Each pattern was suited to the conditions of a given area and was tailored to meet the T'ung-meng Hui's objectives in that area. In Nan-yang, for example, where there were rich Chinese merchants in many centers, the T'ung-meng Hui concentrated on winning over these merchants with an eye to getting financial support. Realizing the fact that in Nan-yang the secret societies were stratified and disorganized and in many places banned by the local authorities because of frequent bloody fightings

---

64. *Ibid.*, p. 280.

65. *Ibid.*, p. 344.

66. *Ibid.*, p. 372.

67. *Ibid.*, p. 323.

between hostile groups, Sun Yat-sen and his followers generally paid less attention to rallying the secret societies as a source of revolutionary strength than in other areas. Instead, efforts were made to woo selected rich merchants at various points and through their influences, to gain popular support for the revolutionay cause and more important, to raise funds. This is well borne out, for example, in the case of Ch'en Ch'u-nan of Singapore and Chuang Yin-an of Saigon. Both were rich merchant's respected and influential in their communities; both became head of the local T'ung-meng Hui branches.

In North America, however, the story was different. There Sun Yat-sen had from the very early days seen the potential strength of the Chih-kung T'ang and was determined to make the best use of it. He not only personally joined the Chih-kung T'ang as a member, associating himself with the leaders of the society, but eventually he was able to merge his T'ung-meng Hui with the Chih-kung T'ang. It would be an exaggeration to say that Sun had succeeded in a complete conversion of the Chih-kung T'ang to the revolutionary cause, but his efforts did pay off nicely, in so far as his chief objective of fund-raising was concerned. The Chih-kung T'ang contributed generously and a special agency was later set up to help in the fund-raising.

Still another pattern was the one employed on the mainland of China. Here the immediate objective was not so much to raise money as to cultivate and build up an opposition force. Thus wherever and whenever possible, the T'ung-meng Hui sought to ally itself with radical groups already in existence or to be organized, as long as there was a common anti-Manchu goal. The New Army, because of its predominant Han composition and because many of its junior officers had been exposed to new ideas, was the chief target of infiltration by the revolutionists. In building up the opposition strength, the revolutionists sought the support of, and utilized, the secret societies whenever possible. However, the strength of the secret societies was in itself very much a myth, disputed not only by many revolutionists, but even by Sun Yat-sen himself.

In general, the revolutionists in their work among different groups of people did not go astray from their avowed intentions, despite the frustrations they had to undergo. There is no denying that from the time the first T'ung-meng Hui members returned to work in China in late 1905 to the outbreak of revolution in October, 1911, the revolutionary activities in China were a growing phenomenon, from sporadic revolts to a nationwide tide. Toward this growth, the efforts made by the revolutionists in various ways cannot be over-emphasized.

FUND–RAISING CAMPAIGNS

We have just alluded to fund-raising campaigns as one of the chief tasks of the T'ung-meng Hui branches abroad. Most of Sun's travels abroad, too, was to raise money, without which military campaigns would not have been possible. Fund-raising drives therefore occupied an important place in the history of the revolution of 1911. Fund-raising campaigns were continuously conducted, but usually an intensified drive was launched before an important military adventure. A case study of one of the fund drives would contribute to a better understanding of the process and the techniques employed by the revolutionists. The campaign carried out just before th April 28, 1911, uprising in Canton offers such an occasion. The correspondence, reports and reminiscences of those who participated in the fund drive combine to paint a vivid picture of a unique aspect of the history of the revolution.

At the outset, a few words should be said about the financial resources of the T'ung-meng Hui. Theoretically, the principal revenue of the T'ung-meng Hui should be membership dues, which were stipulated in the constitution as well as in the charters of various branches. The regulations changed from time to time, but the provisions on membership dues and donations were always included. The constitution of the T'ung-meng Hui first stiuplated an annual membership due of ten silver dollars,[68] but it was later scaled down to one dollar.[69] The constitution of the Singapore branch provided for membership dues of six dollars, in addition to a monthly contribution of one half dollar.[70] The Fukien branch required membership dues of

68 *Hsin-hai ko-ming,* Vol. II, p. 80.

69 *Ko-ming wen-hsien,* Vol. II, p. 238.

70. *Ibid.,* p. 242.

one dollar, and a yearly retaining fee of two dollars.[71] All branches were supposed to be self-sufficient from the membership dues collected, while the expenses of the Tokyo headquarters were shared by those members in Tokyo and all other branches. Apparently the membership dues and regular contributions collected were modest in amount, barely enough to meet routine expenses. For any military campaign, and even for Dr. Sun's travelling, extra funds had to be sought. Particularly in Nan-yang, many T'ung-meng Hui officers were constantly on the move touring various cities to solicit contributions from overseas Chinese.

In the winter of 1907, Sun was in Singapore, seeking funds to aid Huang Hsing, who was still engaging the Manchu troops in battles along the Indo-China borders. Sun had been ordered to leave Indo-China earlier by the local authorities. In October, he wrote to Teng Tse-ju, one of his aides who was head of the T'ung-meng Hui branch in a city in Malaya, pleading with him to help raise money. Teng was an important figure in the fund-raising campaign in the Nan-yang area. After the establishment of the Republic, he was director of a special agency responsible for making payments to those who had contributed to the revolution. Sun said in his letter that "arrangements have already been made with munition dealers of a number of countries" and that the revolutionary army had already occupied Ch'in chow, a port city in Kwangtung, thus making delivery of arms possible. "Arms can be delivered as soon as funds are available," he said, promising "handsome interests" when repayment was made. "For those who make large contributions," he offered "special privileges" in "exploring Chinese natural resources in the future."[72] In another letter to Teng, on March 7, 1908, Sun acknowledged receipt of 1,000 dollars, but said he urgently needed at least 100,000 to 200,000 dollars. The sum, he said, was to be used chiefly for rewards to those government soldiers who would surrender. He was referring to some 4,000 soldiers under the command of General Lu Yung-t'ing, pitched against Huang Hsing's men on the Indo-China borders. Sun claimed that many of Lu's men had

---

71 *WSNWH,* Ser. I, No. 12, p. 90.

72 Letter from Sun to Teng, Teng Tse-ju, *Chung-kuo kuo-min-tang erh-shih-nien shih-chi* (Twenty Years' History of the Kuomintang of China) (Shanghai: Cheng-chung Book Co., 1948), pp. 6-7.

secretly made it known to the revolutionists that they would surrender for a reward. Sun said he promised 100 dollars for each one coming over with arms, to be paid after the capture by the revolutionists of the city of Nanning, a strategic town in Kwangsi privince. The Manchu troops, however, demanded that thirty dollars be immediately paid to each upon surrender. For nearly 4,000 men, the reward would come to more than 100,000 dollars. "It is certainly worthwhile," Sun said, "to win over 4,000 men with 100,000 dollars without firing a shot. . . If Nanning is captured as a base, the revolutionary cause will be greatly enhanced." He added that the current favorable situation was created by the revolutionists after nearly eight months of hard fighting and that the Nan-yang comrades must help so that the fighting would be carried through to its successful end. In particular, he asked Teng to persuade Lu Pi-ch'en, an industrialist, to give. He said Lu had earlier promised to help if the revolution "firmly laid its foundation." Sun added that now "the foundation has apparently been laid."[73] Three weeks later, he again wrote Teng asking him to make another effort to persuade Lu to contribute and promised a "big reward" after the establishment of the Republic.[74] On April 17, Wang Ching-wei was sent to visit Teng, bringing Sun's personal message. He conveyed to Teng Sun's confidence that the better part of south China could be taken and that much would depend on how soon the needed money could be available.[75]

Despite Sun's repeated pleas and Wang's trip, from Teng came very little encouragement. He was able to raise barely another 1,000 dollars. On April 22, Sun sent another letter, repeating his request. With timely financial support, Sun said, uprisings could be staged simultaneously in Kwangtung, Kwangsi and Yunnan provinces to put the "Tartar army in real bad position." Action could also be taken in Fukien, Sun said, and the situation in the seven provinces in south China could be greatly changed. He hopefully predicted: "By then, the Manchu armies in north and central China will come over and my plan for many years will at last be realized." But for the present, the most urgent need was money. "Our old donors are pretty much exhausted footing the long

---

73 *Ibid.*, p.8.

74 *Ibid.*, p. 10.

75 *Ibid.*, p. 11.

campaign in Kwangsi, and I do hope that you will help raise 50,000 to 60,000 dollars," he pleaded with Teng. With the money, Sun continued, "we can hold out long enough to establish a military government, which will be able to tax and borrow from foreign countries." He urged Teng to do everthing possible to help "tide over this most difficult moment," and repeated his promise that contributions would be rewarded four times the original amount after the revolution, and that mining and railroad concessions would be granted to those who contributed most.[76] Prodded by urgent requests from the front and with financial aid not forthcoming, Sun grew increasingly desperate. His desperation was fully reflected in another letter to Teng a month later: "The current financial difficulty our party is facing is unprecedented in the past ten years. Hanoi is pressing me for 100,000 dollars. Where can I get the money?"[77] He said he could think of no one else but Mr. Lu, the industrialist, who might be able to help. "I have asked many people to persuade him and have so far not received a reply. Please keep persuading him until he is moved," Sun pleaded with Teng.[78] To prove the urgent need at the front, he attached the latest Hanoi request to the letter, adding that "the success or failure of our party depends solely on whether or not Mr. Lu will help." If Mr. Lu finally agreed to help, Sun promised, "he will be rewarded with ten years of exclusive mining rights in Yunnan province.[79]

Despite all the efforts made, however, the revolutionists failed to secure the badly needed help from Lu. With ammunition exhausted, Huang Hsing could not hold on and withdrew his demoralized troops to the mountains, after some initial victories at the border town of Hokou. Upon hearing the news, Sun's disappointment was complete. In bitterness, he wrote to Teng on June 19: "As I told you before, our success or failure depended on funds. This is why I repeatedly asked you to try your best to persuade Mr. Lu to help us. As the situation stands now, we can only regret. But for 100,000 dollars we lost Yunnan! Next time, we must first raise all the money needed before

---

76 *Ibid.*, pp. 11-12.

77 *Ibid.*, p. 13.

78 *Ibid.*

79 *Ibid.*

taking any action. We have made a serious mistake in staging the uprising in the hope that money would be available. "[80] Worst of all, the resettlement of the defeated revolutionary soldiers presented Sun with yet another frustration. "Now I need about 20,000 dollars to clear up the aftermath of the campaign. We couldn't even raise enough money when we were winning, how can I get help from others now that we have lost another battle?" He added a desperate plea: "What advice do you comrades have that will enlighten me a bit in my bewilderment?"[81]

Disappointed at the failure of the military adventure from the Indo-China borders and in view of the unfavorable financial situation in the Southeast Asia area, Sun decided on another trip to Europe, partly to seek aid from his foreign friends. In particular, he had in mind M. Domer, the former governor of French Indo-China, who once indicated to Sun he might be able to get some help from French industrialists. But Sun was so short of funds that he had to raise money in order to make the trip. Of the 8,000 dollars needed for the trip, Teng promised to raise 4,000 dollars. As Sun had to tour Kuala Lumpur, Penang and other cities, he sent Wang Ching-wei to Rangoon to raise the rest of the amount. The revolutionists were in such finanical straits that even the 400 dollars needed for Wang Ching-wei to go to Rangoon had to be raised first locally.[82] In May, 1909, Sun sailed for France, but soon after his arrival in Paris, he was informed by Domer that the recent change of government in France had rendered impossible a loan project contemplated earlier by some industrialists. He proceeded to London, where he also made efforts to secure financial help. In a letter to Teng in October, he reported that since one of his British friends was now in America, he was leaving for America in order to carry on the negotiations.[83] While in the United States, Sun kept up his correspondence with Teng Tse-ju, informing the Nan-yang comrades of his activities, particularly the successive establishment of the T'ung-meng Hui branches in New York, Chicago and San Francisco.

---

80 *Ibid.*

81 *Ibid.*

82 *Ibid.*, p. 22.

83 *Ibid.*, pp. 29-30.

In June, 1910, Sun arrived in Japan from America, but the Japanese authorities soon requested his departure when his presence became known. From Japan, he sailed to Nan-yang and arrived in Singapore in July. The revolutionary situation could not have been any worse. Another revolt, this time staged by the New Army in Canton, had been crushed in February. Disappointed at repeated setbacks, Wang Ching-wei resorted to extremist measures by going to Peking to attempt to assassinate the Prince Regent. He failed in his attempt and was jailed in April. Within the T'ung-meng Hui, factionalism was enhanced by military failures and Sun came under open criticism by some prominent members. New efforts were needed to keep the revolutionary flame burning. In August, Sun moved to Penang and set up his temporary headquarters there; new regulations were worked out drastically reducing membership dues in order to recruit more members.

In October, an important meeting was called at Penang to plan a future revolutionary course. Many leaders were present at the meeting, including Huang Hsing, Hu Han-min, Chao Sheng, Teng Tsu-ju and others representing various Nan-yang groups. According to Teng, most of the participants at the meeting, reviewing past failures and looking at the gloomy future, were discouraged, despite Sun's exhortation that "we should not be daunted by this latest failure." After lengthy discussion, all agreed that another military action was needed to boost the morale. But there was also agreement that before attempting the uprising, sufficient funds must be raised. To avoid interference by local authorities, the fund-raising campaign was to be carried out in the name of a charity drive for educational purposes. Canton was decided upon as the place for the next uprising. The fund-raising campaign would be conducted throughout Southeast Asia, with a target set for each area. The British and Dutch colonies were to contribute 50,000 dollars apiece, and the French Indo-China and Siam each 30,000 dollars.[84] The campaign was to be pushed in North America too, although no target was set. The meeting was a successful one, for before it was adjourned, some 8,000 dollars was collected from the participants.[85]

---

84 *Ibid.*, p. 37.

85 *Ibid.*

According to the plan, responsible members were assigned fund-raising areas throughout Southeast Asia and they soon set out to tour their areas, bringing their "charity contribution" books. Teng Tse-ju, for example, had charge of the British colonies, where he distributed a total of seventeen contribution books among the responsible cadres at various points.[86] Meanwhile, Huang and Chao left for Rangoon and Hong Kong respectively to actively prepare for the Canton uprising planned for early the next year. They proceeded to order arms and munitions and to raise a vanguard of 800 men. To kick off the fund-raising campaign, Sun planned to make a speaking tour of various cities in Nan-yang, but soon he encountered difficulties. The Dutch authorities made it clear that all Dutch islands were off limits to Sun; in Indo-China, Siam and Japan, the ban for his entry still stood. Even in Malaya, he soon found himself in trouble. One of the fund-raising speeches he made at Penang got published in a local Chinese newspaper. A translation of the speech subsequently was carried in a local English newspaper, and this immediately alarmed the local govenment. Meanwhile, Sun's opponents lost no time in prodding the local government to order Sun's expulsion, alleging that Sun was a dangerous person, whose presence was detrimental to the maintenance of local law and order. Before the year was out, Sun found himself again on the road, travelling through Europe en route to America. The fund-raising task was entrusted to Hu Han-min and others. Despite Sun's absence, the campaign went on and in time all the money needed for the April 28, 1911 uprising was raised.

The prospect of this fund-raising campaign at first appeared far from bright. Ten days after Sun's departure, Hu Han-min was able to raise only 1,000 dollars, which lagged far behind the original schedule. He called Teng and others to Singapore for another meeting. After the meeting, they set out to continue the fund-raising tour of the Nan-yang cities. On December 4, Teng was in Penang making door to door calls to solicit contributions.[87] The next day, he was in Malacca, where he tried in vain to persuade a rich merchant, T'an Yu-ch'u, to contribute money. Teng later wrote: "When I talked about revolution with him, he

---

86 *Ibid.*, p. 39.

87 *Ibid.*, p. 40.

expressed full agreement. As soon as I mentioned money, his enthusiasm was gone, and he began to complain to me about his poor financial condition."[88] He added that many other rich merchants invariably gave the same answer. On December 31, Huang Hsing returned to Singapore from Rangoon and learned that the fund-raising campaign was not going well. So far in the British colonies, only a little over 10,000 dollars had been raised, far from the original target. He was deeply worried, saying that any delay in getting the money would probably ruin the whole plan. The assigned amount of 50,000 dollars in the British colonies was badly needed for purchasing arms and for other purposes. Even if Sun Yat-sen were able to raise a comparable amount in America, it would probably be too late for the immediate purposes.

Accompanied by Teng and others, Huang embarked on a trip to several important Malayan cities, making an urgent last minute plea to many merchants. At each stop, Huang met local Chinese community leaders, earnestly pleading with them for help. His trip was not made in vain for invariably after each meeting several thousand dollars was raised. In a small town near Kuala Lumpur, Huang scored his biggest success. After a meeting with local Chinese leaders, he was not only able to raise several thousand dollars, but to win other support as well. One local merchant, Cheng Lo-sheng, pledged his railroad holdings in Malaya; another merchant, Li Yuan-shui, decided to sell his mining holdings to help the revolution. In addition, Huang was assured by Cheng that the target amount would be fulfilled by the end of the year. Greatly encouraged, Huang left Nan-yang to proceed to Hong Kong on December 9 to join others in active planning for the uprising.

Meanwhile, in America, a fund drive was also under way. Before he left Singapore, Sun Yat-sen had already written to Feng Tzu-yu in Canada and others in the United States to push the campaign. After his arrival, the pace was stepped up. Within a few months, he was able to raise nearly 50,000 dollars in several major cities in Canada and the United States, thanks to the active cooperation of the Chih-kung T'ang. So enthusiastic was the Chih-kung T'ang in Victoria that it sold its estate for 33,000 dollars and remitted the full amount to Hong Kong. In total, over 150,000 dollars was raised to finance the Canton

---

88 *Ibid.*, p. 41.

uprising.[89] Unfortunately for other reasons, the April 28, 1911 uprising in Canton was again a failure, a failure in which the revolutionists suffered the heaviest losses up to that time. Several hundred young revolutionaries died in action. But the loss of the young revolutionaries at once made the world aware of the turbulent revolutionary tide in China. It also had a great effect on the Chih-kung T'ang in America. Deeply moved by the gallant sacrifices made by the young revolutionaries, the Chih-kung T'ang rallied itself ever closer to Sun's cause. As pointed out earlier, the Chih-kung T'ang eventually cooperated with the T'ung-meng Hui to set up a special agency for the sole purpose of raising funds. With liberal rewards promised, the last few months before the October, 1911 revolution saw the fund-raising campaign reaping remarkable results. The revolutionists kept their promise, for after the birth of the Republic, an agency was established to dispense rewards to those who had contributed, and Teng Tse-ju was appointed head of that agency. According to his report in 1913, total debts amounted to over 1.4 million dollars, of which some 500,000 dollars was repaid as of August 3, 1913.[90]

INTERNAL DISSENSION

From 1907 to 1908, the revolutionary movement reached its high point as far as military actions were concerned. In a period of one year, no less than six revolts, directly under the leadership of the T'ung-meng Hui, were staged. In Nan-yang and elsewhere, the expansion of the organization was in full swing. Ironically enough, despite the busy military adventures in south China and active party expansion, this was also the period that saw the gradual disintegration of the T'ung-meng Hui headquarters in Tokyo. As pointed out earlier, the T'ung-meng Hui at the time of its formation included various radical Chinese groups in Tokyo. On the issue of doing away with the Manchus, there was agreement among them. This issue more than anything else served to unite the membership of the T'ung-meng Hui. However, within the organization provincialism remained a strong factor, because originally

---

89 *Ibid.*, p. 49.

90 *Hsin-hai ko-ming*, Vol. II, p. 82.

the various groups had been formed largely on the basis of the native places of their members. Although Sun Yat-sen was head of the T'ung-meng Hui by popular choice, leaders of the various groups continued to command the respect if not loyalty of their followers. A potential source of personality clashes between Sun and them was thus always in existence. This, for example, was precisely the case between Sun and the leaders of the Hunan group, particularly Huang Hsing and Sung Chiao-jen. Some passages in Sung's diary will shed light on this point.

On January 4, 1907, Sung recorded in his diary that Huang Hsing was leaving for Hong Kong the next day to prepare for a new uprising. Huang, who was head of the important general affairs department of the T'ung-meng Hui, a post next only to that of Sun's, asked Sung to act in his behalf during his absence. Sung agreed. Later that evening Sung went to see Sun Yat-sen for instructions about his new duty, but "Sun spoke very little at the meeting."[91] On February 15, Huang returned from Hong Kong. On February 27, Sung went to Sun and told him that since Huang was now back in Tokyo, he (Sung) would be glad to see Huang assume the general affairs department post again. Sun appeared rather indifferent, according to Sung, and replied that he was leaving for Nan-yang shortly himself, and that Sung had better talk about the matter with Huang.[92] Sung went to talk to Huang the next day. At first he found Huang very silent. After a long while, Huang suddenly spoke, declaring that he was planning to withdraw from the T'ung-meng Hui. This did not take Sung completely by surprise, for he knew something had been brewing between Sun and Huang for some time. The most recent squabble between them was over the design of the flag of the future republic. Sung recorded this incident in his diary as follows: "Sun designed the flag all by himself. When Huang Hsing at a meeting expressed objections to certain features of it and asked for changes, Sun not only stubbornly insisted on his own idea, but spoke to Huang in a rude manner. Thereupon Huang rose angrily and stalked out of the meeting in the presence of all others."[93]

---

91 Sung Chiao-jen, *O chih li-shih,* pp. 198-99.

92 *Ibid.,* pp. 314, 319.

93 *Ibid.,* p. 319.

Whatever difference over such a relatively unimportant matter as the design of a flag, Sung said, did not seem to warrant the display of open defiance by Huang in front of all others. He sensed that the "flag affair" was merely an accidental occasion seized upon by Huang to serve as an outlet for his accumulated grievances. Bad feelings, according to Sung, "have been in existence between the two for some time." Sung recorded his own feelings in these words: "Now that Huang has displayed his displeasure in front of all of us and the cleavage has all but come into the open, there appears little that can be done to patch it up."[94] Sung added that personally he had been bothered by the squabbles and jealousies among the members ever since the founding of the T'ung-meng Hui and that he was now "seriously considering going my own way."[95] The next day, he saw Sun again and despite Sun's reluctance, he turned over "all the documents" to Sun to make it clear that he, Sung, was no longer acting head of the general affairs department.[96]

The next episode came at the time of Sun's departure from Japan in March, 1907. When the Japanese government politely ordered Sun to leave Japan, it gave Sun several thousand *yen* as travelling expenses. In addition, Sun also accepted a sum of 10,000 *yen* from a sympathetic Tokyo stock broker, Suzuki Shisagoro.[97] Leaving behind 2,000 *yen* for the maintenance of the *Min Pao,* Sun left Japan with Hu Han-min and others for Singapore en route to Hanoi, where he was to set up his headquarters to direct several campaigns launched from the Indo-China borders during the next year. The departure of Sun, Hu, Huang and others left the Tokyo headquarters with no leaders of comparable stature. Moreover, the Tokyo office, already stripped to a skeleton staff, was further weakened by the fact that military campaigns in the ensuing months were planned and carried out from Indo-China under the personal direction of Sun, with the Tokyo office playing very little part. Beside the publication of the *Min Pao,* which was now edited by Chang Pin-lin, the Tokyo office seemed to be doing little else at this

94 *Ibid.,* pp. 319-20.

95 *Ibid.*

96 *Ibid.*

97 Feng Tzu-yu, *Chung-hua-min-kuo k'ai-kuo-ch'ien ko-ming shih,* Vol. I, P. 210.

time. However, Sun's acceptance of the gift from the Japanese friend soon became a subject of criticism by some members.

Among Sun's most vociferous critics were Chang Ping-lin, Sung Chiao-jen and Chang Chi. After several military setbacks in Kwangtung and along the Indo-China borders, the criticism grew in intensity. At one point, Chang Ping-lin and others went so far as to demand Sun's ouster as leader of the T'ung-meng Hui.[98] Although the proposal did not get through, the internal squabble in Tokyo continued to grow. Liu Kwei-i, now head of the general affairs department who was acting as head of the Tokyo office, had to write to Hu Han-min and Feng Tzu-yu, suggesting that they solicit an apology from Sun about accepting the money from the Japanese in order to quiet down the heightening resentment among the Tokyo members. Feng and Hu approvingly forwarded the suggestion to Sun, but Sun categorically rejected it. He said the internal strife could only be quieted down by successful future military actions, and that he owed apologies to no one.[99]

As a result of the attitude of the Tokyo members, Sun put little confidence in them. In 1907, for example, he wrote Miyazaki Torazo from Hanoi, empowering him to be a T'ung-meng Hui agent with special responsibility for purchasing arms. He urged Miyazaki to keep the arrangement secret, even from the knowledge of the Tokyo headquarters.[100] Meanwhile, Chang Ping-lin and T'ao Ch'eng-chang kept up their attack on Sun. They distributed an open message among the Chinese in Japan and in Nan-yang, and charged that when Sun was in Nan-yang, he claimed that all Chinese students in Tokyo were T'ung-meng Hui members; when he came to Tokyo, he boasted that all business leaders in Nan-yang were aiding the revolution. If he had large contributions from Nan-yang businessmen, why did he not spare some of the money for the *Min Pao* when it was in deep financial difficulty? they asked. In adition, they charged that Sun discriminated against those who were not from his native Kwangtung province.[101]

---

98 *Ibid.*, p. 201.

99 *Ibid.*, p. 202.

100 Marius Jansen, *op. cit.*, p. 124.

101 *Hsin-hai ko-ming*, Vol. II, p. 44.

The internal squabbles among the Tokyo comrades on the whole did not seriously affect the military campaigns which were carried out largely without an active role of the Tokyo office. But the repeated military setbacks did have an adverse effect on the morale of the revolutionists. In April, 1910, after the failure of the New Army uprising in Canton, Wang Ching-wei, deeply frustrated, slipped to Peking in an attempt to assassinate the Prince Regent in order to dramatize the revolutionary movement. After the failure of the April 27, 1911 uprising in Canton, an uprising in which the revolutionists suffered the heaviest loss, many members were so upset that they proposed to shift the revolutionary activities to central China. Their efforts culminated in the formation of the T'ung-meng Hui central China chapter in July, 1911.

This organization, with its headquarters in Shanghai, was established by those T'ung-meng Hui members who were openly dissatisfied with the efforts made in south China so far, and were trying to stage revolts in the Yangtze valley. Leaders of this organization did not go so far as to repudiate the mother organization, but they made little effort to conceal their disappointment with the leadership of the party. This sentiment was clearly expressed in a manifesto they issued, as we shall see a little later. Although this group did not exist long enough to be of any real significance in influencing the course of the revolution, it is nevertheless worth noting in view of its nature and the important leaders connected with it. In a sense, it represented the first organized dissident group within the mother organization. Among the important leaders of the T'ung-meng Hui central China chapter were Sung Chiao-jen, Ch'en Ch'i-mei and T'an Jen-feng.

Prior to the Wuch'ang revolution of October, 1911, military adventures by the revolutionists had been confined to south China. But in central China, the revolutionists were working covertly, infiltrating the New Army and rallying the secret societies. Ch'en Ch'i-mei, who joined the T'ung-meng Hui in 1906 while studying at the Police Academy in Tokyo, returned to Shanghai in 1908 as the T'ung-meng Hui man responsible for the revolutionary work in the Yangtze valley.[102] He was assisted by T'an Jen-feng, who traveled a great deal

102. *WSNWH*, Ser. I, No. 12, p. 155.

up and down the Yangtze valley and between Shanghai and Hong Kong, acting as a liaison. Sung Chiao-jen was in Hong Kong briefly, in April, 1911, just before the abortive April 27 Canton uprising, and took part in its planning.[103] Before the uprising, opinions were divided as to the locale for staging this latest adventure. Sung and T'an favored a place in the Yangtze valley, preferably Nanking, but they were overruled by Huang Hsing and Hu Han-min who at the time held much real power and were commanding an unmistakable majority in the T'ung-meng Hui.[104] After the Canton failure, Sung went to Shanghai, and joined Ch'en, T'an and others in active planning for the formation of a T'ung-meng Hui branch devoted to revolutionary work in central China. The idea of setting up a center to direct and coordinate the work in central China had been discussed by Sung, T'an and others in Tokyo the previous year,[105] but the failure of the Canton uprising undoubtedly accelerated its birth. The central China chapter was established on July 31, 1911 in Shanghai.[106] T'an wrote its manifesto and Sung drafted the constitution. The abortive Canton uprising inevitably increased the bitterness of many T'ung-meng Hui members. Tan, for one, began openly castigating Huang Hsing, blaming the failure on Huang's stubborness and rashness. He was so bitter and discouraged that he once told a colleague of his intention to quit the revolutionary cause.[107]

In the manifesto he drafted, T'an openly criticized the many shortcomings in the revolutionary movement. The manifesto summed up the failure of the revolution in these words: "Although there is a mutually agreed upon goal, there is no mutually agreed on plan; although there are able men, there is no efficient organization."[108] Without solving these two problems, it continued, apparently referring to the latest failure in Canton, "any hasty action against the

---

103 Wu Hsiang-hsiang, *Sung Chiao-jen: Chung-kuo min-chu hsien-cheng ti hsien-ch'u* (Sung Chiao-jen: Forerunner of Chinese Democracy and Constitution) (Taipei: Book World Co., 1964), p. 96.

104 *WSNWH,* Ser. II, No. 1, pp. 14-21.

105 Wu Hsiang-hsiang, *op. cit.,* p. 97.

106 *Ibid.,* p. 98.

107 *WSNWH,* Ser. II, No. 1, pp. 14-21.

108 *Ibid.,* p. 12.

government, using undisciplined new recruits, would have little hope of success." Apart from sacrificing lives, it would only waste the money raised from all sources, the manifesto said. It is "with these problems in mind that the central China chapter has been established."

The chapter chose Shanghai as its site "because of Shanghai's strategic location and communication facilities which will provide better coordination and liaison with points in other provinces." The manifesto stated that the chapter would set up branches in various provinces sharing the responsibility in a collective manner; that it would "adopt a majority vote system at the headquarters to forestall dictatorship," and that it would "leave open for the time being the post of chairman for a truly deserving man."[109] Although the specifics were not spelled out, it is at once clear that all these were thinly veiled criticisms of the mother organization. The general tone of the document was crystal clear: Here was a group of revolutionists who saw the weakening of the T'ung-meng Hui as a result of internal dissension and the lack of good organization, who were not satisfied with the present leadership, and who declared their intention to do something about the situation.

Although the group went on record about its "loyalty" to the T'ung-meng Hui headquarters in Tokyo, there was evidence that under the general banner of revolution, its organizers intended to make the group somewhat independent in many ways. The evidence is both explicit and implicit in the constitution drafted by Sung Chiao-jen and adopted at the founding meeting in Shanghai. According to article XVIII of the constitution of the T'ung-meng Hui, "regulations of all regional chapters must be adopted by the general headquarters and approved by the Tsung-li (President)." The same article also stipulated that the "head of regional chapter shall be appointed by the Tsung-li."[110] However, these restrictions were disregarded by the newly formed chapter.

Article I of the constitution of the central China chapter said that the chapter was formed "by those members of the T'ung-meng Hui who

---

109 *Ibid.*

110 *Ko-ming wen-hsien,* Vol. II, p. 240.

have expressed agreement."[111] There was no mention of authorization from the general headquarters or, for that matter, from Sun Yat-sen as president of the T'ung-meng Hui. Article II set forth the goals of the chapter as "overthrowing the Manchu government and establishing a democratic and constitutional form of government."[112] The word "republic" which appeared in practically all important T'ung-meng Hui documents and oaths, was conspicously missing. In the absence of any explanation either by Sung or in any contemporary sources, the significance of this omission can only be conjectured in the light of later developments. After the birth of the republic, Sung emerged as the most prominent party organizer, who was largely responsible for uniting the T'ung-meng Hui with other political factions to form the Kuomintang (Nationalist Party) and maintaining a Kuomintang majority in the parliament. A dedicated and undaunted worker of parliamentary democracy, he fought Yuan Shih-k'ai courageously, until his assassination by the ambitious and authoritarian Yuan. There is no question that Sung was for a republic; but there is a good reason to believe that he attached more importance to genuine democracy through parliamentary processes, a cause for which he eventually gave his life. All this, coupled with his earlier criticism of Sun Yat-sen, seemed to suggest that Sung's using of the phrase "democratic and constitutional form of government" was deliberate and it, if anything, at least in some measure showed Sung's displeasure of Sun. Article III provided for the establishment of branches "in other places" than Shanghai, a stipulation again not fully in accord with the assigned role of a regional chapter. Article V went even further, setting up the chapter's own membership requirement. It declared: "Any T'ung-meng Hui members, who have joined this chapter according to its regulations, will be considered members of this chapter."[113] The chapter "pays respect" to the Tokyo headquarters as the "mother organization," but it regarded the south China T'ung-meng Hui office in Hong Kong, headed by Hu Han-min, as a fraternal organization."[114]

After the founding of the chapter, members soon began their efforts

111 *WSNWH,* Ser. II, No. 1, p. 3.

112 *Ibid.*

113 *Ibid.*

114 *Ibid.*, p. 12,

to organize branches in Hunan, Hupeh, Szechuan, Shensi and Anhwei provinces. Sung and others were contemplating these ambitious plans aimed at capitalizing on the popular opposition in the Yangtze valley provinces to the government's plan to nationalize railroads, and to organize simultaneous revolts in these provinces. Although the central China chapter took upon itself to push the project, there was cooperation with the south China office of the T'ung-meng Hui. Sung informed Huang Hsing of his plan and Huang, writing back from Hong Kong, praised Sung's "farsightedness" and expressed the belief that the planned move in central China, if carried out, "may well lay the foundation for national restoration."[115] However, the central China chapter hardly had an opportunity to begin in earnest its ambitious project when the Wuch'ang uprising broke out and revolutionary flames soon swept over many parts of the country. To the revolutionists in Wuch'ang, who looked to the T'ung-meng Hui leaders for guidance and help, whether it was the central China chapter or south China office did not seem to make any difference. Just before the outbreak of the revolution, for example, they sent representives to Shanghai to ask for help and through Shanghai, they urged that Huang Hsing come to Wuch'ang to command the revolutionary force.

As to the role played by the central China chapter in the Wuch'ang uprising and during the months immediately following the outbreak of the revolution, there are different interpretations. Hu Han-min, for example, spoke of the south China office's orders to Sung Chiao-jen and Ch'en Ch'i-mei before the April 27, 1911 Canton uprising to prepare for synchronizing actions in Yangtze valley, but he made no mention of their work prior, during, and after the Wuch'ang uprising. In fact, he did not even mention the existence of the central China chapter at all.[116] On the other hand, another contemporary went so far as to declare that the Wuch'ang uprising was the handiwork of the central China chapter. Tseng Po-hsing, who in 1911 was a high school teacher in Ch'angsha, capital of Hunan, and who had taken part in the revolutionary work in Hunan, particularly praised T'an Jen-feng's work

---

115. Huang Hsing, *Huang ko-ch'iang hsien-sheng shu-han mo-chi* (Correspondence and calligraphy of Mr. Huang Hsing) (Taipei: Committee for Compilation of Party History, 1956), p. 77.

116. *Ko-ming wen-hsien,* Vol. II, pp. 413-14.

in organizing the revolutionary force in the Yangtze valley from Szechuan in the west to Kiangsu in the east. He mentioned that the Wuch'ang uprising was staged under the direction of the central China chapter, and that the successive declaration of independence of the Yangtze valley provinces owed much to the groundwork laid earlier by the central China chapter.[117] Both theories, however, are less than candid. Hu's total disregard of even the existence of the central China chapter was apparently a personal bias; while Tseng has, on the other hand, for whatever reason, indeed exaggerated the role of the central China chapter. The central China chapter was founded only two and a half months before the outbreak of the Wuch'ang uprising, with the declared purpose of coordinating and organizing the revolutionary forces in the Yangtze valley. To fulfill this different task in such a vast region, whatever could be accomplished within the short space of two and a half months was bound to be on a rather limited scale.

When the Yangtze valley provinces successively declared their independence from the Peking government after the Wuch'ang uprising, Chien Ch'i-mei was made governor of Shanghai. The revolution spread throughout the country like wild fire and less than two months later, the Republic of China was proclaimed. In the revolutionary torrents, whatever differences there were became temporarily buried. The central China chapter came into being because of previous failures in the revolutionary movement; it now disappeared with the birth of the republic.

---

117. *WSNWH,* Ser. II, No. 1 pp. 14-21.

Chapter VI

RELATIONS WITH THE KUANG-FU HUI

Before the birth of the T'ung-meng Hui in Tokyo in 1905, the Kuang-fu Hui, together with the Hsing-chung Hui headed by Sun Yat-sen and the Hua-hsing Hui headed by Huang Hsing, were the three most important revolutionary organizations. In terms of strength and the calibre of the leaders, the three stood out among other Chinese revolutionary groups. This was particularly true before 1905 in Tokyo, where there were numerous radical groups of Chinese students loosely organized according to their native provinces. Both the Hua-hsing Hui and the Kuang-fu Hui had their origin in the Chun Kuo-min Chiao-yu Hui (Citizen's Society for Military Education), which had been formed in Tokyo earlier primarily for the purpose of training the revolutionists in the techniques of assassination. The Hua-Hsing Hui was strong among the natives of Hunan province in central China, while the Kuang-fu Hui members came largely from the two coastal provinces of Chekiang and Kiangsu. After Huang Hsing decided to join forces with Sun Yat-sen to form the T'ung-meng Hui in 1905, all his followers became members of the T'ung-meng Hui and the Hua-hsing Hui thus ceased to exist. The case with the Kuang-fu Hui, however, was different. Although many important members of the Kuang-fu Hui joined the T'ung-meng Hui, the Kuang-fu Hui continued to exist and in fact carried out revolutionary activities independent of the T'ung-meng Hui. For some time, people did not bother to distinguish between members of the T'ung-meng Hui and Kuang-fu Hui as they were all called revolutionists or rebels. Indeed for some time even some revolutionary leaders made no attempt to draw a clear line between the two organizations, so long as revolutionary activities were carried out. The situation with the local revolutionaries in Chekiang province, however, was a little different. Apparently due to poor communications, many Kuang-fu Hui members there, according to one revolutionary leader, did not know immediately about the formation of the T'ung-meng Hui in Tokyo, in August, 1905, and continued to carry on their work under the name of Kuang-fu Hui [1]

With the repeated setbacks suffered by the revolutionists and the development of factionalism in the T'ung-meng Hui headquarters in Tokyo after the departure of Sun Yat-sen and Huang Hsing in 1907, it was the Kuang-fu Hui members who were largely responsible for the worsening of the squabbles within the T'ung-meng Hui. Many important leaders of the Kuang-fu Hui, although they were at the same time prominent in the T'ung-meng Hui, openly began to attack Sun Yat-sen. The attack grew in intensity and at times seemed seriously to threaten the unity among the factions and to hamper revolutionary activities. Prominent leaders of the Kuang-fu Hui even tried to ally themselves with radical exiles of other countries in Tokyo rather than actively take part in uprisings in China at a time when the T'ung-meng Hui was plotting one revolt after another.

The feuding between members of the T'ung-meng Hui and the Kuang-fu Hui, particularly the attack on Sun by some prominent Kuang-fu Hui leaders, continued even after the republic was born. In one of his first statements as provisional president of the new republic, Sun Yat-sen had to appeal openly to the Kuang-fu Hui members to bury the hatchet and join hands with their fellow revolutionists to work for the future of the nation. In view of the relationship between the two revolutionary organizations and particularly the Kuang-fu Hui's contribution to the revolutionary work in the Chekiang and Kiangsu provinces, the whole episode of the Kuang-fu Hui merits close examination.

THE BEGINNING OF THE KUANG-FU HUI

The man who initiated the Kuang-fu Hui was a student from Chekiang province named Kung Pao-ch'uan. However, not too long after the formation of the Kuang-fu Hui, he sank into obscurity as

1. T'ao Ch'eng-chang, "Che-an chi-lueh" (A Brief Account of the Uprisings in Chekiang), *Hsin-hai ko-ming,* Vol. III, p. 17.

others took over and became its active leaders. In 1904, Kung was among the Chinese students in Japan and belonged to the Chun Kuo-min Chiao-yu Hui. In early 1903, when Russia reneged on her promise to evacuate from Manchuria and the Manchu Court seemed unable to do anything about it except to acquiesce in the face of Russian intransigence, patriotic Chinese students in Japan were deeply disturbed. Some impatient students in Japan organized themselves into a volunteer corps for military training, planning to return to China to fight the Russians. However, their attempt was thwarted by the Japanese authorities, who took measures to ban students from engaging in such extra-curricular activities.

Meanwhile, student representatives were sent back to China to persuade the government not to "sell" out Manchuria to the Russians. When word came to Tokyo that the Manchu Court, instead of accepting the petition of the students, was trying to arrest them, the radicals in Japan were so furious that many immediately decided to return to China to resort to violence against the Manchus. Kung Pao-ch'uan was among the students who returned to China. This was sometime in the summer of 1904.

With several fellow students from the Chekiang province, Kung first organized a secret assassination ring with the avowed purpose of killing a few prominent Manchu officials as part of the larger military action against the Manchus. The secret organization was based in Shanghai with only a handful of members observing very strict discipline and regulations. This group soon came to the knowledge of Ts'ai Yuan-p'ei, who was at the time the head of the Chung-kuo Chiao-yu Hui (China Education Soceity). A man of established intellectual stature but also harboring deep anti-Manchu sentiments, Ts'ai immediately asked to join the secret organization. Members of the organization were overjoyed at Ts'ai's request and welcomed him in. With the addition of Ts'ai, the group was strengthened.

Meanwhile, a reorganization was effected and the group became known as the Kuang-fu Hui (Restoration Society); Ts'ai was elected its first chairman. The initial membership, according to Sun Yat-sen in

1912, was somewhere between forty to fifty persons.[2] The exact date of the formal establishment of the Kuang-fu Hui was not available. From various sources, it appears that it was sometime in the winter of 1904. Probably the most authoritative source was T'ao Ch'eng-chang, a veteran revolutionist from Chekiang province, who had worked on behalf of the revolutionary cause in his native province prior to his joining the Kuang-fu Hui and who later became one of the Kuang-fu Hui's most important leaders. According to T'ao, there were two groups of members of the Chun Kuo-min Chiao-yu Hui who returned to China from Japan in 1904. The group led by Huang Hsing went to Hunan, became known as the Hua-hsing Hui, and later fled to Shanghai after the abortive uprising in Hunan. The other group comprised members from various provinces, who lived in Shanghai following their return from Japan. They organized an assassination ring. Later Ts'ai joined this group, which became known as the Kuang-fu Hui. T'ao said the Kuang-fu Hui was formed at the time of the attempted assassination of the former governor of Kwangsi, Wang Chih-ch'un, by a revolutionary named Wan Fu-hua. This would put the date somewhere between October and November of 1904.[3] T'ao's reference to the approximate date of the establishment of the Kuang-fu Hui was the most authoritative, because of his work was first published as early as 1909, within less than five years of the emergence of the Kuang-fu Hui. His view has been accepted by most historians.[4]

Soon after the establishment of the Kuang-fu Hui, T'ao, after more than a year's work in Chekiang and Anhwei provinces among the local secret society members, arrived in Shanghai on his way to Japan. Ts'ai approached him and asked him to join the Kuang-fu Hui, knowing his connections with the secret societies which Ts'ai thought might be helpful to the revolutionary cause. It was in Shanghai that T'ao joined the Kuang-fu Hui and then he proceeded to Japan.[5] Meanwhile, Ts'ai Yuan-k'ang, Yuan-p'ei's younger brother, went to Shaohsing to work among the schools and business circles on behalf of the Kuang-fu Hui.

---

2 Feng Tzu-yu, *Chung-hua min-kuo k'ai-kuo-ch'ien ko-ming shih,* Vol. II, p. 32.

3 T'ao Ch'eng-chang, *op. cit.*, p. 16.

4 Feng Tzu-yu, *op. cit.*, Vol. II, p. 20; *Chung-kuo Kuo-min-tang ch'i-shih-nien ta-shih nien piao,* p. 10.

5 T'ao Ch'eng-chang, *op. cit.*, p. 17.

When he announced that T'ao had already joined the Kuang-fu Hui, many followed T'ao's lead and the Kuang-fu Hui was greatly strengthened. A little later, Hsu Hsi-lin, who was to play an important role, also joined the Kuang-fu Hui.

IMPORTANT LEADERS AND ACTIVITIES

Among the Kuang-fu Hui leaders, T'ao Ch'eng-chang was one of the most important. A native of Shaohsing, Chekiang province, he had been known as a child prodigy. At the age of fifteen, when he began to read new books and to come under the impact of reform ideas, he was already well-versed in the Chinese classics. In his late teens, he served as a tutor. As he came to realize how the Han people were oppressed, his hatred for the Manchus deepened. During the height of the Boxer Rebellion, he slipped into Peking in an attempt to assassinate the Empress Dowager. In 1902, he went to Japan, but soon returned to China when the Chinese student counselor, a Manchu official, promised him a position in the army. After he returned, however, he found that the promise could not be realized. Later, when the two Chinese student representatives, Niu Yung-chien and T'ang Erh-ho, returned from Japan to China to petition the government to resist the Russians in Manchuria and they failed in their mission, some even suspected that T'ao, who had returned to China earlier for a promised army post, might have played an obstructionist role. Kung Pao-ch'uan, who also returned to China at this time, was assigned to watch over T'ao. However, Kung came to know T'ao as a righteous man and the two became good friends.[6] Through Kung, T'ao came to know many secret society leaders and other radicals in Chekiang. For the next two years (1903-1904), T'ao toured various cities in Chekiang to meet local secret society leaders to plot for revolution. In the winter of 1904, he joined the Kuang-fu Hui, not long after its founding.

---

6 Chang Huang-ch'i, "Kuang-fu Hui ling-hsiu T'ao Ch'eng-chang ko-ming shih" (The Revolutionary History of T'ao Ch'eng-chang, Leader of Kuang-fu Hui), *Hsin-hai ko-ming*, Vol. I, p. 522.

As far as the Kuang-fu Hui's military activities were concerned, Hsu Hsi-lin was the most important figure. Hsu was also a native of Chekiang province. As a boy, he was a problem child for he loved to destroy things. Often punished by his father, he once left the family and shaved off his hair to become a monk in a temple in a neighboring town though he was only twelve. However, his father found him and brought him back. He had little formal education, but was said to be gifted in mathematics. At the time of the Boxer Rebellion, he tried to organize a militia to protect his village. Later he became a mathematics teacher in the public school in Shaohsing, a large city in his native province. He was soon discovered by the mayor of the city, who made him deputy principal of the school. He stayed on that job for four years and was well-liked by the students. In 1903, he went to Japan to visit a trade fair in Osaka, and later went to Tokyo. It was the time when the Chinese students there were trying to organize volunteers to return to Manchuria to fight the Russians. Caught in the student agitation, he met many student leaders, including T'ao and Kung, and soon became closely associated with them, mainly because they were all from Chekiang province. After he returned to China, he set up a school and a bookstore in his native village and started his anti-Manchu campaign.

In the winter of 1904, he went to Shanghai on a business trip, and there he met T'ao again. At the suggestion of T'ao and Ts'ai Yuan-p'ei, he joined the Kuang-fu Hui, which had just come into existence. Upon returning to his village, he added to the curriculum of his school the subject of military science. Meanwhile, he travelled in the neighboring counties, making acquaintances with local radical elements. After two months of travelling, he was greatly encouraged at having become acquainted with a number of what he described as "comrades."[7]

In the autumn of 1905, Hsu started another school, this time in the city of Shaohsing, with a far more ambitious purpose in mind. The school, named Ta-t'ung, was ostensibly a specialized school of physical education but actually was a training ground for revolutionary cadres. In order to avoid official suspicion, Hsu, with the assistance of T'ao Ch'eng-chang, even tried to get official sanction for the school. For this

---

7. T'ao Ch'eng-chang, *op. cit.*, p. 56.

purpose, T'ao went to the provincial capital city of Hangchow and presented his views to the authorities. He told the Manchu officials that in many Western countries, the militia system had become very popular. Citizens with preliminary military and physical training were serving as militiamen while going about their usual professions but were ready for call-up on short notice. With a little additional training after the call-up, they could be assigned to military duties. While the militia system was lacking in China at that time, he said, the trend was toward eventual adoption of the system. It was only natural to be prepared for that eventuality and the Ta-t'ung school was established precisely for that purpose. It would admit students who had completed six years of elementary schooling for six months of intensive military and physical education, and upon completion of the six-month course, the students would return to their hometowns to serve as volunteer militiamen, ready for call-up in the future. The authorities became interested in his ideas, and granted him permission to start the school.[8]

With the official sanction obtained, T'ao, accompanied by Kung and one other comrade, returned to Shaohsing to report the news to Hsu. On their way home, they made side trips to various cities to meet with local secret society leaders, asking them to come to Shaohsing to attend the Ta-t'ung school. Meanwhile, Hsu openly bought guns and ammunition from Shanghai for "training" use at the school. The enrollment of the Ta-t'ung school was quite impressive, with the secret society leaders from several neighboring counties all coming to it. Upon T'ao's suggestion, a secret ruling was put into effect that all graduates of the school would automatically become members of the Kuang-fu Hui.[9] With the Ta-t'ung school becoming a meeting ground for the secret society members, many of whom were known to local community leaders as unscrupulous people, some grumbling voices were heard from the public, but in the face of the official sanction, local opposition or dissatisfaction never became too strong, and more secret society members kept coming to the Ta-t'ung school.

Hsu and T'ao had yet another way to enchance the prestige of the school and to allay the dissatisfaction of the local community. Using

---

8 *Ibid.*, p. 27.

9. *Ibid.*, p. 28.

the official sanction to the best advantage, Hsu managed to have the official seal of the Shaohsing prefecture and those of the several counties under its jurisdiction affixed on the student's diplomas. In addition, at each commencement exercise, local officials and prominent community leaders were invited to attend the ceremony and pose for pictures with the students. Thus both the officials and local community leaders were deeply involved in the school. This trick paid off later, for the school was to withstand many difficulties, and some former students even received protection in one form or another from local officials who feared their own fate after revolts had taken place.[10]

Prior to the establishment of the Ta-t'ung school, the inculcation of revolutionary ideas in Chekiang province was largely due to the work of T'ao and a few others. Traditionally, Chekiang had been a province known for its intellectual standing. As a coastal province, it stood at the forefront of Western impact. Anti-Manchu feeling had already been growing even before organized opposition appeared. For several years before the emergence of the Kuang-fu Hui, T'ao and others had concentrated their work on the secret societies. Aside from personally contacting the secret society leaders and attempting to unite them for the anti-Manchu cause, T'ao paid special attention to propaganda work. Radical publications, including journals and booklets, some originating from Tokyo and others done in China, were widely disseminated, particularly among the lower social strata, where some revolutionary pamphlets written in colloquial style were very popular. The secret societies were never a unified force, but their rekindled anti-Manchu feeling was a source of strength to the revolutionists. Toward rekindling this feeling T'ao had contributed much, and it was chiefly relying on the assumed strength of the secret societies that Hsu Hsi-lin and others later staged daring revolts.

With the Ta-t'ung school established, Hsu and others were busy thinking about the next step in the revolutionary plot. According to T'ao Ch'eng-chang, it was he who first proposed that they should go to Japan to study military science in order to join the army upon their return and occupy important posts in it. T'ao was of the opinion that in

---

10 *Ibid.*

11 *Ibid.*

order to expand their revoltuionary activities, they must try to make use of the army. He believed that it was not enough merely to operate a school to train a limited number of local revolutionaries, who possessed no real knowledge of a professional soldier. Hsu agreed with him. With the help of a wealthy local merchant, who contributed a sizable amount of money, Hsu bribed the governor of Chekiang, Shou Shan, into approving the applications of Hsu and four others to go to Japan to study military science. They included T'ao and Kung Pao-ch'uan, the man who was among the first to organize the Kuang-fu Hui. In early 1906, they arrived in Japan. The original goal of studying military science was never realized, however, because Hsu was refused admission by both the military academy and the quartermaster school owing to his nearsightedness. Hsu wound up in the police academy, and stayed there only a few months before returning to China. Meanwhile, T'ao, accompanied by Kung, also returned to China, recuperating from a foot injury in Hangchow.

Returned students from Japan in those days were looked upon with special favor, more so if one knew people in high places. With his connections among high officials, Hsu won the post of associate director of the police academy in Anking, capital of Anhwei province. This was in the winter of 1906. For a young returned student, this was quite a high post and Hsu was apparently satisfied with it. Ostensibly he worked so hard that the governor of Anhwei, En Ming, a Manchu, came to regard him as a confidant. Actually, using his position as a cover, Hsu was actively plotting a revolt to be staged simultaneously in Anhwei and Chekiang.

It is to be recalled that at the time of the departure of Hsu and T'ao for Japan, the Ta-t'ung school was temporarily left without an able leader. For a short while, it was managed by a few local prominent educators at the urging of Hsu. Shortly after, however, the school had an able head in the person of a lady revolutionist, Ch'iu Chin, the first and best known heroine of the 1911 revolution. Under her direction, more secret society members were recruited from neighboring counties. She even started a girl's class to train girls in the use of small arms in the name of "physical education." This was far ahead of her time in China and there were criticisms among local community leaders. Meanwhile, as more secret society members came to town, there were unruly elements among them, including those known to others as bandits and ringleaders. Their appearance often incurred the wrath of local community leaders. However, as the Ta-t'ung school was sanctioned by the government, the local people were able to do very little about it.

Ch'iu Chin, a native of Shaohsing, was born to a scholar-gentry family. In her youth, she showed qualities that set her quite apart from other girls. She loved to read chivalrous stories, rode on horseback and was quite at home with liquor. Shunning femininity, she liked to wear men's clothing and to act like a man. Her admiration for masculine qualities was so strong that after she joined the T'ung-meng Hui, she even changed her name to Ching Hsiung, which literally means "competing with the male."

At the age of eighteen, she was married to Wang Yen-chun and moved to Peking, where Wang served in the government. However, her marriage was not a successful one – she later was separated from her husband, after bearing him two children, a boy and a girl. By her own admission, the reason for their separation was that their personalities were so different and their interests so diverse that to continue co-habitation would have been unbearable to both. Divorce or separation was rare in the traditional Chinese society in those days. Forbearance was regarded as a virtue with regard to matrimony, and this virtue was often particularly urged upon the wife. It took a courageous woman like Ch'iu Chin to break this tradition. She received a sizable amount of money after the separation from her husband, and with the money she went to Japan to study, in early 1904.

Soon after her arrival in Japan, she started to make friends among the radical students. While studying the Japanese language before entering formal school, she and ten other Chinese students organized a secret society. In the winter of 1904, T'ao Ch'eng-chang went to Japan, where Ch'iu met him. Because they both were natives of Chekiang, they became very close. Having finished her language course, she planned to return to China to visit her family briefly. Before her departure, she asked T'ao about the revolutionary activities which T'ao and others had carried out in Chekiang. T'ao told her everything, and wrote two letters for her, introducing her to Ts'ai Yuan-p'ei and Hsu Hsi-lin. With the letters in hand, she sailed for Shanghai, where she met Ts'ai and Hsu, who later initiated her into the Kuang-fu Hui.[12] This was in June, 1905. Two months later, she was back in Japan and was enrolled in a girl's school.

While in Tokyo, she was busy with anti-Manchu agitation among the students. She was so active among the students that according to one of her biographers, she attended all meetings of the students and rose to speak at each meeting.[13] When Sun Yat-sen organized the T'ung-meng Hui in Tokyo in 1905, she was one of the two Chekiang members at the founding meeting and later, when she returned to China, she was chief of the T'ung-meng Hui branch in Chekiang.[14] At the time she joined the T'ung-meng Hui, she was the first women to join the organization.

After her return to China, she first lived in Shanghai, where she secretly made home bombs with a few other comrades. An explosion took place one day, wounding one comrade and Ch'iu narrowly escaped injury. Fortunately, they got away from the police. After the incident, she abandoned the bomb-making business and started a journal in Shanghai called *Chung-kuo Nu Pao* (Chinese Women's Journal). The publication was short-lived, because she soon closed it down and returned to Shaohsing to join the Ta-t'ung school. This was in early 1907. Meanwhile, she travelled between Shanghai and Hangchow, making contacts with the military and school circles through comrades who were secret society members. By this time, she had already turned the Ta-t'ung school into a revolutionary center. Efforts to organize opposition and to win comrades were pushed in earnest in many cities, and in some cases, rich merchants were converted to the revolutionary cause.[15]

---

12 T'ao Ch'eng-chang, *op. cit.*, p. 61.

13 Ch'en Ch'u-ping, "Chien-hu nu-hsia Ch'iu Chin chuan" (A Biography of Ch'iu Chin), *Hsin-hai ko-ming,* Vol. III, p. 184.

14 Feng Tzu-yu, *op. cit.*, p. 21.

15 One Liu Yao-shun, a rich merchant in Wuyi, for example, promised to finance a revolutionary army. T'ao Ch'eng-chang, *op. cit.*, p. 62.

Ch'iu's plan called for an uprising in Kinhua in Chekiang province to induce the Manchu troops from Hangchow, the capital, to come to the aid of Kinhua, so that the revolutionary force from Shaohsing could move in to take the provincial capital. Failing that, the revolutionaries from Shaohsing would consolidate with the forces from the neighboring cities to move westward to join force with Hsu Hsi-lin in Anking. The date for the uprising was first set for July 17, then changed to July 30. However, the Manchu authorities got wind of the plot and started to raid local revolutionary groups before the set date. It was claimed that the local revolutionary forces, several thousand strong, were organized in eight columns known as the Kuang-fu Chun (Restoration Army), with Hsu Hsin-lin as commander and Ch'iu as one of the deputies. Meanwhile, a "dare-to-die" detachment of thirty-two men went to Hangchow to await order to move.[16] However, with Hsu's failure in Anking, Ch'iu's plan fell to the ground and she found herself in a hopeless situation.

Hsu Hsi-lin's uprising in Anking was a daring venture. He had only two close associates working with him, Ch'en Po-p'ing and Ma Chung-han. Ch'en was a student of his, while Ma was a fellow native from Chekiang. Taking advantage of his position as associate director of the Police Academy, Hsu believed that the cadets under his command could be an asset. His plan for revolt was almost unbelievably rash; but in a way it does suggest the intensity of the anti-Manchu feelings on the part of the radical revolutionists. Hsu's plan called for the uprising to be staged on July 17, the day when the commencement exercises would be held at the Police Academy. With all ranking officials including the governor of Anhwei province, En Ming, at the Police Academy for the occasion, Hsu decided to kill En Ming on the spot and take control of the situation by manipulating the cadets. In one stroke, he hoped to take over the provincial administration. Meanwhile, in Shaohsing, Ch'iu Chin was to time her revolt with Hsu's move, so that the two provinces of Anhwei and Chekiang could be taken simultaneously before news of the uprising could reach Peking and government troops were rushed in. Local forces, supposedly well-coordinated by Ch'iu, at the same time would also raise the standard of rebellion to seize control of several

16 Ch'en Ch'u-ping, *op. cit.*, p. 185.

important cities. However, in Shaohsing, for reasons unexplained, Ch'iu had already postponed the date for the uprising to July 30, and this was done apparently without the knowledge of Hsu.

On the day of the commencement exercises, the graduating cadets were all gathered in the hall, waiting for the arrival of the governor. Hsu, in his capacity as associate director of the academy, was the grand marshal for the occasion. At one point, he would come very near the governor to hand over to him the student roster for the governor to make a roll call. That was the moment Hsu had chosen to kill En Ming. The place was in a room just behind the main hall.

The governor arrived on time. Dutifully, Hsu approached him ostensibly to hand over the roster to him. At a distance of only a few feet, Hsu suddenly drew two pistols from his long boots and fired at En Ming point blank. Because of his near-sightedness and understandable nervousness, he emptied both his pistols to make sure that En Ming was hit. The room was immediately in commotion, with everyone running for cover. Ch'en Po-p'ing, standing beside Hsu, also started to shoot, with Ma Chung-han at the door to keep other officials from fleeing. Having reloaded his guns, Hsu turned toward the main hall, and announced that the governor had been shot by an assassin, and then commanded the deeply shocked cadets to follow him out to search for the assassin. With Ch'en and Ma guarding behind, Hsu forced the unarmed cadets to march toward the nearby arsenal. Knowing that something went wrong, suspicious and fearful, many cadets fled on the way. When the procession reached the arsenal, only forty to fifty cadets were left. Fully aware of what was happening now, the cadets, however, could do very little but follow Hsu's orders to get hold of fire arms in the arsenal and were assigned guard duties. Soon the Manchu troops arrived. Hsu, Ch'en and Ma led the cadets to resist arrest, but several were killed in the ensuing battle, including Ch'en. Seeing that there was little hope, Hsu and Ma retreated inside, and then fled through the back door. A little later, Ma was caught by the pursuing soldiers, without knowing that Hsu had already been captured. En Ming died of wounds that afternoon, and Hsu was executed the next day. For all practical purposes, the uprising was over.

The Anking episode ended just as abruptly as it took place. Before

Hsu was executed, he wrote a testimony, boldly admitting his anti-Manchu plot. His testimony, together with that of Ma Chung-han's, was the only direct source of information about the incident, for which very few details were otherwise available. The voluminous memorials and reports by the Manchu officials in the aftermath of the uprising were primarily based on the two testimonies. The authenticity of the two documents is beyond doubt, not only because they contain some minute details of the events which could not be known to others, but also, as in the case of Hsu's testimony, because of the fiercely anti-Manchu tone that runs through each passage.

In his testimony, Hsu admitted that he was the leader of the "revolutionary party," apparently meaning the Kuang-fu Hui. He declared that he came to Anking solely for anti-Manchu purposes, taking the official post so that he would not be suspected.[17] Assailing the Manchus for having "persecuted the Han race for nearly 300 years," he expressed particular indignation at the decision of the Manchus to adopt constitutional monarchy, which he termed "nothing but a trick to deceive the people in order to further increase the power of the central government." Knowing that he was soon to die, Hsu explained his motive:

> I have decided that once the opportune moment presents itself, I would kill off all Manchus. . . I had intended to proceed slowly with my plan. But lately the governor has been enforcing strict orders to arrest all revolutionists and he has in fact ordered me in person to do the job. Fearing that any delay would only hurt my plan, I decided to take his life first and then force all officials at Anking to surrender. Thereupon, I would lead my force to proceed to Nanking and fulfill my greatest ambition.[18]

Referring to the cadets, Hsu said they were all innocent and knew nothing of his plans. "You can kill me, but do not hurt the innocent students, who were forced at gun point to follow me to the arsenal."[19] He asserted that the revolutionary party "has a large number of

---

17 T'ao Ch'eng-chang, *op. cit.*, p. 80.

18 *Ibid.*,

19 *Ibid.*, p. 81.

followers, but in Anking, I am the only leader, with my helpers Ch'en and Ma." At the end of his testimony, Hsu revealed his difference with Sun Yat-sen: "My objectives are different from those of Sun Wen's and he is not qualified to ask me to make this assassination attempt."[20] By saying this, Hsu might have intended simply to protect Sun.

While Hsu in his testimony referred to Ma Chung-han as one of his two assistants in Anking, Ma's own testimony does not seem to bear that out. In his testimony, Ma, apparently under great strain and fear and trying to protect himself, pictured himself as an innocent man involuntarily involved in the case. Since Ch'en Po-p'ing was killed at the arsenal, Ma was the only alleged revolutionists aside from Hsu. He was thus held for lengthy questioning. The testimony might not have been entirely given freely by Ma, but it was revealing and it did present the intimate aspects of the planning of the Anking episode. It was therefore worth extensive quoting.

Ma, who was twenty-four at the time of his arrest, first recounted his acquaintance with Hsu and Ch'en in early 1906 aboard a ship homebound from Japan. Ch'en, who came from the same village as Ma, was in a third class cabin. Through Ch'en, he came to know Hsu who was travelling aboard the same ship as a first class passenger. He recalled that Hsu talked about anti-Manchu revolution and wanted him to join in the movement. "I promised on the surface, but not convinced in my heart," he said in his testimony.[21] In early 1907, he met Ch'en again in Shanghai, and was asked by Ch'en to go to Anking with him to see Hsu, who was then the associate director of the Police Academy there. Reluctantly, he related, he followed Ch'en to Anking, and lived at Hsu's residence. One day, after he overheard Hsu and Ch'en talk about revolution, he was scared. Then, one night, Hsu and Ch'en came to his room and Hsu told him of the assassination plan in the following conversation as recorded in Ma's testimony:

---

20 *Ibid.* In Tsou Lu, *Chung-kuo Kuo-min-tang shih-kao,* the official historian of the Kuomintang gives a somewhat different version of the same passage: "My objectives are different from those of Sun Wen's, and he did not ask me to commit this assassination," p. 738.

21 T'ao Ch'eng-chang, *op. cit.,* p. 81.

Hsu: The governor will be at the academy tomorrow. We shall kill him and start our revolution.

Ma: I am afraid it is impossible.

Hsu: Everything has already been arranged, and you don't have to be afraid. Since you are already in this, you are not free to say no.[22]

According to Ma, Hsu said that after killing the governor, he, Hsu, would be the governor and everybody would then obey him. Hsu then continued, as Ma told in his testimony:

> After we kill the governor, we'll take control of the arsenal, the telecommunications office and the training headquarters. They can do nothing because they will have neither arms nor communications facilities at their disposal. By the time the news reaches Nanking, we'll be in Nanking already. My only worry is that the cadets will escape at the time the governor is shot. We must keep the door closed and our success will be assured.[23]

Ma testified that the manifesto of the Kuang-fu Hui, copies of which were uncovered after the assassination, was drafted by Ch'en while the accompanying disciplinary regulations for the revolutionary army were written by Hsu. Ma recalled that some forty to fifty copies of the manifesto were printed on the eve of the uprising and that he helped with the printing. After the printing was done, Ma said, Ch'en produced five pistols, and loaded each with five rounds of ammunition. Ch'en handed one over to Ma, two to Hsu, and kept two himself. The next morning at the Police Academy, when Hsu was with the governor, Ma and Ch'en were waiting in a side room. Suddenly they heard shots and Ch'en immediately dragged Ma out toward the next room. When Ch'en started shooting, Ma said he was too afraid to shoot. At this time, the governor was already fatally wounded and the cadets in the hall were thrown into consternation. According to Ma, Hsu ordered the cadets to follow him to the arsenal, with Ch'en at the rear of the procession. En route, many cadets fled, and upon arrival only about twenty to thirty

---

22 *Ibid.*, p. 82.

23. *Ibid.*

were left. Hsu then ordered several cadets to guard the front gate under the command of Ch'en. Soon, shots were heard. Seeing that the soldiers were approaching, Ma with several students slipped out through the back door, scaled the wall and escaped. Within an hour, however, he was captured. It was not until two days later when he was asked to identify two bodies that he realized that Ch'en had died at the arsenal and that Hsu was executed after arrest. At the end of his testimony, Ma pleaded that he was only following Hsu's orders and that he had never heard of such a revolutionary party as the Kuang-fu Hui.

In general the two testimonies were in substantial agreement about the episode. Ma's detailed testimony such as how he was told of the plot at the last minute, how he was given the pistol, and how he helped to print the manifesto, tended to substantiate Hsu's admission that he, Hsu, was the principal plotter. This seemed to support Hsu's contention that the cadets were innocent and that he had no accomplices except Ch'en Po-p'ing and Ma Chung-han, for nowhere in Ma's testimony was another name or any number of persons mentioned. However, whether Ma was really so innocent as to know nothing of the plot before hand, as he so claimed in his testimony, is highly doubtful. It was at this point that his confession apparently contradicted Hsu's testimony. Ma's claim that he did not even know of the existence of such a revolutionary party as the Kuang-fu Hui was even more difficult to believe, in view of the fact that he had been so close to Hsu. The circumstances would strongly suggest that Ma had lied in an attempt to prove his innocence. However, whatever plea Ma had made came to no avail. He was executed after a short imprisonment.

From Ma's confession that only forty to fifty copies of the manifesto were printed and that the printing was done on the eve of the uprising, it was clear that the uprising attempt was ill-planned and was on a limited scale. Hsu was naive in believing that once the governor was killed, everything would go his way. The only force he relied on for starting the revolt was the cadets, whom he apparently either had not succeeded in converting to the cause of the revolution, or, as Ma's confession would suggest, Hsu did not disclose his plot to them at all.

After the defeat of Hsu's plot, the government forces moved quickly against Ch'iu Chin in Shaohsing. When Hsu's death became known, some of Ch'iu Chin's followers had urged that the date for the uprising be moved ahead of schedule, but Ch'iu, probably by then already disheartened, turned a deaf ear to the plea. Because of the apparent hopeless situation, many left the Ta-t'ung school at the last moment for good. Ch'iu's plan never had a chance, for on July 24, government troops came in force and surrounded the school. After a brief resistance, all the remaining revolutionists at the school, including Ch'iu, were rounded up. Two days later, Ch'iu was executed.

After the Ch'iu Chin case was over, the governor of Chekiang, Chang Tseng-yang, collected all the documents relating to the case, including the confessions of the accused and all their correspondence and memorials, compiled them into a single volume and submitted them to the Chun-chi Ch'u (General Staff Office) for permanent custody. Two documents in this collection were of particular relevance. One was Ch'iu Chin's testimony; the other was a joint memorial submitted by the prefect of Shaohsing and the magistrates of the two counties under the jurisdication of the Shaohsing prefecture.

In her testimony, Ch'iu had said she was twenty-nine years of age at the time of her arrest. However, other sources put her age variously at thirty-one or thirty-three.[24] Ch'iu admitted that on the day the soldiers raided the Ta-t'ung school, she was trying to flee, carrying a pistol and a brief case containing secret papers. However, it was too late to do so. Admitting that the pistol and the seized papers belonged to her, she refused to answer any further questions. Her testimony closed with this statement: "As for other details of the revolutionary party, there is no point for you to pursue further now that I already made the above admission."[25]

The joint memorial submitted by the Shaohsing prefect and the magistrates of the Shanyin and Kuaichi counties contained a brief recount of the case. In it, the local officials claimed that they had

---

24 T'ao Ch'eng-chang, *op. cit.*, p. 31. T'ao puts Ch'iu's age at 31. In an epitaph, Hsu Tzu-hua puts her age at 33 at the time of her death.

25 Ku-kung Tang-an Kuan (Palace Archives), "Che-chiang pan-li Ch'iu Chin ko-ming ch'uan-an" (Complete File on Ch'iu Chin's Revolutionary Case in Chekiang), *Hsin-hai ko-ming,* Vol. III, p. 195.

knowledge of Ch'iu's July 30 uprising and moved quickly to foil it. According to their information, Ch'iu and Chu Shao-k'ang, a local secret society leader, had several thousand followers. The memorial said that every precautionary measure was taken before the raid was staged against the Ta-t'ung school. The officials reported in the memorial:

> Secretly, we called in troops and on the fourth day of the sixth moon (July 24), with important points of the city posted with guards, a detachment was sent to the Ta-t'ung school to arrest the culprits. Some opened fire to resist arrest, and the soldiers were obliged to fire back, wounding two of the bandits. Ch'iu Chin was captured together with six others, and a pistol and a diary were found on her. Arms seized at the Ta-t'ung school included 41 nine-shot mauser guns, one 13-shot sub-machine gun, five one-shot mauser gun, one front loading gun, and 6,200 rounds of ammunition.[26]

In substantial agreement with Ch'iu's testimony, the memorial said that Ch'iu, when asked about the number of followers in the "bandit party," persisted in not saying anything. "With the concrete evidence in hand and in view of the fact that rumors have filled the area causing general unrest, we sought, and were granted, permission by the governor to have Ch'iu Chin executed to prevent unpredictable happenings," the officials said in the memorial, adding that 1,000 silver dollars had been offered for the arrest of Chu Shao-k'ang, Ch'iu's accomplice, who was in hiding.[27]

The failure of both Hsu and Ch'iu in their respective plots greatly shocked the provincial authorities and measures were subsequently taken to clear up their followers in various localities within the two provinces of Chekiang and Anhwei. Meanwhile, the local rebel leaders, among whom T'ao Ch'eng-chang and others had worked, were grieved over the loss of Hsu and Ch'iu. One after another, they raised the banner of rebellion. However, these disorganized and undisciplined local rebel groups were no match for the government troops and the scattered revolts were eventually put down. Within less than one year of the Anking and Shaohsing uprisings, revolutionary resistance in Chekiang all but disappeared, at least on the surface. Casualties on both

---

26 *Ibid.*, pp. 192-93.

27 *Ibid.*

sides were heavy, although no large-scale engagements were ever fought throughout the year-long unrest. Many rebels died in action, others were rounded up by the authorities in the aftermath, many of whom were either executed or given jail terms.

According to T'ao Ch'eng-chang, who now had a price on his head, several hundred Kuang-fu Hui members died in action, while local rebels killed numbered several thousand.[28] On the government side, the loss was equally heavy. The governor of Anhwei, En Ming, was killed, so were several prefects, magistrates and military officers. Junior officials and soldiers lost in action, according to T'ao, numbered as many as 3,000.[29] In addition, several high officials, including the governor of Chekiang and prefect of Shaohsing, were dismissed as a result of the incidents.[30] The casualty figures cited by T'ao were surprisingly high, considering the fact that no large-scale engagements ever took place in the two provinces during the period under consideration. Unfortunately there is as yet no other known source to verify T'ao's statements. Records concerning the Kuang-fu Hui are scanty, and T'ao's work is the most authoritative source in existence.

As a leader of the Kuang-fu Hui, T'ao probably exaggerated about the scale of the rebellions led by or connected with the Kuang-fu Hui. Moreover, it can be said that the casualties suffered by the local rebels in a number of scattered revolts cannot possibly be accurately known even to the participants. However, one thing is certain: in the two provinces of Chekiang and Anhwei, although organized resistance was weak, the popular anti-Manchu feeling was high at the time, and in the actual rebellions, there was wide participation by the local people, particularly by the members of secret societies. It is true that the rebels were disorganized, and the immediate result of the rebellion was disastrous, but in the whole revolutionary picture, this was undoubtedly another step forward in undermining the authorities of the Manchus and consequently contributing to the spread of the revolutionary flames across the land.

---

28 T'ao Ch'eng-chang, *op. cit.*, p. 45.

29 *Ibid.*, p. 46.

30 *Ibid.*

ORGANIZATION AND PROGRAMS

There is no known source about the exact membership of the Kuang-fu Hui at any time or the details of its organization. While much is unknown, judging from the activities of the leaders of the Kuang-fu Hui, it appears that the organization was never a tightly knit one, or as well established as the T'ung-meng Hui. The leaders of the Kuang-fu Hui, especially T'ao Ch'eng-chang, Hsu Hsi-lin and Ch'iu Chin, were pretty much on their own in carrying out anti-Manchu activities, with very poor planning or coordination. All of them relied heavily on the secret societies, which proved to be a highly questionable source of support. As already mentioned, T'ao had started to work among the secret societies in Chekiang even before the Kuang-fu Hui was formed. Whether T'ao himself was a member of one of the secret societies cannot be readily established, but perhaps this is an inconsequential point. What is known is that he once did have wide contacts among the various local groups and there is evidence that he had particularly close connections with a certain sect known as the Lung-hua Hui (Dragon Flower Society). T'ao once wrote a lengthy manifesto in the name of the Lung-hua Hui and a ten article by-law of the society.[31] No reference was made to the Kuang-fu Hui in this manifesto, but presumably the Lung-hua Hui had close relations with it because of T'ao. As to the Kuang-fu Hui itself, there exist today several documents bearing its name. Among them two are significant: one is a manifesto, issued in Hsu Hsi-lin's name; the other is a statement on the organization of the Kuang-fu Chun (Restoration Army), attributed to Ch'iu Chin. These documents in similar way tell of the violent anti-Manchu feelings of the Kuang-fu Hui leaders, but at the same time also raise interesting questions about the aims of the Kuang-fu Hui and the claims of the leaders about the strength of their followers.

To begin with, the manifesto of the Lung-hua Hui written by T'ao appears to show that T'ao was trying to reorganize the Lung-hua Hui, whose anti-Manchu origin can be traced to the downfall of the Ming Dynasty. The document was dated February, 1904, with no exact date given. This was nearly one year prior to the formation of the Kuang-fu

---

31 T'ao Ch'eng-chang, "Chung-kuo pi-mi she-hui shih" (The History of Chinese Secret Societies), *Hsin-hai ko-ming,* Vol. I, pp. 534-44.

Hui, at the time when T'ao was known to be working among the secret societies. The document was written in colloquial style presumably to suit the poorly educated secret society members. It showed T'ao's political ideas, which were naive and incoherent. Borrowing from Confucius and other sages in Chinese history to justify his anti-Manchu stand, T'ao called for a revolution to overthrow the Manchus and restore the rule to the Han people. Beyond this, his political ideas became less clear and it appears doubtful if T'ao at this stage had formulated any concrete political ideas at all. He declared his opposition to both constitutional monarchy and republicanism, but he did not spell out just what kind of political system he would advocate.[32] He spoke of the day when taxes would be cut, the number of soldiers reduced, the fabulous rich would disappear, no one would go hungry, and peace and tranquility would reign, but he had not a single word on how to make all this a reality.[33] In Article I of the by-laws, he drafted, T'ao stated that the purpose of the Lung-hua Hui was to "drive out the Tartar royal family" and to "restore the Ming Dynasty." He seemed to show some interest in socialism, for the same article declared that land was to be owned by all, rich and poor, so that all could be assured a decent living.[34] Quite naturally, he attached great importance to the military, outlining the organization of "five viceroyships" each with subordinates down the line laid out in detail.[35] Other articles of the by-laws contained provisions concerning promotion and punishment, duties and membership requirements. Following the traditions of the secret societies, members were to address each other as "elder brother" or "younger brother," according to their seniority.[36] However, as T'ao later joined the Kuang-fu Hui and the T'ung-meng Hui, there was little further evidence to show that he had actually reorganized the Lung-hua Hui according to this plan.

There is one other source that refers to T'ao's efforts at organizing a rebellion. Chang Huang-ch'i, one of T'ao's biographers, said that in the

---

32 *Ibid.*, p. 538.

33 *Ibid.*

34 *Ibid.*, p. 540.

35 *Ibid.*, pp. 540-41.

36 *Ibid.*, p. 544.

summer of 1906, T'ao organized the revolutionaries in the provinces of Anhwei and Fukien and called himself viceroy of five provinces. It was claimed that he had organized "ten regiments" in the provinces of Chekiang, Fukien, and Anhwei but that soon he went into hiding after his plot was uncovered by the local authorities.[37] The claim was never substantiated, and T'ao's activities, as far as is known, give little credence to such a wild claim. It is possible that the "ten regiments" referred to T'ao's plan to organize the "five viceroyships," as told in the Lung-hua Hui manifesto, but T'ao's biographer puts the time at 1906 rather than 1904.

The Kuang-fu Hui manifesto was one of the documents seized by the Manchu officials after Hsu Hsi-lin's assassination of En Ming, governor or Anhwei. According to Ma Chung-han's testimony, it was drafted by Ch'en Po-p'ing but issued in Hsu's name. In much the same manner as the Lung-hua Hui manifesto, it vehemently attacked the Manchus for their oppression and persecution of the Han people. The document also showed Hsu's basic distrust of the Manchus in their attempt to adopt a constitutional monarchy. Hsu charged in the manifesto: "Recently, under the pretext of preparing for constitutional monarchy in an attempt to further their power, the Manchus have stepped up their tyrannical rule by denying freedom to the people, killing off progressive elements and enforcing other repressive measures.[38] Hsu not only shared with T'ao the same suspicion of the Manchus' attempt to adopt constitutional monarchy, but he had doubts as to whether China at that time was up to the level of constitutionalism. In his testimony after his arrest, he had this to say: "I feel that the Chinese people are not up to the level of genuine constitutionalism. . . . It will not be too late for the Han people to strive for genuine constitutionalism" after the Manchus were overthrown.[39] However, the similarity of Hsu's and T'ao's political ideas ends here. While T'ao spoke of his opposition to both "constitutional monarchy and republicanism" and advocated "restoring the Ming Dynasty," Hsu spoke of the overthrow of the Manchus in order to "assure our people

---

37 Chang Huang-ch'i, *op. cit.*, p. 524.

38 T'ao Ch'eng-chang, "Che-an chi-lueh," p. 76.

39 *Ibid.*, p. 80.

of the blessings of republicanism in the future."[40] It is indeed surprising to see the two most important leaders of the Kuang-fu Hui speak of diametrically opposed goals of their revolution.

There is another evidence showing Hsu's commitment to a future republic form of government for China. The manifesto issued in his name was dated "the 2752nd year of the Republic." Presumably, this is reckoned from the time in Chinese history when the empire was indeed a "republic" for a brief period of time. It was in the year 841 B.C., during the reign of the 10th emperor of the Chou Dynasty, Emperor Li, who was known as a bad ruler. He was overthrown in a rebellion in that year, and several dukes took over and declared a "republic." However, the "republic" was short-lived and a successful restoration was effected a few years later.There is apparently a discrepency in Hsu's calculation, however. The manifesto was seized in 1907, which then should have been the 2748th, not 2752nd year, of the "republic."

Following the manifesto, there were five articles listing five categories of people who would be given the death penalty. They included those who refuse to surrender, those who should oppose the revolutionary army, commit looting, spread rumors or otherwise disturb public order, or serve as traitors.[41]

The statement on the organization of the Kuang-fu Chun (Restoration Army) is attributed to Ch'iu Chin. As far as the anti-Manchu tone is concerned, the statement is not different from those by T'ao and Hsu. However, while Hsu wanted to see "genuine republicanism" in China and T'ao wanted to "restore the Ming Dynasty," Ch'iu urged the people to "act to avenge the wrongs of the past 200-odd years" and to "rebuild a new empire of our own." An "empire" certainly was not a republic, and a "new empire" would not be a mere restoration of the Ming Dynasty. Thus Ch'iu advanced yet another goal of the Kuang-fu Hui, leaving the readers bewildered as to just who was the authoritative spokesman of the Kuang-fu Hui, or indeed whether the Kuang-ful Hui had a clear objective at all. The diverse statements of the Kuang-fu Hui leaders suggested that the organization did not have a coherent body of political ideas guiding its followers.

---

40 *Ibid.*, p. 76.

41 *Ibid.*, p. 88.

Ch'iu worked out a set of regulations governing what she described as the Kuang-fu Chun, consisting of "eight regiments," with Hsu Hsi-lin as commander. It included such details as organization, ranks of officers, insignias, design of flag, and secret codes. However, all this existed on paper only, for there was little evidence to show that the Kuang-fu Chun was actually organized, or even if it was organized, had made any show of force against the Manchus.

In terms of organization and program, the weakness of the Kuang-fu Hui was evident when compared with the T'ung-meng Hui. It had no elaborate program to speak of. Aside from the anti-Manchu sentiment, there was no Kuang-fu Hui leaders who went a step further to expound seriously a post-revolution program for the nation. Its most important leaders did not even agree on just what the goals of the Kuang-fu Hui should be, and they made no attempt to reconcile their differences. The Kuang-fu Chun, with its claimed "eight regiments," was more a myth than a reality. Despite the Kuang-fu Hui leaders' claimed strength in the secret societies, the strength proved to be largely ineffective when faced with the government troops. The Kuang-fu Hui never was a tightly organized group. With the crush of the attempted rebellions in Anking and Shaohsing and the death of Hsu Hsi-lin and Ch'iu Chin, it continued to exist largely on the strength of its few surviving leaders and the remaining members who managed to persist in the revolutionary activities, both in association with the T'ung-meng Hui and independently.

RELATIONS WITH THE T'UNG-MENG HUI

The relations between the Kuang-fu Hui and the T'ung-meng Hui were a mattter of controversy from the beginning. While the establishment of the Kuang-fu Hui was ahead of the T'ung-meng Hui by nearly one year, many important leaders of the Kunag-fu Hui later joined the T'ung-meng Hui after the latter's formation. But in China, particularly in Chekiang province, the Kuang-fu Hui continued to exist and many local revolutionaries were unaware of the T'ung-meng Hui and at least one important leader of the Kuang-fu Hui, Hsu Hsi-lin, refused to join the T'ung-meng Hui.[42] In the first few years, the relationship between

42 Feng Tzu-yu, *Chung-hua-min-kuo k'ai-kuo-ch'ien ko-ming shih*, Vol. II, p. 2.

the two organizations was smooth and, as we have already pointed out, the revolutionists did not bother to distinguish between the Kuang-fu Hui and the T'ung-meng Hui. However, as time went on, and particularly after the failures of the Kuang-fu Hui-led uprisings, differences began to develop and the inter-party struggle persisted even after the birth of the Republic.

With the failure of the Anking and the Shaohsing uprisings, the Kuang-fu Hui received a fatal blow from which it was never to recover. Hsu and Ch'iu, two of the most important leaders, were dead. The remaining leaders, now on the Manchu wanted list, fled the country. Scattered armed resistance in the two provinces was put down. For a while, it looked as though the Kuang-fu Hui had come to an end. However, while the military action ceased, political bickering began. The exiled leaders of the Kuang-fu Hui, T'ao Ch'eng-chang and Chang Ping-lin, both members of T'ung-meng Hui, started to air their differences with the T'ung-meng Hui and in particular they aimed their attack at Sun Yat-sen.

The first open attack on Sun as head of the T'ung-meng Hui made by Chang Ping-lin, then editor of the *Min Pao,* took place even before the Kuang-fu Hui uprisings. In March, 1907, the Japanese government, under pressure from of the Chinese legation in Tokyo, requested Sun to leave Japan but gave him some money for travelling expenses, which Sun accepted. Meanwhile, Sun also received a contribution of 10,000 *yen* from a friendly Japanese stock broker, Suzuki Shisagoro, part of which he left for the *Min Pao* before he sailed for Southeast Asia. Chang Ping-lin openly assailed Sun for impropriety in accepting the gifts of money; he was apparently unhappy because Sun left only a small portion of the money for the *Min Pao,* which was then in financial difficulties.[43] As a gesture of his displeasure, he removed Sun's picture from the office of the *Min Pao* and sent it to the Hong Kong office of the T'ung-meng Hui.[44] A few months later, when T'ao arrived in Tokyo after the Chekiang and Anhwei uprisings, he and

---

43 CF. p. 136.

44 Hu Han-min, "Nan-yang hua-ch'iao yu Chung-kuo ko-ming" (Chinese in Southeast Asia and the Chinese Revolution), Feng Tzu-yu, *Ko-ming i-shih* (Reminiscences of the Revolution), (Taipei: The Commercial Press, 1965), Vol. V, p. 212.

Chang joined the exiled radicals from India, French Indo-China, and Burma to organize the Tung-ya Wan-kuo T'ung-meng Hui (Pan-East Asia Revolutionary United League) with Chang as chairman.[45] The next year, T'ao left Japan for Southeast Asia. He first stayed briefly in Rangoon, serving with a newspaper run by the pro-revolutionist overseas Chinese there. He then toured the British and Dutch islands to raise funds. It was said that T'ao once asked Sun Yat-sen, who was then in Penang, to write to local comrades in his behalf, but Sun refused his request. When T'ao started his fund-raising campaign without Sun's help, the animosity between the two deepened.[46] Sun was said to have accused T'ao of working for the royalists, and allegedly even contemplated to assassinate him[47] Together with one Li Hsieh-ho, who was also a member of both the T'ung-meng Hui and the Kuang-fu Hui and likewise dissatisfied with Sun's leadership, T'ao wrote a letter to the Tokyo T'ung-meng Hui headquarters requesting that Sun be replaced by Huang Hsing as chairman of the T'ung-meng Hui.[48]

In 1910, Chang Ping-lin and T'ao revived the Kuang-fu Hui in Tokyo and they were elected chairman and vice chairman respectively. Meanwhile, many T'ung-meng Hui branches in the Dutch islands which Li Hsieh-ho had helped to establish previously, were now converted to Kuang-fu Hui branches with the reactivation of the Kuang-fu Hui in Tolyo.[49]

While the inter-party bickering continued and an open split appeared likely at times, the revolutionary activities nevertheless went on without interruption. T'ao and Li, for example, continued to work actively. After the Wuch'ang uprising in 1911, they led the Kuang-fu Hui members to participate actively in the revolutionary work in Kiangsu and Chekiang. In particular, they were credited with playing an important role in the capture of Shanghai and other cities in the two provinces. So significant was the role played by T'ao that he was once

45 Chang Huang-ch'i, *op. cit.*, p. 524.

46 *Ibid.*, p. 525.

47 *Ibid.*

48 Kung I-hsing, "Kuang-fu Chun chi" (Records of the Restoration Army), *Hsin-hai ko-ming,* Vol. I, p. 532.

49 Kung I-hsing, *op. cit.*, p. 532.

offered the post of chief of staff to the new governor of Chekiang when that province declared independence from the Manchu, and that he was later mentioned as a possible choice for governorship of the same province.[50]

At the height of his revolutionary career, T'ao was suddenly assassinated in Shanghai, apparently a victim of power struggle. Death came to him on the night of Jan. 13, 1912. He was thirty-five. While the mystery of T'ao death may never be solved, it is plain that the loss of T'ao was a fatal blow to the already weakened Kuang-fu Hui. The death meant that the Kuang-fu Hui lost its last energetic leader and as a result, it practically ceased to operate as an organization. Deeply shocked by the assassination, some Kuang-fu Hui members who now commanded the revolutionary forces in various provinces turned the wrath on the T'ung-meng Hui members. The feud was particularly serious in the Kwangtung province, where members of both parties held equally important military posts. An open break was threatened, with the prospect of bloodshed. Sun Yat-sen, in his capacity as the provisional President of the new Republic, had to issue an open plea for reconciliation between the two factions. In a message to the governor of Kwangtung for transmission to the feuding comrades in early 1912, Sun said the Kuang-fu Hui and the T'ung-meng Hui were originally brotherly groups both dedicated to the same revolutionary goals and there was no appreciable difference in their respective objectives. He acknowledged the contribution of the Kuang-fu Hui in the capture of Shanghai and Nanking and Chekiang province. He urged that amity between the two groups should not be adversely affected by the differences of opinion of one or two leaders, presumably meaning Chang and T'ao. In conclusion, he pleaded with the comrades to bury the hatchet and to work for the unfinished revolutionary task.

---

50 Chang Huang-ch'i, *op. cit.*, p. 527.

Chapter VII

MILITARY CAMPAIGNS

Any revolt against an established order would, in the final analysis, inevitably rely on military force. Curiously enough, until the year before the outbreak of the revolution, the T'ung-meng Hui practically had no military force of its own. Even during the year prior to the birth of the Republic, when the T'ung-meng Hui leaders were keenly aware of the importance of having an organized military force, and made efforts to organize one, the actual size of such a force was still quite small. Its main strength was almost wiped out in the uprising in Canton in early 1911, during which several hundred youths died in action. Heretofore the revolutionists primarily relied on two sources for their strength, the secret societies and the New Army. This continued to be true right up to the time of the birth of the Republic. Almost all uprisings were carried out by either one, or a combination of the two.

Of the ten revolutionary attempts which Dr. Sun spoke of prior to the successful revolt at Wuch'ang on Oct. 10, 1911, two were launched in 1895 and 1900 respectively, while eight took place from 1907 to 1911, after the formation of the T'ung-meng Hui, and were carried out under its direct leadership. The first two were negligible in scale, and the first one actually did not go beyond the planning stage when it was foiled by the authorities. Of the remaining eight, six took place between 1907 and 1908, two of the busiest years as far as the T'ung-meng Hui's military activities were concerned. These revolts all occurred along China's south and south-western borders. Secret society members constituted the bulk of the revolutionary force, while units of the New Army were also involved in some cases. After these came the New Army revolt in Kwangtung in 1910, and the April 27 uprising in 1911, a daring military effort that for the first time saw the participation of the T'ung-meng Hui's own force. The uprising in Wuch'ang on October 10, 1911, that precipitated the downfall of the

Manchu Dynasty, and the secession of many provinces from the Manchu regime after the Wuch'ang uprising were in no small measure attributable to the role played by the New Army.

Whatever the significance of the series of military campaigns in terms of their contribution to the overthrow of the Manchu Court, the role played by the secret societies and the New Army in these military campaigns cannot be ignored. Indeed there would be little to tell in the way of military campaigns had it not been for the secret societies and the New Army, and it would be doubly difficult for the revolutionists to oppose the Manchus without the two sources upon which they could draw their strength.

This chapter purports to examine the role played by the societies and the New Army in so far as they affected the course of the revolutionary movement. In doing so, efforts will be made to probe the mysterious origins of the secret societies and how the revolutionists made use of them. Equal attention will be paid to the history of the New Army and the process by which the revolutionists infiltrated into the New Army to convert the soldiers to the anti-Manchu cause. It is hoped that an examination of these two factors will help put the military campaigns in perspective, and enable us to better evaluate the importance of these campaigns.

SECRET SOCIETIES AND THE REVOLUTION

The Chinese secret society is a fascinating subject that has attracted the attention of many scholars. However, it remains the least studied subject. The primary difficulty lies in the secrecy that shrouds the secret society in regard to its origin, nature, organization, rituals, etc. The earliest beginning of the secret societies cannot be readily ascertained – some people trace it to the Yellow Turbans as far back as the last years of the Han Dynasty (207 B.C. – 220 A.D.) and other quasi-religious sects in Chinese history. However, these organizations are beyond the scope of the present inquiry, which is concerned with the secret societies that were connected with the 1911 revolution. These secret societies were known by different names both within and outside China, but they can all be traced to the same origin in the Hung Meng (The Hung League), a loosely organized secret society established at the end of the Ming Dynasty in south China. According to the commonly accepted version, the original goal of the society was nationalistic: to support the cause of the deposed Ming Dynasty and to overthrow the Manchus, who were regarded as alien conquerors. Loyalist Chinese of the Ming Dynasty, the traditional theory goes, fearing that nationalism would be lost under the Manchu rule, secretly organized the society among the uneducated masses in order to preserve nationalism.

The Manchus were a minority. Upon coming to power in China, in order to control effectively the majority of Chinese, they had to adopt various repressive measures. Rebellions were ruthlessly suppressed and discriminatory treatment was given the Chinese as a conquered people. In regard to the intellectuals, whom the Manchus knew well that they must win over in order to consolidate their rule, both high-handed coercion and material inducement coupled with ideological indoctrination were used. The result was virtual disappearance of oppsoition among the intellectual class, with many intellectuals recruited into the officialdom. Seeing that the intellectuals were no longer "reliable," Ming loyalists turned to the uneducated masses to try to keep Chinese nationalism alive among them by organizing the Hung Meng secret society. Explaining the deliberate design of the Ming loyalists, Sun Yat-sen said theirs was like the rich men hiding their treasures in the earth when the bandits came.[1]

While there is general agreement on the anti-Manchu revolutionary nature of the secret society, there is, however, disagreement about the time the society was founded, and on who were the founders. On these important points, even the documents of the secret society itself did not make clear and members of the society seemed to care little, content with blindly following the myth and fairy-like tales as handed down through the years by the elders.

According to the popular version of the traditional history of the secret society, the Hung Meng, which to outsiders was known as the

---

1. Sun Yat-sen, *San Min Chu I,* pp. 58-59.

T'ien-ti Hui (Heaven and Earth Society), was founded in the 13th year of the reign of Emperor K'ang Hsi (1674 A.D.), the second emperor of the Manchu Dynasty, by a sect of militant Buddhist monks of the Shao-lin Monastery in the P'u-t'ien district of Foochow prefecture of the Fukien province. The monks, well-trained in arms, were said once to have helped the government repel the invading western tribes. After they had returned to their monastery from the expedition, the Emperor was said to have become so alarmed at the strength of the monks that on the advice of an official, Teng Sheng, the emperor decided to get rid of the monks as a potential source of trouble.[2] A large number of troops were sent to P'u-t'ien to attack the monastery. Caught completely unprepared, so the story goes, most of the monks were killed. Only five of them were able to escape. They later fell in with a certain former high official, Ch'en Chin-nan, who had been dismissed from office by the emperor for daring to memorialize the throne, criticizing the massacre at the Shao-lin Monastery. Living as a recluse, he invited the monks to stay with him in a small temple known as the Red Flower Pavilion.[3] It was there that the five monks, together with Ch'en, organized the T'ien-ti Hui and vowed to avenge the Manchu outrages. They adopted the slogan "Overthrow the Manchu and Restore the Ming."[4] The five monks have since been worshipped by members of the secret society as "five ancestors." As to why the name Hung was adopted, there were said to be two reasons. First, this was the first character of the given name of the founder of the Ming Dynasty, Chu Hung-wu. The other reason is the inner hidden meaning of the character Hung, which means flood or inundation. For as the Hung Meng ritual says:

> May the Hung League sweep the world with all the blessings of the primary virtues, humanity, righteousness, propriety, wisdom and faith. So every man who in his heart believes in Heaven above and Earth beneath, and who intends sincerely the liberation of his fellow men from tyranny and immorality, is in fact a member of the Hung League, and his influence is therefore great – boundless like an inundation.[5]

---

2 Hsiao I-shan, "T'ien-ti Hui ch'i-yuan k'ao" (A study of the Origins of the T'ien-ti Hui), *WSNWH,* Ser. 1, No. 2, p. 313.

3 L. F. Comber, *Chinese in Malaya* (New York: J. J. Augustin Inc., 1959), p. 6.

4 *Ibid.,* p. 2.

5 Carl Glick, *Swords of Silence* (New York: McGraw-Hill, 1947), p. 52.

However, all this was based on the traditional version as handed down by the members and there is little historical evidence to back it up. Written records are very scanty, and whatever is in existence today is told by the elders. Fantastic as some of the claims may sound, they are, however, accepted by the secret society members as authentic history.

Serious historians have questioned the traditional history of the Hung Meng as well as the popular interpretation of the Chinese word Hung. Hsiao I-shan, an authority on the history of the Manchu Dynasty, believes the word 洪 (Hung) is an intentionally simplified form of the word 漢 (Han), which originally means the Han Dynasty but has traditionally been used to mean the Chinese people or the Chinese race. Hsiao claims that he learned from a Hung Meng elder that when the last Ming loyalists retreated to Taiwan and attempted to reconquer the mainland overrun by the Manchus, they organized the secret society by adopting the word 洪 which is the word 漢 less its middle part, 𡈼. 𡈼 can be separated into two other words, 中土, meaning "middle land" or "mainland." This, according to the elder, whose interpretation Hsiao endorsed, served as a reminder to all members that the middle land was lost to them and it was incumbent upon them to recover it.[6] Furthermore, it was pointed out that among the Hung Meng members, it was a general practice to omit part of those words that referred to the Manchus. The word for the Manchu Dynasty, 清, was written as 消, omitting the part 主, which means "master." The word for Manchu, 滿, was wirtten as 㴐, without the part 廿 on the upper right corner, implying cutting off the head of the Manchus.[7]

Hsiao also put the date of the T'ien-ti Hui sixty years later than the traditional version at 1723, or the 12th year of the reign of Emperor Yung Cheng. According to the T'ien-ti Hui records as told by the elders, now kept at the British Museum in London, the repulsion of the invading barbarians by the monks took place in the twelfth year of Emperor K'ang Hsi (1674), but after that, there was a prolonged period

---

6 Hsiao I-shan, *op. cit.*, p. 298.

7 *Ibid.*

of peace and it was not until the twelfth year of the reign of Yung Cheng that the Shao-lin Monastery was attacked.[8] He further believed that since there was no record in official history of the Manchu Dynasty about the barbarian invasion in the twelfth year of Emperor K'ang Hsi's reign, the whole story about the monks in the Shao-lin Monastery and the "five ancesters" may well be fiction.[9]

Another historian believed that the T'ien-ti Hui was actually established by Cheng Ch'eng-kung, who at the end of the Ming Dynasty retreated to Taiwan to continue the Ming Dynasty and tried to stage a comeback to recover the mainland. It was from Taiwan that the T'ien-ti Hui spread across the Taiwan Strait to the coastal provinces in south China.[10] This argument was supported by the fact that in the sixtieth year of the reign of Emperor K'ang Hsi (1721), an anti-Manchu rebellion took place in Taiwan, and its leader, Chu Kwei-i, largely relied on the strength of the T'ien-ti Hui.[11] This would suggest that the T'ien-ti Hui had already been in existence before the rebellion. T'ao Ch'eng-chang, the revolutionist who had close contact with the secret societies, also named Cheng Ch'eng-kung as the founder.[12]

While the mysterious history of the secret societies is not of immediate concern to the present inquiry, the general agreement as to the revolutionary nature of the societies is significant. After spreading to the southern coastal provinces of Kwangtung and Fukien and northward to the Yangtze valley, the secret society became known by different names. In the south, it was known as the T'ien-ti Hui, or San-ho Hui or San-tien Hui (Triad Society); in the Yangtze valley, it was called Ko-lao Hui (Elders and Brothers Society). Although among themselves, members were all known as belonging to the Hung Meng, in

---

8 Hsiao I-shan, "Chin-tai pi-mi she-hui shih-liao" (Materials on Modern Secret Societies), *WSNWH*, Ser. 1, No. 2, pp. 304-305.

9 *Ibid.*

10 Lien Heng, *T'ai-wan t'ung-shih* (General History of Taiwan) (Taipei: Chung-hua Book Co., 1955), V. 1, p. 47

11 Ibid.

12 T'ao Ch'eng-chang, "Chiao-hui yuan-liu k'ao" (A Study of the Origins of Religious Sects and Secret Societies), *Hsin-hai ko-ming* Vol.: II, p. 101.

different localities, however, they were organized into various groups, maintaining no close relations with each other, and sometimes even engaged in armed clashes.

Gradually, the original revolutionary nature was lost and the groups became more in the nature of fraternities and mutual help organizations, although the secrecy about membership, rituals, and other details remained. The changed nature of the secret societies was particularly noticeable among the overseas Chinese in Southeast Asia. The exigencies of living abroad among other people apparently helped to cement the ties of the Chiese, and in tying the Chinese together, the role of the secret societies was very important. The local authorities in Southeast Asia gradually became aware of the secret societies among the Chinese. Discoveries were made from time to time, and the results added up to a startling revelation of the existence of many powerful and sometimes notorious organizations.

The existence of the secret societies among the overseas Chinese was not known to the Western world until 1825, when the British and Dutch secret services launched an investigation in the British colonies of the Straits Settlements in connection with a local incident. The result was a report written by the Rev. Dr. Milne, principal of the Anglo-Chinese College in Malacca, entitled "Some Account of a Secret Society in China Entitled 'The Triad Society,' " which was later read at the Royal Asiatic Society of Great Britain and Ireland. He found that the society, supposedly a mutual-aid and protective association for Chinese living abroad, was in reality "a band of blackmailers, cutthroats, thieves, murderers and criminals that terrorized the Chinese community."[13] The next report came in 1840, when a paper, co-authored by two British army officers, Lt. Newhold and Maj. Gen. Wilson of the Madras Army, was again read at the Royal Asiatic Society. More was known about the secret society in the British colonies, including some of its rituals, secret signs, and passwords.[14] The most detailed exposé, however, was made by a Dutchman, Gustave Schlegel, whose work, based on seized documents, was published in

---

13 Glick, *op. cit.*, p. 11.

14 *Ibid.*, p. 12.

1866.[15] While Schlegel's work is still the standard authority today, another comprehensive work on the same subject by two Britons was published in 1925.[16] Battles between rival factions in the secret societies took place in Singapore in 1854 and in Penang in 1867.[17] The Thai government started to pay attention to the secret societies in the 1900's.[18]

As noted previously, Sun Yat-sen was the first to note the importance of the secret society as a potential source of support for the revolution. He joined the Hung Meng in Honolulu as early as 1903. Throughout his revolutionary career, Sun had received aid from the secret societies in various forms, from financial contribution to direct participation in military action. His reliance on the secret societies was heavy, particularly during the early years. Huang Hsing, Sun's chief military aide who personally led most of the uprisings, agreed with Sun that the secret societies, although unreliable in the long run, were useful in the initial stage of an uprising.[19]

The T'ung-meng Hui had no army of its own; in many uprisings, the revolutionary force was composed solely of secret society members or men hastily recruited through the help of the secret society. This was especially true of the six uprisings stated in south China in 1907-08. The uprising that took place in May, 1907, at Huangkang in northern Kwangtung, a traditional stronghold of the San-ho Hui, was led by Hsu Hsueh-ch'iu, an overseas Chinese from Singapore, who was a leader of the secret society and a member of the T'ung-meng Hui. Returning to his native place from Singapore, he led a force of several thousnad secret society members to attack the local government offices and the garrison troops in Huangkang. The preparation for this uprising was largely made by the T'ung-meng Hui office in Hong Kong with Sun Yat-sen giving instructions from Indo-China, where he resided at the

---

15 Gustave Schlegel, *Thiam Ti Hui, or Heaven-Earth* League (Batavia, 1866).

16 J. S. M. Ward and W. G. Sterling, *The Hung Society* (London, 1925).

17 Victor Purcell, *The Chinese in Southeast Asia* (London: Oxford University Press, 1965), p. 114.

18 Kenneth P. Landon, *The Chinese in Thailand* (London: Oxford University Press, 1941), p. 149.

19 Hsueh Chun-tu, *op. cit.*, p. 57.

time. Overwhelming the garrison troops by a surprise attack, the secret society members were able to take full control of the town of Huangkang in the first day of the uprising.[20] Public notices were posted throughout the town proclaiming the revolution in Sun's name.[21] However, after the initial victory, the field commanders were divided on the next target. Before a final decision was reached on the next move, government troops were rushed to the scene in force. Faced with the superior fire power of the government troops, the rebels soon were defeated. Many were captured, others fled to the mountains. In less than a week, the revolt was practically over and Hsu and other surviving leaders fled to Hong Kong. Thus came to an end what Sun Yat-sen called his third revolutionary attempt. (The first was a rebellion planned for 1895 but not carried out. The second was the Huichow uprising in 1900).

Informed of this failure, Sun immediately ordered another attempt in Huichow, another stronghold of the secret society, among whose members the revolutionists had built up some strength. As in the Huangkang uprising, the revolutionists scored some initial victories. However, the military action was hampered by a lack of supplies as a badly needed shipment of arms and ammunition could not reach Huichow because of the close watch the government troops kept on coastal shipping. With their ammunition exhausted and the arrival of government reinforcements, the revolutionists had no choice but to end the revolt by disbanding the secret society members. Sun called this uprising his fourth setback. Teng Tzu-yu, the man who led this uprising, fled to Hong Kong but was later arrested on charges of robbery. He was later handed over to Manchu authorities in Canton and executed.[22]

CAMPAIGNS ON THE SOUTHWESTERN BORDERS

After these two failures in Kwangtung, Sun turned his attention to the Southwest and for the next year or so, four uprisings were staged

20 Feng Tzu-yu, *Chung-hua-min-kuo k'ai-kuo-ch'ien ko-ming shih,* Vol. II, p. 155; Tsou Lu, *Chung-kuo Kuo-min-tang shih-kao,* p. 730.

21 Feng Tzu-yu, *op. cit.,* p. 154.

22 *Ibid.,* p. 168.

on the borders adjoining Indo-China. Huang Hsing personally led all the campaigns, in which fierce fighting took place in the treacherous mountains. In one revolt, Sun Yat-sen was present at the battle scene.

The first of a series of revolutionary attempts, from the Indo-China borders started out with a peasant rebellion against heavy taxation in the summer of 1907 in the border city of Ch'inchow. It soon spread to the neighboring city of Lienchow, where a food riot was in progress. Government troops, numbering near 4,000, were rushed to the scene. This presented the revolutionists with a golden opportunity: the anti-government revolt could be utilized; and the troops rushed to the area were New Army units, whose commanders the revolutionists hoped to win over to their side. Sun Yat-sen, aided by Huang Hsing and others, immediately set to work. On the one hand, they contacted local secret society and community leaders to raise an army to prepare for an uprising. On the other hand, a Japanese follower of Sun's, Kayano Chochi, was sent to Japan with money to purchase arms. Meanwhile, Sun sent men to the New Army camp to sound out the commanders, Chao Sheng and Kuo Jen-chang, on possible collaboration. Favorable response was received on the promise of a cash reward for those soldiers coming over to the revolutionary side.

In August, 1908, the revolutionists decided to take action. A band of several hundred men was sent to join forces with the local rebels to attack Fangch'eng, a city on the Indo-China border. After taking the city, the rebels proceeded to attack the nearby city of Ch'inchow, which was heavily guarded by government troops, among which were New Army units led by Kuo Jen-chang. Huang Hsing was at the time staying with Kuo, actively persuading him to lead the New Army troops to join the revolutionists. Kuo was wavering, partly because the promised reward had not arrived, and partly because he himself had already come under the suspicion of his superior, Wang Hu, prefect of Ch'inchow.[23] Consequently, the original plan, which had called for Kuo to open the city gate on a certain evening to let the rebels in to join a mutiny by Kuo's units, was never carried out.

---

23 *Ibid.*, p. 177.

Unable to take Ch'inchow, the rebels turned to attack another city, Lingshan, in the hope that Chao Sheng, the other New Army commander, would come to their aid as previously planned. However, Chao, apparently influenced by Kuo Jen-chang's inaction, also decided to play it safe by holding up his troops. The lack of the vital support from Kuo and Chao was further compounded by the failure of Kayano Chochi's mission to Japan to purchase arms. The arms deal was sabotaged as a result of the factionalism in the T'ung-meng Hui Tokyo headquarters.[24] With more government troops coming to the scene, the rebels found the situation hopeless and dissolved themselves into small groups and fled into the mountains on the southwestern Chinese borders. So ended Sun's fifth uprising.

Undaunted by the setback, Sun, from his headquarters in Hanoi, directed Huang Hsing to lead some one hundred revolutionaries, together with their French instructors, to mount a surprise attack on Chen-nan-kuan, a strategic pass on the Indo-Chinese border, in late November. With the help of the local tribesmen, the revolutionists seized control of one wing of the pass, together with its powerful guns. The garrison troops, numbering some one hundred, eventually surrendered and were incorporated into the revolutionary forces. Sun Yat-sen for the first time in his revolutionary career was present on the battlefield.[25] Three gun emplacements were now in the hands of the revolutionists, each equipped with a 120 mm Krupp cannon, a 70 mm gun, a heavy machinegun, four 75 mm guns and a number of mortars, with several thousand rounds of ammunition.[26] For a while, the Manchu troops were unable to mount an effective attack on the pass. In intermittent artillery exchanges that lasted seven days and nights, the Manchus suffered heavy casualties from the salvos fired from the pass with deadly accuracy under the directions of the retired French officers. While the situation appeared stalemated, Sun and Huang knew that with their limited stock of ammunition, they could not hope to hold the pass for too long. The only alternative was to break through the siege by attacking the government forces from the flanks and the

---

24 *Kuo-fu ch'uan-shu,* p. 26.

25 *Ibid.,* Feng Tzu-yu, *op. cit.,* p. 193.

26 Feng Tzu-yu, *op. cit.,* p. 195.

rear. In doing so, they badly needed small arms. Sun and Huang therefore left the pass and returned to Hanoi to try to buy arms. Before Sun could get the arms deal through, however, news came that the pass already fell into the hands of the government troops. This was Sun's sixth setback.

Meanwhile, the fighting on the southwestern borders shocked the Manchu Court in Peking. French papers in Indo-China widely reported the military exploits of the revolutionists. Knowing that the rebels mounted their attacks from Indo-China across the border and that Sun's headquarters were based in Hanoi, the Peking government lodged a strong protest with the French governor-general, requesting Sun's immediate departure from Indo-China. Entrusting the military responsibilities to Huang and Hu Han-min, Sun left Hanoi for Singapore in early March, 1908.

Before Sun's departure, he ordered Huang to make another attempt at Ch'inchow and Lienchow on the Indo-Chinese border. With some 200 men under his command, Huang was able to roam the countryside for several months, inflicting casualties on the government troops with a series of attacks. However, laboring under difficult conditions resulting from poor logistic support and limited amount of available ammunition, Huang could not mount a concentrated attack on any of the cities he set out to take. After several months, he had to call off the hit-and-run operation and return to Hanoi.

Meanwhile, another band of revolutionaries, commanded by Huang Ming-t'ang, had seized control of Hokou, killing the garrison officers and taking many soldiers prisoners. Together with the surrendered soldiers and local armed militia, the revolutionaries grew into a sizable force, which prompted Hsi Liang, viceroy of Yunnan and Kweichow, to send urgent cables to Peking for help. He reported that Sun Yat-sen's rebel force was substantial in number, equipped with modern weapons and amply supplied.[27] Informed of the initial success in Hokou, Sun immediately instructed Huang Hsing to proceed to the scene to assume

---

27 Hsi Liang to Chun-chi Ch'u (General Staff Office) and Wai-wu Pu (Foreign Ministry), May 3, 4, 1908, Ku-kung Tang-an Kuan (Palace Archives), *Hsin-hai ko-ming,* Vol. III, p. 269.

command. Huang, who since returning to Hanoi from his last military venture had grown a mustache in order to hide his identity from the local authorties, left Hanoi immediately. Before he could cross the border, he was mistaken by the French border guards as a Japanese and arrested for not possessing proper identification papers. Hokou fell again into the hands of the Manchus in early May, and the revolutionaries, with some 600 men remaining, retreated into Indo-China. These men later were deported to Singapore upon Sun Yat-sen's representation. Sun called Huang Hsing's failure to take Ch'inchow and Lienchow and the Hokou campaign his seventh and eighth setbacks.

With the removal of Sun from Hanoi and the successive departure of Huang, Hu Han-min and others, Indo-China ceased to be a staging area for the revolutionists. Six setbacks in a little over one year in the same area were enough to convince the revolutionists that for future revolts, they must shift to new locations. The role of secret society members and local armed bands, who practically constituted the bulk of the revolutionary force up to now, was also reappraised. A new source of strength apparently was needed as well as a new location for future action. After some serious rethinking and planning, the next few uprisings were staged in Canton, and the main attention was shifted to the New Army.

NEW ARMY AND THE REVOLUTION

After repeated humiliations suffered at the hands of the Western powers in the 19th century, many leaders in China had come to the conclusion that in order to cope with the superior military might of the Western powers, China must build a strong national defense. Despite traditional contempt for foreign ways, coupled with xenophobia resulting from the recent humiliating experiences, it became painfully clear to many people that for China to stand up, or even to hold herself in the face of foreign encroachment, the only way was to learn from the West, particularly in technology and armament. To be sure, conservative opposition to modernization was strong at all times, and this largely accounted for the slow progress of reform in any field. While such modern techniques as shipbuilding and arms manufacture were being slowly developed in a local basis, the final impetus for the training of a modern, Western-style army did not come until after China's defeat by Japan in 1895. The man whose name was most closely linked with what was later known as the New Army was Yuan Shih-k'ai, who eventually became one of the most powerful men in modern Chinese history.

After China's defeat by Japan in 1895, Yuan, then a progressive army officer, was asked by Jung Lu, viceroy of Chihi and the most influential military leader of the time, to study ways and means of adopting Western training methods for the organization of a modern army. The result of Yuan's study, in which he advocated German training, not only won approval by the government, but also won him the appointment to command the first brigade designated to undergo the new training. In December, 1895, Yuan proceeded to Hsiao-chan, a small town near Tientsin in northern China, to assume his new command.[28] Hsiao-chan, like the name Yuan Shih-k'ai, also became a name of historical significance in the military annals of modern China.

Plans for the building of a new Western-style army were soon afoot. The target was set for a total of thirty-six divisions to be stationed in various parts of the country. By the end of 1906, details concerning organization, ranks, pay scales and reserve units were worked out.[29] Although the New Army was to be a national army, the actual responsibility for recruiting, organization and maintenance fell on the shoulders of the local viceroys. Creation of the New Army thus not only became an effort at the provincial level, but also a matter of competition among the viceroys, many of whom were ambitious men, who regarded the New Army strength as their political assets and stressed personal loyalty rather than patriotism. This was particularly true of Yuan Shih-k'ai, who was later responsible for the building of the six New Army divisions in north China, since known as the Peiyang Army. The Peiyang Army had a head start over other planned divisions, which were slow in coming into being and some in fact were never

---

28 Ralph Powell, *The Rise of Chinese Military Power, 1895-1912* (Princeton: Princeton University Press, 1955), p. 75.

29 *Ibid.*, p. 198.

actually organized. According to one estimate, on the eve of the revolution, only fourteen divisions of over two-thirds strength and twenty brigades varying from 2,000 to 6,000 men each were actually formed, falling considerably short of the original target.[30]

From the very beginning, winning over the New Army had been the objective of the revolutionists. It was of course not an easy task, and the revolutionists in their work had met with varying degrees of success with different units. By and large, with the exception of the Peiyang Army which was primarily loyal to Yuan Shih-k'ai, the revolutionists had considerable success in infiltrating the other units. One startling fact was that after the Wuch'ang uprising in October, 1911, all the New Army troops, except the Peiyang Army, quickly cast their lot with the revolutionary forces. While it may be argued that opportunism on the part of those who controlled the New Army units in central and south China may have had a decisive effect on their defection, the successful infiltration of the New Army by the revolutionists certainly was a major factor that should not be overlooked.

Several factors were at the time working in favor of the revolutionists. Some of the factors were not of the revolutionists' making, but they were quick to take full advantage of them. To begin with, the revolutionists often found the growing discontent in the New Army a favorable situation to exploit. The New Army, despite its modern organizational setup and the new method of training, had nevertheless inherited many bad features of the old-style armies, such as failure to pay the troops in full or on time, harsh treatment, favoritism, and partiality for men who came from the commander's native province. These potential sources of trouble, abetted by revolutionary propaganda, often resulted in mutinies, which the revolutionists naturally were glad to see happen.

Secondly, the New Army, because of its favored position and preferential treatment, was often envied by other provincial troops. Consequently, bad feeling developed between them and friction was frequently reported in many places, sometimes resulting in bloodshed. Such friction the revolutionists did their best to promote whenever

---

30. *Ibid.*, p. 288.

possible. In at least one case, a minor dispute, instigated by the revolutionists, actually grew into a large-scale rebellion. Thirdly, in organizing and training the New Army troops, officers, particularly lower ranking officers, were in critical shortage. The local viceroys competed with each other in sending youths abroad, mainly to Japan, for military training. On the other hand, returned students were wooed by the local viceroys. Often they were offered tempting posts even before they completed their schooling abroad, and many cut short their education to return to China. This was where the best opportunity for the revolutionists lay. Most of the students were liberal-minded, and many of them had actually already joined the revolutonary movement while abroad. Their participation in the New Army greatly faciliated the revolutionary work.

With the creation of the New Army, military schools were established in many provinces to train junior officers. The establishment of these schools, like that of the New Army, was also largely done by the local viceroys. In north China, for example, the military school in Tientsin was closely identified with Yuan Shih-k'ai's Peiyang Army. This school, under Yuan's direct supervision, had both German and Japanese instructors.[31] Its graduates went exclusively to serve in the Peiyang Army and in time rose to high positions. Many of the well-known warlords in the post-revolution era were among the proud alumni of this school. Their unswerving loyalty to Yuan Shih-k'ai was one of the main reasons why the revolutionists failed to infiltrate the Peiyang Army. Because of the Peiyang Army, north China remained firmly under the control of Yuan after the 1911 revolution. With a strong military force led by his own "boys," Yuan was ultimately able to become the real beneficiary of the revolution, although only briefly.

The military schools established in other provinces were not so richly endowed as the Tientsin school. While a few foreign instructors were hired here and there, these schools chiefly had to rely on returned students from abroad to serve as instructors. Having been exposed to Western influence and revolutionary propaganda, these young officers became increasingly dissatisfied with the backwardness and corruption

---

31. Wen Kung-chih, "Hsin-hai ko-ming chung chih hsin-chun" (The New Army in the Revolution of 1911), *Hsin-hai ko-ming,* Vol. III, p. 325.

at home. The blame naturally was laid to the Manchu Court, which many of them wanted to overthrow in favor of a republic. These young officers were not only commanding the New Army troops at the lower echelons, but were training future leaders of the New Army. On the eve of the 1911 revolution, there were said to be some 800 officers serving in the New Army who had been trained in Japan and most if not all of whom were pro-republican.[32]

The most important factor, of course, was revolutionary propaganda. Both the revolutionists and those who were inclined to the revolutionary cause continued to carry on their activities after joining the New Army, from secretly contacting the T'ung-meng Hui offices to lecturing their men on nationalism and democracy. The literacy rate among the junior officers in the New Army was higher than that of the old-style army and other local troops; propaganda literature thus was widely circulated among them, particularly if the commander was pro-republican in thinking. Extra-curricular activities of the New Army included the free organization of clubs and associations, nominally for study or fraternity purposes but often they turned out to be fronts of the revolutionists. In addition, the secret societies to which many soldiers belonged also played a role in enhancing revolutionary sentiments in the New Army.

On the propaganda front, the Manchus were in an embarrassingly disadvantageous position. They had to discourage the expression of nationalism even at a time when China was suffering from serious foreign encroachment. This attitude stemmed from the fear of the Manchu Court that the Manchus were themselves a minority race and thus any feeling of nationalism on the part of the Chinese people, even expressed in patriotic terms, could easily be turned on the Manchus. Indeed, this was precisely the case, for the revolutionists were quick to see this propaganda advantage they had.

In their propaganda work within the New Army, the revolutionists strove to "awaken" the "nationalistic consciousness" of the junior officers and enlisted men. This was also the main theme of most of the

---

32. Powell, *op. cit.*, p. 291.

revolutionary pamphlets and tracts popular in the New Army, and often of the lectures of the pro-revolution junior officers. This persistent propaganda, coupled with the discontent caused by the evils inherited from the old-style army and carefully nurtured by the revolutionists, plus the friction between the New Army and other local troops, turned the New Army into a powder keg. Organized to defend the country, the New Army now became a potential source of danger itself. While such claims that the New Army divisions in south and central China were the backbone of the republican forces[33] were exaggerated, one may say that the creation of the New Army, instead of helping the Manchu Court, only hastened the downfall of the Manchu Dynasty. It is true that save on two occasions, the New Army troops had not engaged in large-scale rebellions against the Manchu Court. What was of vital importance to the revolutionary cause was the fact that soon after the outbreak of the 1911 revolution in Wuhan, itself a handiwork of certain New Army units there, practically all New Army troops in central and south China went over to the republican side as one province after another seceded from the helpless Manchu Court. This move of the New Army certainly hastened the demise of the Manchu Dynasty.

NEW ARMY UPRISING, CANTON, 1910

One campaign before 1911 involving the New Army was the uprising in Canton in February, 1910. The uprising grew out of a minor incident, and the revolutionists immediately seized upon the opportunity to make a move against the Manchu Court. It was the first uprising involving a sizable number of New Army troops.

Because of the proximity of Canton to Hong Kong, where the revolutionists had their headquarters, the New Army units stationed in Canton were more deeply infiltrated by the revolutionists than units in other areas. By 1910, revolutionary ideas had permeated the three New Army regiments stationed in the suburbs of Canton.[34] On the night of

---

33 T'ang Leang-li, *The Inner History of Chinese Revolution,* p. 59.

34 Ch'en Ch'un-sheng, "Keng-hsu kuang-chou hsin-chun chu-i chi," (The New Army Uprising in Canton in 1910), *Hsin-hai ko-ming,* Vol. III, p. 347.

February 9, 1910, a soldier by the name of Wu Ying-yuan, from the Third Battalion of the First Regiment, got into an argument with a store-keeper over some minor matters. A police officer intervened and the argument soon became one between the soldier and the police officer, who tried to arrest him. As the argument grew heated, several New Army soldiers happened to pass by. They immediately came to the aid of Wu, while police reinforcements also sped to the scene. A fist fight broke out, resulting in the arrest of several soldiers by the police who outnumbered them.[35] That night happened to be New Year's Eve according to the Chinese calendar. The next day, New Year's Day, was a holiday. Resentful that their comrades were arrested by the police, several hundred New Army soldiers from the Third Battalion came to the police station to seek vengeance. They rescued their comrades, injured several policemen and sacked the police station before returning to their camps in the suburbs.

This mob action shocked the governor of Kwangtung, Yuan Shu-hsun, whose office was in Canton, the provincial capital. He immediately alerted the garrison troops, the navy and the police. He also ordered the city gates closed to bar the New Army soldiers from entering and decreed a curfew. Meanwhile, orders went out to the New Army units that due to the incident, the three-day New Year holiday was cancelled and that all soldiers were confined to their barracks. Garrison troops in the city were posted in strategic positions ready for any contingency as the governor was informed that revolutionists were actually behind the incident.

Meanwhile in the New Army camp, indignation was running high. Confined to their barracks, soldiers from the First Battalion went to the camps of the Second and Third Battalions openly to air their grievances and to agitate for action. The result was that the soldiers later stormed the armory and raised the banner of rebellion.

Behind all this was a prime moving force, a man named Ni Ying-tien. Ni, a graduate of the army and artillery school in Anhwei in central china, had served in the cavalry units in Anhwei but had been dismissed because of his revolutionary activities. He later came to

---

35. *Ibid.*, p. 347.

Kwangtung, changed his name, and joined the New Army as a platoon leader in the artillery unit. But before long, he was again dismissed on account of his overt extra-curricular activities. However, this time he did not leave Canton; he stayed on and travelled between Canton and Hong Kong, acting as a liaison between the T'ung-meng Hui headquarters and the New Army units. Ni and the T'ung-meng Hui leaders were originally planning a New Army revolt in late 1910, but the incident forced a change of the date. Taking advantage of the situation, Ni went to work among his old comrades in the New Army. Eventually, Ni assumed command of the mutinous troops, described as over 1,000 strong.[36]

The governor of Kwangtung later in a statement to the press claimed that the mutineers numbered several thousand.[37] The mutineers killed the New Army commander and met the garrison troops in pitched battle. Ill-prepared and disorganized and without sufficient arms, the mutineers soon proved to be no match for the garrison force which was rushed to the scene in overwhelming numbers. After three days of fighting, the rebels were completely defeated and Ni was killed in action. Casualties were heavy on both sides. Many rebels were captured and some later confessed that revolutionists were behind the uprising. A captured sergeant, named Wang, admitted under questioning, that he was a revolutionist, and that the T'ung-meng Hui headquarters in Hong Kong did not have foreknowledge of the uprising. He confessed that it was only after the outbreak of the incident that urgent requests were sent to Hong Kong for arms and ammunition, which never came. He also confessed that the uprising was originally planned for June, but that it was moved ahead of schedule because of the incident.[38] This abortive rebellion Sun Yat-sen called his ninth revolutionary attempt.

In retrospect, one can see that this uprising once again showed the weakness of the revolutionists in actual action. As a rule, they had no force of their own and had to depend on outsiders who proved unfit for making a successful revolt. Poor planning, lack of leadership and

---

36 *Ibid.*, p. 352.

37 *Ibid.*, p. 356.

38 *Ibid.*, p. 375.

inadequate coordination and logistical support all worked to doom the revolt. However, the revolutionists were undaunted by their first failure at utilizing the New Army for revolts after all previous setbacks. Their work within the New Army continued. And if they learned any lesson from this defeat, it was that they must have a force of their own, a well-trained force to serve as a hardcore in future revolts. Such a force was eventually raised, and one year later, another revolt took place in Canton.

CANTON UPRISING, APRIL 27, 1911

The Canton uprising of April 27, 1911, was the first and only campaign involving an "army" raised, trained and commanded by the revolutionists. This campaign surpassed all previous ones in scale. It was planned long in advance by the best brains in the revolutionary movement headed by Sun Yat-sen, and it was supported by the most extensive fund-raising campaign ever conducted by the revolutionists.

The uprising was first planned at a secret meeting in Penang in November, 1910, attended by many important leaders, including Huang Hsing, Chao Sheng, the New Army officer whom Huang had courted two years previously on the Indo-China borders and who had since joined the revolution; and Hu Han-min, who had been responsible for the Hong Kong branch of the T'ung-meng Hui for the past two years. Among other things, it was decided at that meeting that a force of 500 revolutionaries was to be organized into several Hsuan Feng (Selected Vanguards) groups to start the uprising,[39] to be assisted by units of the New Army, local patrol force and militia which the revolutionists were supposed to have won over. Detailed military planning was left to Huang Hsing, who was in complete charge of the uprising, with Chao Sheng serving as his deputy. As Huang, Chao and Hu returned to Hong Kong to work on the details of the operation, orders went to Japan, Rangoon, Hanoi and other places for the purchase of arms and ammunition.[40] Emissaries were dispatched to the Yangtze valley to coordinate supporting action there.

---

39 Tsou Lu, *Chung-kuo Kuo-min-tang shih-kao,* p. 801.
40 *Ibid.,* p. 804.

While the 500 Hsuan Feng, known popularly as the "dare-to-dies," were to serve as the vanguards of the uprising, the bulk of the support, according to the calculation of the revolutionists, was expected to come from many New Army units and units of the patrol force and the militia. The loyalty of the New Army troops had long been suspected by the Manchu authorities. Even before the revolt in February, 1910, the authorities in Canton had begun to take precautionary measures, one of which was to control the ammunition allowed the men. On the eve of the revolt, the authorities not only took the ammunition away from the soldiers, but even removed the triggers from some of the rifles stored in the armory.[41] After the revolt in February, 1910, even more stringent measures were taken. Soldiers of the three mutinous regiments were disbanded and replaced with new recruits. Many revolutionists again managed to infiltrate into the newly formed units.[42] However, the newly formed units were closely watched by the authorities, and the recruits were not allowed any ammunition.

The plan for the new uprising, as it was finally worked out, called for simultaneous attacks on the governor's office and other key points of the city of Canton by ten groups of "dare-to-dies" led by able leaders. Once the revolution began, according to the plan, friendly units in the New Army, the patrol forces and the militia were to converge on the city to aid the revolutionaries. After taking the city Huang and Chao were each to command a column to proceed northward to the Yangtze valley, where they were supposed to join forces with other units already won over to their side.

Once the plan was set, preparations were pushed ahead in earnest. An atmosphere of crisis permeated the city of Canton as the authorities stepped up security measures. The revolutionists used various tricks to avoid detection by the authorities: many contact points were set up in the city disguised as stores or clubs; arms and ammunition were shipped into the city hidden in trunks as dowry with female comrades posing as brides. However, as the preparations proceeded, secrets were leaked here and there. Some comrades were arrested, and a shipment of bombs was seized at the Canton customs. The provincial authorities were so

---

41 Ch'en Ch'un-sheng, *op. cit.*, p. 350; Hu Han-min, "Tzu Chuan," p. 33.

42 Hu Han-min, *op. cit.*, p. 36.

alarmed that a door to door check which would almost certainly bare the revolutionary plot, was ordered throughout the city.[43] After several changes of date, Huang Hsing, in desperation, decided to move on the afternoon of April 27.

The planned "dare-to-dies" groups were reduced to four,[44] with Huang himself leading one to attack the governor's office. Killing off the guards at the gate, the revolutionaries stormed into the office only to find that the governor and all high officials were gone. Meanwhile, the other groups fighting their way to the pre-set destinations, all encountered heavy resistance. As night fell on the city, the provincial capital was in a state of complete chaos with shots falling wild in the streets. The revolutionaries, already overwhelmed by government forces and sustaining heavy casualties, suffered many handicaps. Wearing no identification except a white cloth band on their arms, the revolutionaries at times fought with friendly forces. What proved fatal to the revolutionists, however, was the failure of the expected assistance to come from the New Army, the patrol force and the militia. The revolutionists later blamed bad communication and the fact that the city gates were tightly closed. Huang, in a long letter to all the comrades after the uprising, particularly accused several persons with failure in their liaison work.[45] However, Hu Han-min, who also signed the letter, later said investigation showed that Huang's accusation was not justified. Huang was apparently too emotional at the time the letter was written.[46]

The only group from the patrol force headed by a friendly junior officer that rushed to the aid of the revolutionists encountered the badly beaten revolutionists in retreat near the south gate of the city. Not recognizing each other, the two sides opened fire, killing the leaders of both sides and many others.[47] As the night wore on, it became apparent that the uprising was again a failure. The groups scattered and lost contact with each other; they fought while retreating

---

43 Tsou Lu, *op. cit.*, p. 804.

44 *Ibid.*, p. 807.

45 *Ibid.*, pp. 822-23.

46 Hu Han-min, *op. cit.*, p. 39.

47 Tsou Lu, *op. cit.*, p. 808.

with decreasing numbers of men. Huang Hsing narrowly escaped death. When he fled to Hong Kong the next morning, he had an injured arm and had lost two fingers on his right hand. Most of the 500 "dare-to-dies," the cream of the revolutionary force, were either killed in action or captured and later executed. When the revolt was all over, seventy-two bodies were found in the streets and later buried en masses at Huang-hua-kang (Yellow Flower Mound) in the suburbs of Canton. Since the establishment of the Republic, the place has been preserved as the Martyr's Shrine and the day of the uprising has been observed as the Martyr's Day.

The revolutionists had thrown in all that was at their command for what appeared to be a life-and-death gamble, and the setback was so damaging to the revolutionists that the whole movement, never a unified one from the beginning, was threatened by a serious internal dissension. Comrades in central China blamed the failure on the Hong Kong comrades and set up their own organization. The dissension at this critical juncture was a further blow to the revolutionary cause.

However, the failure of this latest revolt was in some way compensated. The Manchu Court, which hitherto regarded the revolutionary movement as an insignificant subversive campaign, was literally shocked by the size of the revolt and particularly by the bravery displayed by the revolutionaries. Other countries also became aware of the existence of a strong revolutionary force in China. The young revolutionaries had not died in vain. To the revolutionary elements in other parts of China, this sacrifice accentuated the revolutionary movement and further dramatized their cause. To many others, this sacrifice was a shining example to follow. The repercussion of this uprising reached far and wide. Although the T'ung-meng Hui sustained a heavy loss in this failure, the whole nation appeared in the grips of an ever-rising revolutionary tide. The Manchu Court was still in power on the surface, but the popular basis of its support was fastly deteriorating. The local viceroys, though not necessarily in favor of the revolution, had by now lost confidence in the dying Manchu Court. All that was needed was another strike to put it to an end. That strike soon came, and proved fatal to the Manchus.

WUCH'ANG UPRISING, OCTOBER 10, 1911

Next to Canton in south China, Wuhan in Hupeh province in central China was the place where the revolutionists were most active in military circles. Wuhan is the combined name for the three cities of Wuch'ang, Hankow and Hanyang, straddling the Yangtze River some 800 miles upstream from sea coast in central China. The strong revolutionary influence, ironically, was largely attributable to the policies of the former viceroy of Hupeh, Chang Chih-tung, one of the prominent leaders of the modernization movement in the closing days of the Manchu Dynasty. Chang, a champion of Western technology, was instrumental in the building of the New Army in Hupeh province and the establishment of modern military schools and one of China's first modern arsenals. Under Chang's liberal policies, many young students were sent abroad to receive military education. Upon return, they were given various military posts. They brought back not only modern technology and training methods, but also revolutionary ideas that came to permeate most of the military units in the area.

The bulk of the New Army units in Wuhan comprised the Eighth Division and the Twenty-first Mixed Brigade, with supporting engineering corps, artillery corps and cavalry corps, totalling about twenty-five battalions. The total strength was estimated at between 15,000 to 18,000 men.[48] The commanding general of the Eighth Division was Chang Piao, the highest ranking military officer in the area. The Twenty-first Mixed Brigade was commanded by Li Yuan-hung, who later unexpectedly found himself at the top of the rebel forces. These units were infiltrated by the revolutionists to varying degrees. In each unit, there was invariably a hard core of revolutionists. On the eve of the uprising, two regiments, which had the largest numbers of revolutionists, were ordered to leave for Szechuan to pacify that strife-ridden province in southwestern China. The impending departure of the two regiments was one of the factors that precipitated the revolt because the revolutionists feared that the drastic reduction of their strength would adversely affect their plans.

---

48 Hsueh Chun-tu, *op. cit.*, p. 108.

The overall leadership of the revolutionary elements in the Wuhan area was weak, and at times confusing. There apparently lacked a man with enough stature who could command all the revolutionists. This was shown by the fact that Li Yuan-hung was forced to assume command of all the rebel forces after the initial victory of the rebellion. Despite the poor overall leadership, the work done by the hard core revolutionists in each of the New Army unit was effective, and the coordination among them at the time of the revolt was surprisingly smooth considering the circumstances. This effective leadership at the lower level was in no small measure due to the work of two subversive organizations in the New Army, the Wen-hsueh She (Literary Society) and the Kung-chin Hui (Common Advance Society).

Various groups had been organized by junior officers and the men in the New Army in Wuhan at one time or another. Some were bent on revolution, others were less subversive in nature, but all were dissatisfied with the Manchu Court and harbored republican sentiments. After the disbanding of one organization by the authorities, another soon sprang up. By 1911, two stood out among others as the most prominent, each commanding a sizable following in the New Army. The Kung-chin Hui was a front organization of the T'ung-meng Hui, set up by students who returned from Japan. Its members all belonged to the T'ung-meng Hui. Among its leaders were Sun Wu and Liu Kung, both educated in Japan, and Chu Cheng, who was later prominent in the Kuomintang. They maintained close relations not only with the leading T'ung-meng Hui members, but with the central China chapter of the T'ung-meng Hui as well. As a matter of fact, at the time of the outbreak of the Wuch'ang revolution, Chu Cheng was on a mission to Shanghai to contact Sung Chao-jen and Ch'en Ch'i-mei about buying arms, while at the same time urgent requests were sent to Hong Kong asking Huang Hsing to proceed to Wuhan to assume command.

The other organization was the Wen-Hsueh She which, because of its longer history in Hupeh, perhaps had more followers than the Kung-chin Hui. Most of its ranking members had been educated in China rather than abroad, although many of them were also T'ung–meng Hui members. The chairman of the society, Chiang I-wu, a junior officer in the New Army, for example, was himself a member of the

T'ung-meng Hui.[49] This organization eventually decided to cooperate with the Kung-chin Hui to stage an uprising.[50]

Plans for the uprising were laid out at a secret meeting at the secret headquarters of the Kung-chin Hui on September 24, 1911, attended by over sixty representatives from virtually all the units of the New Army.[51] Chiang I-wu, chairman of the Wen-shueh She, who happened to be out of town that day because his unit had been transferred to a nearby city a few days earlier, was chosen commander of all the rebel forces at the motion of Sun Wu, the Kung-chin Hui leader, who was chosen chief of staff.[52] The date for the uprising was tentatively set for October 6, but was later postponed at the request of the comrades in the neighboring Hunan province who needed more time to prepare for raising the standard of rebellion simultaneously.[53] Meanwhile, word was sent to Chiang I-wu asking him to return to Wuch'ang to assume the command.

On the morning of October 9, a bomb accidentally exploded in one of the revolutionists' secret hideouts in the Russian concession of Hankow. The place was searched by the police, resulting in the arrest of several comrades and the capture of many secret documents, including name lists of many rebels.[54] Sun Wu, who was wounded in the accident, narrowly escaped arrest. With the discovery of the plot, the authorities clamped down on the revolutionists and started mass arrests of suspects. The revolutionists, in desperation, decided to move before it was too late. Chiang I-wu, who was just back in town, immediately gave order to start off at midnight.[55] Actual action began in the

---

49 Hu Tsu-shun, "Wu-ch'ang k'ai-kuo shih-lu" (Veritable Record of the Wuch'ang Uprising), *Ko-ming wen-hsien,* Vol. IV, p. 462. Hu, a member of the Kung-chin Hui, took part in the uprising. His residence in Wuch'ang was the secret headquarters of the Kung-chin Hui.

50 *Ibid.*

51 *Ibid.*, p. 21.

52 *Ibid.*

53 *Ibid.*

54 *Ibid.*, p. 25.

55 Chang Yu-k'un, *Wen-hsueh She Wu-ch'ang shou-i chi-shih* (Veritable Account of Wen-hsueh She in Wuch'ang Uprising) (Peking: San-lien Bookstore, 1952), p. 40.

evening of October 10, with the two engineering battalions in Wuch'ang first raising the banner of rebellion.

With the first shots fired, the situation in Wuch'ang soon became one of complete chaos and disorder. Not long after the beginning of the Wuch'ang uprising, Chiang I-wu fled the scene, while Sun Wu was in hiding, nursing the wounds he received from the bomb explosion. Virtually without a head, the rebels, however, moved with remarkable swiftness, thanks to the hard core revolutionary leaders in each of the New Army units. In addition, the revolutionists were greatly helped by the cowardice displayed by the viceroy, Jui Cheng, and Chang Piao, the top military commander in Wuhan. After the outbreak of the uprising, the two men, instead of taking quick action against the rebels with the still overwhelming number of loyal troops under their command, elected to flee aboard a boat in the Yangtze River.[56] Deserted by their superiors, most of the New Army troops joined the rebels while scattered loyalist troops fled across the river to Hankow. Before noon the next day, the rebels were in complete control of Wuch'ang. Within a few days, Hankow and Hanyang were taken. The rebels thus won the strategic Wuhan area practically by default. Even Sun Yat-sen later stated that had it not been for the flight of Jui Cheng and Chang Piao, Wuhan would not have been so handily taken and the revolt may well have been another failure like the one in Canton the previous year.[57]

After Wuch'ang was taken, the rebels were without a leader and urgently in need of one. Among the leading comrades from various units, all of whom junior officers, none was capable of commanding all the rebel forces. In desperation, they had to force a reluctant and bewildered Li Yuan-hung, commander of the Twenty-first Mixed Brigade, many of whose junior officers were now rebel leaders, to accept the title of governor-general of the newly proclaimed military government.

From his ship, Jui Cheng dispatched urgent reports to the government in Peking, requesting troops to quell the rebellion. Large

---

56 Hu Tsu-shun, *op. cit.*, p. 46.

57 Li Chien-nung, *op. cit.*, Vol. I, pp. 299-304.

numbers of troops were soon ordered to the Wuhan area, first commanded by the Manchu general Yin Ch'ang and then by Yuan Shih-k'ai, who was given the title of imperial commissioner. The counter-attacking government forces made a good showing, putting heavy pressure on the rebels. The rebel troops, then commanded by Huang Hsing who had rushed to Wuhan, fought back valiantly. However, the rebel troops exhibited little organization or discipline and were obviously not ready for prolonged fighting. Besieged by overwhelming enemy troops and under heavy enemy gunfire, they were forced to retreat. By November 2, Hankow fell to the government troops and the rebels recrossed the river to Wuch'ang. Two weeks later, Hangyang was also retaken by the government forces despite the bitter resistance put up by Huang Hsing.

While the military situation in Wuhan appeared very bad for the revolutionists at this time, a greater part of the country quickly changed colors during the weeks in which Huang fought hard in an desperate attempt to hold Hankow and Hanyang. Before Hankow was lost, five provinces had declared independence. By the time Hanyang was recovered by the government troops, ten more provinces joined the secession list. Virtually all provinces of China, save for Chihi, where the imperial court was located, and the Manchuria area, had by now withdrawn their allegiance from the Manchu Court. The question now facing the Peking government was no longer how to defeat the rebels at Wuhan, but how to reassert authority over all the secessionist provinces.

Yuan Shih-k'ai, who became premier in November, had perhaps already sensed the demise of the Manchu Dynasty. He was a man who had no reason to like the Manchus but who had great personal ambitions. He saw no reason to stake the Peiyang Army, his great political asset which was virtually int:ct, for the sake of saving a falling Manchu Dyasty. On the contrary, his greatest hope apparently lay in striking a bargain with the revolutionists using the strong army under his command to strengthen his hand. This was precisely what he did, thereby forcing the abdication of the Manchu emperor.

Meanwhile, a rapid succession of events took place in central and south China. By December, Nanking had been lost to the rebels, a truce reached, and a republican government proclaimed in Nanking. On

Janurary 1, 1912, Sun Yat-sen, who had rushed back from the United States, was installed as the Provisional President of the new government. The man who had started out seventeen years before on a one-man rebellion against the Manchus now saw the consummation of his life-long goal.

With the establishment of the Republic, there was no longer any need for the T'ung-meng Hui to remain a secret revolutionary organization. Agitations were growing among the members that it be reorganized into an open political party. It may be recalled that since the development of factionalism in the headquarters in Tokyo in 1908, the T'ung-meng Hui had practically no central organization. As a preliminary step toward reorganization, a national congress was called in Nanking, the site of the provisional government, on January 22, 1912. Over 2,000 members representing all eighteen provinces in China attended the congress, and Wang Ching-wei was elected chairman of the party so as to enable Sun Yat-sen to concentrate on his work as Provisional President of the Republic. However, Wang, in deference to Sun, never assumed the post.[58] Since negotiations were still under way with the Peking government and the Manchu emperor had yet to abdicate, it was decided that another congress of the T'ung-meng Hui be convened as soon as the "over-all situation is stabilized."[59] On March 3, the second congress was called in Nanking, at which the T'ung-meng Hui was declared an open political party.[60] Since he had handed over the presidency of the republic to Yuan Shih-k'ai, Sun Yat-sen was chosen chairman of the party.

Meanwhile, a number of political parties sprang up during the first year of the republic. Some were organized by those who had formerly served under the Manchus but now were in the new government; others were formed by dissident groups in the T'ung-meng Hui; still others were former local groups which were active in the constitutional movement during the closing days of the Manchu Dynasty. The parliament in Peking for a while was split among so many parties that

---

58 Hu Han-min, "Tzu Chuan," p. 435.

59 Wu Hsiang-hsiang, *op. cit.*, p. 160.

60 *Ibid.*, p. 161.

none could muster a clear majority. Largely due to the efforts of Sung Chiao-jen, the T'ung-meng Hui eventually merged with four other small parties to become the Kuomintang (Nationalist Party). The merger was made official in a joint declaration issued by the five parties on August 13, 1912, and twelve days later the Kuomintang was formed at the founding meeting held in Peking.[61]

61 *Ibid.*, p. 203.

Chapter VIII

CONCLUSION

The downfall of the Manchus was perhaps inevitable. After more than 200 years in power, the Manchu Court by the turn of this century had shown every sign of a dynasty coming to its end. However, one factor that set the demise of the Manchu Dynasty apart from those of the previous dynasties and made it unprecedented in Chinese history was the revolutionary movement aimed at changing the centuries-old monarchical system. In this revolutionary movement, the T'ung-meng Hui provided the leadership in the most crucial years and played a vitally important role.

It is true that the T'ung-meng Hui was not the only revolutionary organization then in existence. There were many at one time or another. But as the foregoing has shown, it was the most important organization compared with all the others. In terms of its size, its expansion at home and abroad, the revolutionary ideas and programs espoused by its leaders, and the military campaigns carried out under its direction, the T'ung-meng Hui clearly stood out among other groups.

The inception of the T'ung-meng Hui in Tokyo in 1905 was designed to effect a grand union of many diverse groups. The Hua-hsing Hui and the Kuang-fu Hui, two groups with the largest followings, became merged with the T'ung-meng Hui, as did other splinter groups. Although the Kuang-fu Hui continued to exist, its influence was declining, and it could not rival the T'ung-meng Hui in any sense. To the extent that it provided a rallying center for all the anti-Manchu Chinese radicals, first in Japan and then in China and many other parts of the world, The T'ung-meng Hui fulfilled its first goal.

To be sure, there were many other groups scattered in China dedicated to the revolutionary cause, but they either looked to the

T'ung-meng Hui for leadership, such as the Wen-hsueh She and the Kung-chin Hui in Hupeh, or otherwise affiliated with the T'ung-meng Hui. None, however, had the resources of the T'ung-meng Hui, nor had any of them carried out anti-Manchu activities on as large a scale. The revolutionary movement admittedly was not a unified movement, but in the diverse and at times confusing waves of events, the T'ung-meng Hui was always in the mainstream. It provided the inspirational leadership by promulgating a revolutionary program and by widely circulating numerous pamphlets and tracts. It also persistently carried out more revolts against the Manchus than any other group.

All this, however, does not mean that the T'ung-meng Hui as a revolutionary organization was so successful that there is nothing to criticize. On the contrary, it left very much to be desired. It is appropriate that we briefly sum up what we have covered in the foregoing chapters to put the role played by the T'ung-meng Hui in perspective.

First, it was undeniable that the T'ung-meng Hui at its inception had an impressive organization, complete with a general headquarters with various working departments and branches in all of China's provinces. More significant was the fact that the best brains in the revolutionary movement, save for a few individuals, all became members of the T'ung-meng Hui. Despite criticisms from some quarters, such men as Sun Yat-sen and Huang Hsing were held in high esteem by most of the revolutionists. On their part, these leaders, by words and deeds, proved themselves worthy of their names. However, the actual organization of the T'ung-meng Hui was far from being effective, as some of the departments soon disappeared. Moveover, internal factionalism painfully hindered its function.

While the headquarters in Tokyo showed signs of disintegration, however, the T'ung-meng Hui enjoyed a rapid expansion both in China and in other countries, thanks to many dedicated workers. The expansion of branches in China was largely done through alliance with the secret societies, while the growth overseas was attributable to the efforts of many leaders of overseas Chinese communities. The domestic branches took part in action, while the overseas branches concentrated on fund-raising. All branches, of course, consistently spread revolutionary propaganda. By the time the revolutionists stepped up their activities after 1907, first along the southwestern border and then in Canton in south China, the Tokyo headquarters practically ceased to function. The center for directing the revolution tended to follow Sun Yat-sen, wherever his travels took him, or to move to where the action was. Admittedly, the T'ung-meng Hui as a secret revolutionary organization was anything but a tight-knit one. The hierarchy as worked out at the inception existed largely on paper only. It was the vigorous personal leadership shown by Sun and others, rather than organizational efforts, that largely accounted for the continued functioning and growth of the T'ung-meng Hui.

Secondly, in terms of ideology, a good case can be made of the T'ung-meng Hui. What the T'ung-meng Hui advocated was unequivocally clear: It wanted the Manchu monarchy overthrown and a republic form of government established in its place; it also wanted democracy in place of monarchical despotism. Not only were these goals set forth, but detailed programs were worked out for their attainment. It is all too easy for us today to take republicanism and democracy for granted, but we must remember the circumstance under which the revolutionists advocated such goals if we are to appreciate their courage and far-sightedness properly. They asked for a change which was unprecedented in China's long history, and they advocated what was regarded as the most advanced political system. It was for the purpose of "educating" the Chinese people in democracy that the controversial "tutelage" system was included in the T'ung-meng Hui's program. Although debatable in many respects, the program still surpassed in sophistication all that the other revolutionary groups had to offer. A case in point was the Kuang-fu Hui, which had only ill-defined goals and practically no working program to speak of.

In defense of republicanism against constitutional monarchy, the revolutionists carried out a spirited debate with the royalists. The importance of the debate lay not only in its offering the revolutionists a chance to articulate what they stood for, but also in the fact that the T'ung-meng Hui's cause was enhanced as a result, particularly among the intellectuals. The debate also touched upon another important aspect of the T'ung-meng Hui's program, namely, its economic policy. The controversy centered around the issue of socialism, specifically on the land policy of the T'ung-meng Hui. Admittedly, the T'ung-meng Hui's stand on this issue was rather vague. Sun Yat-sen often spoke of the "equalization of land ownership" and this was in fact listed as one of the four slogans of the T'ung-meng Hui. But on the other hand, *Min Pao,* the organ of the T'ung-meng Hui, openly advocated "nationalization of land." Whether Sun's "equalization" meant nationalization was the focal point of the dispute. However, Sun's idea was evolving, and as time went on, he increasingly spoke of using heavy taxation to eliminate landlords instead of outright nationalization of land.

Thirdly, the T'ung-meng Hui persistently carried out military campaigns against the Manchus. To be sure, the T'ung-meng Hui–directed campaigns were not the only ones – there were others launched by other groups, such as the Kuang-fu Hui and the Hua-hsing Hui revolts, but the fact remains that the T'ung-meng Hui directed most of the revolts, and each of a larger scale than the previous one. Lacking an army of its own, the T'ung-meng Hui relied on two sources for its strength, namely, the secret societies and the New Army. However, neither, in a military sense, proved to be a reliable force for rebellion. Moreover, the revolutionists were shown to be poor conspirators, for in many cases their plots were discovered and foiled by the authorities.

In view of all this, it would appear that one might well question the military importance of these campaigns. Indeed, the significance of these campaigns did not lie in their military importance. In a purely military sense, their significance was minimal. But these campaigns had a much larger political significance, for they served as a persistent political demonstration against the Manchu Court, and they also served to erode the authority of the Manchu rulers. Above all, they served to awaken the Chinese people to the dawning of a revolutionary era. The downfall of the Manchu Dynasty was not effected by military action – even the revolutionists do not make such claim. Rather, it was the result of the interaction of a number of factors. A situation seemed to have obtained in which the demise of the centuries-old monarchical system was all but sealed. Toward the creation of such a situation, the contribution of the series of military campaigns should not be overlooked.

Establishment of a republican form of government, however, did not bring immediate order to the country. The solution to all the problems of the fallen old empire called for far more than just the proclamation of a republican form of government. The country had yet to be unified. Yuan Shih-k'ai, with real power, controlled north China. Sun Yat-sen was soon forced out of office. After assuming the presidency, Yuan built his personal power and plotted for the restoration of the monarchy by installing himself as emperor. After he failed and died of frustration, the country was again plunged into chaos, with warlords fighting each other. It is true that the Manchu Court was overthrown, but now it looked as though the net result of the downfall of the Manchus was the disruption of the established order and the creation of a void at the place where power traditionally belonged. The monarchical system, over two thousand years old, was overthrown, but what could be established in its place appeared by no means certain. For the people, life had not become easier in the republic than in the former monarchy. On the contrary, civil war and internal strife only brought added woes to them. As is always the case in time of unrest and general disorder, it is the mass of people who ultimately suffer the most, and the lot of the Chinese in the early years of the republic was hardly an exception.

In foreign relations, China did not fare better either. The inability of the Manchu Court to cope with the situation caused by foreign encroachment had been effectively exploited by the revolutionists in the propaganda campaign against the Manchus, but the dawning of the republican era did not bring about a lessening of the same danger. On the contrary, it saw the aggravation of the situation, particularly in relations with Japan. In short, both domestically and externally, the revolution did not seem to have done any real good to the country.

It follows that one might be tempted to question whether the revolution should be regarded as "successful" in a real sense. To such questioners, the best answer perhaps can be found through an examination of the motives of the revolutionists and a realistic recognition of the limitations of the circumstances. As far as the motives of the revolutionists were concerned, there is no doubt but that most of the revolutionary leaders were selfless men, who acted on patriotic impulse and strove for what they sincerely believed was the best course for the nation. They may have been ahead of their time, particularly in adovcating a system for which the old empire of China was all but unprepared for, but their sincerity could not be questioned. Politically, republicanism was the most advanced system. Economically, socialism was popular as an ideology around the turn of this century. And it should be noted that despite their insufficient understanding of the diversified and sometimes confusing manifestations of socialism as an ideology and a system, the revolutionists did not elect to follow its most radical wing, but only advocated the milder features of socialism for China.

The fact that the political and economic programs of the revolutionists could not be effectively put into practice immediately after the revolution should not be totally blamed on the revolutionists. The circumstances under which the revolutionists labored must be realistically appraised. The revolutionists, after all, could not and should not have been expected to perform miracles. Practical limitations should be taken into consideration. Indeed there were many factors at work which were beyond the control of the revolutionists. When the Manchu Court finally collapsed, not as a result of the military action of the revolutionists, but rather largely of its own weight, it was too much to expect the revolutionists, now all of a sudden with the heavy responsibilities thrust upon them, to cure a country of its multiple ills overnight. Above all, it must be noted that what the revolutionists inherited was anything but a unified country, with north China practically beyond their reach. Moreover, the revolutionists had no military force of their own, and this proved to be the most serious handicap of all. They could not unify the country without military force, and consequently they really did not have a chance to put their program in practice.

Realizing the sincere motives of the revolutionists and the complex situation with which they had to cope by means of their limited capability, we might perhaps become a little more charitable in our assessment of the revolution and of the T'ung-meng Hui's role in the revolution. In particular, we may be able to avoid using argument gained *ex post facto* in our judgement. Events that took place after the revolution should not be used to discredit the T'ung-meng Hui's role. Above all, if we consider the 1911 revolution a success – it succeeded in overthrowing the Manchus and establishing a republic – then it is only fair to say that the role played by the T'ung-meng Hui in guiding the course of the revolutionary movement in the six crucial years prior to the Wuch'ang uprising was vitally important. Indeed it is not an overstatement to say that had it not been for the T'ung-meng Hui and for all it had done, the 1911 revolution would not have taken place.

BIBLIOGRAPHY

PRIMARY SOURCES

Chang, Chi. *Chang P'u-ch'uan hsien-sheng ch'uan-chi* (張溥泉先生全集 Collected Works of Chang Chi). Edited by the Committee for the Compilation of Materials on the Party History [of the Kuomintang,] Taipei, 1951.

_______________. *Chang P'u-ch'uan Hsien-sheng ch'uan-chi pu-pien* (張溥泉先生全集補編 Collected Works of Chang Chi: A Supplement). Edited by the Committee for the Compilation of Materials on the Party History [of the Kuomintang], Taipei, 1952.

Chang, Hsiang-wen. *Nan-yuan ts'ung Kao* (南苑叢稿 Collected Works of the South Study). Peking, 1929.

Chang, Kuo-kan. *Hsin-hai ko-ming shih-liao* (辛亥革命史料 Source Materials on the Revolution of 1911). Shanghai, 1958.

Chang, Ping-lin. *Chang Ping-lin tzu-ting nien-p'u* (章炳麟自定年譜 Autobiographical Chronology of Chang Ping-lin). Chungking: *Kuo-min Kung Pao* (Citizen's Daily), 1943.

_______________________. *Chang-shih ts'ung-shu* (章氏叢書 Collected Works of Chang Ping-lin). Reprint, Taipei, 1958.

Ch'en, T'ien-hua. *Ch'en T'ien-hua chi* (陳天華集 Collected Works of Ch'en T'ien-hua). Chungking: China Cultural Service, 1944.

The China Yearbook. London: George Routledge & Sons, 1912.

Chu, Cheng. *Hsin-hai cha-chi mei-ch'uan jih-chi ho-k'an* (亥辛劄記美全日記合刊 Diary and Random Notes of 1911, Published in One Volume). Reprint, Taipei, 1956.

Chung-hua-min-kuo k'ai-kuo wu-shih-nien wen-hsien (中華民國開國五十年文獻 Materials on the Fifty Years of the Republic of China). Edited by the Committee for the Compilation of Materials on the First Fifty Years of the Republic of China, Taipei: Cheng-chung Book Co., 1963–.

Chung-kuo Kuo-min-tang ch'i-shih-nien ta-shih nien-piao (中國國民黨七十年大事年表 Chronology of Major Events of the Kuomintang During the Past Seventy Years). Edited by the Committee for the Compilation of materials on the Party History [of the Kuomintang], Taipei, 1964.

Chung-kuo Kuo-min-tang wu-shih chou-nien chi-nien t'e-k'an (中國國民黨五十週年紀念特刊 Special Commemoration Issue on the Fiftieth Anniversary of the Founding of the Kuomintang). Edited by the Committee for the Compilation of Materials on the Party History [of the Kuomintang], Chungking, 1944.

Harvard University, Committee on International and Regional Studies, ed. *Biographies of Kuomintang Leaders,* Cambridge, 1948, mimeographed, 3 vols.

Hsin-hai ko-ming (辛亥革命 The Revolution of 1911). Edited by Ts'ai Te-keng, *et al.* for the Chinese Historical Society, Shanghai: People's Publishing House, 1957, 8 vols..

Hsin-hai ko-ming ch'ien-shih-nien chien shih-lun hsuan-chi (辛亥革命前十年間時論選集 Selected Essays During the Ten-year Period Prior to the Revolution of 1911). Edited by Chang Nan, *et al.,* Hong Kong: San-lien Bookstore, 1962, 4 vols.

Hsin-hai ko-ming hui-i lu (辛亥革命回憶錄 Reminiscences of the Revolution of 1911). Edited by the Committee on Materials, National People's Political Consultative Conference, Peking: Chung-hua Book Co., 1961, 2 vols.

Hsin-hai ko-ming shou-i lu (辛亥革命首義錄 Reminiscences of the Uprising of 1911). Edited by the National People's Political

Consultative Conference, Hupeh Committee, Wuhan: Hupeh People's Publishing House, 1957, 2 vols.

Hsin-hai ko-ming tzu-liao (辛亥革命資料 Materials on the Revolution of 1911). Edited by the Institute of Modern History, National Academy of Sciences, Peking: Chung-hua Book Co., 1961.

Hu, Han-min. *Hu Han-min hsien-sheng yen-chiang chi* (胡漢民先生演講集 Collected Speeches of Mr. Hu Han-min). Shanghai: Min-chih Book Co., 1937, 3 vols.

Hu,Shih. *Liu-hsueh jih-chi* (留學日記 Diary of a Student in the United States). Shanghai, 1947.

Huang, Hsing. *Huang K'o-ch'iang hsien-sheng shu-han mo-chi* (黃克強先生書翰墨跡 Correspondence and Calligraphy of Mr. Huang Hsing). Edited by the Committee for the Compilation of Materials on the Party History [of the Kuomintang], Taipei, 1956.

Hummel, Arthur W., ed. *Eminent Chinese of the Ch'ing Period.* Washington: Government Printing Office, 1943-44.

Ko-ming wen-hsien (革命文獻 Materials on the Revolution [of 1911]). Edited by the Committee for the Compilation of Materials on the Party History [of the Kuomintang], Taipei, 1953-58, 7 vols.

Kuan-tu-lu (pseud. of Wu T'ing-fang), ed. *Kung-ho kuan-chien lu* (共和關鍵錄 A Record of the Peace Negotiations That Were Crucial to the Republic). Shanghai, 1912.

Liang, Ch'i-ch'ao. *Yin-ping-shih wen-chi* (飲冰室文集 Collected Works of the Ice-drinker's Studio). Shanghai: Chung-hua Book Co., 1936.

Shao-nien Chung-kuo Ch'en Pao wu-shih chou-nien chi-nien chuan-k'an (少年中國晨報五十週年紀念專刊 Fiftieth Anniversary Special Commemorative Collection of the *Young China Morning Paper.*).

San Francisco: Young *China Morning Paper,* 1960.

Sun, Yat-sen. *Kuo-fu ch'uan-shu* (國父全書 Complete Works of the Founding Father). Taipei: National War College, 1960.

____________. *Tsung-li ch'uan-chi* (總理全集 Complete Works of the President [of the Kuomintang]). Taipei: China Cultural Service, 1953.

____________. *San Min Chu I* (三民主義 Three Principles of the People). Trans. Frank W. Price, Chungking: Ministry of Information, 1943.

____________. *Sun Yat-sen, His Political and Social Ideals.* A Source book compiled and translated by Shihlien Hsu, Los Angeles: University of Southern California Press, 1933.

Sung, Chiao-jen. *O-chih li-shih* (我之歷史 My History). Reprint, Taipei: Book World Co., 1962.

Tang-shih shih-liao ts'ung-k'an (黨史史料叢刊 Collected Materials on Party History). Edited by the Committee for the Compilation of Materials on the Party History [of the Kuomintang], Shanghai: Cheng-chung Book Co., 1945.

Tsou, Lu. *Chung-kuo Kuo-min-tang shih-kao* (中國國民黨史稿 Draft History of the Kuomintang). Reprint, Taipei: Commerical Press, 1965.

____________. *Tsou Lu wen-ts'un* (鄒魯文存 Collected Works of Tsou Lu). Peking: Pei-hua Book Co., 1930.

Wang, Ching-wei. *Wang Chao-ming keng-hsu pei-tai kung-tz'u* (汪兆銘庚戌被逮供詞 The Testimony of Wang Ching-wei When Arrested in 1910). With post script by Chang Ts'ang-hai, n. p., 1934.

———————. *Wang Ching-wei wen ts'un* (汪精衛文存 Collected Works of Wang Ching-wei). Canton: Min-chih Bookstore, 1926.

Yun-nan Kwei-chow hsin-hai ko-ming tzu-liao (雲南貴州辛亥革命資料 Source Materials on the Revolution of 1911 in Yunnan and Kweichow). Edited by the Institute of History, Academy of Sciences of China, Peking, 1959.

BOOKS

Amann, Gustav. *The Legacy of Sun Yat-sen: A History of Revolution.* Trans. Frederick Philip Grove, New York: L. Carrier, 1929.

Bate, Don. *Wang Ching-wei: Puppet or Patriot?* Chicago: R. F. Seymour, 1941.

Bland, J.O.P. *Recent Events and Present Policies in China.* Philadelphia: J. B. Lippincott, 1912.

———————. *Li Hung-chang.* New York: Henry Holt, 1917.

Bland, J.O.P. and Backhouse, E. *China Under Empress Dowager.* Philadelphia: J. B. Lippincott, 1910.

Buck, Pearl. *The Man Who Changed China: The Story of Sun Yat-sen.* New York: Random House, 1953.

Cameron, Meribeth E. *The Reform Movement in China, 1898-1912.* Stanford: Stanford University Press, 1931.

Cantlie, James. *Sun Yat-sen and the Awakening of China.* London, 1912.

Chang, Ch'i-yun. *Tang-shih kai-yao* (黨史概要 An Outline History of the Kuomintang). Taipei: China Cultural Service, 1954.

Chang, Nan-hsien. *Hu-pei ko-ming chih-chih lu* (湖北革命知之錄 An Account of the Revolutionary Movement in Hupeh). Chungking, 1945.

Chang, Yu-k'un. *Wen-hsueh She Wu-ch'ang shou-i chi-shih* (文學社武昌首義紀實 A Factual Account of the Wuch'ang Revolution Initiated by the Literary Society). Peking: San-lien Bookstore, 1952.

Chang, Yung-fu. *Nan-yang yu ch'uang-li min-kuo* (南洋與創立民國 Overseas Chinese in Southeast Asia and the Establishment of the Republic). Shanghai, 1933.

Ch'en, Hsi-hao. *Kuo-ch'u san-shih-wu nien chih Chung-kuo Kuo-mintang* (過去三十五年之中國國民黨 The Kuomintang in the Past Thirty-five Years). Shanghai: Commercial Press, 1929.

Ch'en, Hsu-lu. *Hsin-hai ko-ming* (辛亥革命 The Revolution of 1911). Shanghai, 1955.

Ch'en, Jerome. *Yuan Shih-k'ai*. Stanford: Stanford University Press, 1961.

Chen, Stephen and Payne, Robert. *Sun Yat-sen: A Portrait*. New York: John Day, 1946.

Chiang, Kai-shek. *China's Destiny*. Trans. Wang Ch'ung-hui, New York: Macmillan, 1947.

Chiang, Monlin. *Tides from the West: A Chinese Autobiography*. New Haven: Yale University Press, 1947.

Chou, Fu-hai. *San-min-chu-i li-lun ti t'i-hsi* (三民主義理論的體系 The Theoretical System of the Three People's Principles). Shanghai: *New Life Monthly*, 1928.

Comber, Leon F. *Chinese Secret Society in Malaya*. New York: J.J. Augustin Inc., 1959.

DeBary, William T., *et al. Sources of Chinese Tradition.* New York: Columbia University Press, 1960.

Dingle, Edwin J. *China's Revolution, 1911-1912.* New York: McBride, Nast & Co., 1912.

Fairbank, John K. *United States and China.* Cambridge: Harvard University Press, 1962.

Farjenel, Fernand. *Through the Chinese Revolution.* New York: Frederick A. Stokes, 1916.

Feng, Tzu-yu. *Chung-hua-min-kuo k'ai-kuo-ch'ien ko-ming shih* (中華民國開國前革命史 History of the Revolution before the Founding of the Republic). Taipei: World Book Co., 1954, 2 vols.

————. *Ko-ming i-shih* (革命逸史 Reminiscences of the Revolution). Taipei: Commercial Press, 1965, 5 vols.

————. *Hua-ch'iao ko-ming k'ai-kuo shih* (華僑革命開國史 The Overseas Chinese, the Revolution, and the Creation of the Republic: A History). Chungking: Commerical Press, 1946.

————. *Chung-kuo ko-ming yun-tung erh-shih-liu nien tsu-chih shih* (中國革命運動二十六年組織史 A History of the Organizations Connected with the Chinese Revolutionary Movement During the Last Twenty-six years). Shanghai: Commerical Press, 1948.

Glick, Carl and Hong, Sheng-hwa. *Swords of Silence: Chinese Secret Societies.* New York: McGraw-Hill, 1947.

Green, Owen Mortimer. *The Story of China's Revolution.* London: Hutchinson & Co., 1945.

Holcombe, Arthur N. *Chinese Revolution.* Cambridge: Harvard University Press, 1931.

Hatano, Kenichi. *Chugoku kokuminto tsushi* (A History of the Chinese Nationalist Party). Tokyo, 1943.

Hirayama, Shu. *Chung-kuo pi-mi she-hui shih* (A History of Chinese Secret Societies). Shanghai: Commercial Press, 1935.

Hsu, Hsueh-erh, et al. *Sung Yu-fu* (宋漁父 Sung Chiao-jen). Shanghai, 1913.

Hsu, Shih-ying. *Mien-tien Chung-kuo T'ung-meng Hui k'ai-kuo ko-ming shih* (緬甸中國同盟會開國革命史 Revolutionary History of the T'ung-meng Hui Branch in Burma). Rangoon, 1932.

Hsueh, Chun-tu. *Huang Hsing and the Chinese Revolution.* Stanford: Stanford University Press, 1961.

Hu, Han-min. *San-min-chu-i ti lien-huan-hsing* (三民主義的連環性 The Cyclical Character of the Three People's Principles). Shanghai: Min-chih, Bookstore, 1928.

Hu, O-kung. *Hsin-hai ko-ming pei-fang shih-lu* (辛亥革命北方實錄 A Factual Account of the Revolution in North China). Shanghai, 1948.

Hua, Lin-i. *Chung-kuo Kuo-min-tang shih* (中國國民黨史 History of the Kuomintang of China). Shanghai: Commercial Press, 1928.

Huang San-teh. *The History of Hung League Revolution.* San Francisco, 1936.

Hughes, E. R. *The Invasion of China by the Western World.* New York: Macmillan Co., 1938.

Kayano, Chochi. *Chuka minkoku kakumei hikyu* (Private Sources for the Chinese Republican Revolution). Tokyo, 1940.

Ko, Kung-chen. *Chung-kuo pao-hsueh shih* (中國報學史 A History of Chinese Journalism). Shanghai: Commerical Press, 1927.

Ko-ming Chi-nien Hui (Revolutionary Memorial Society), ed. *Kwang-chou san-yueh erh-shih-chiu-jih ko-ming shih* (廣州三月二十九日革命史 History of the Uprising in Canton on the 29th Day of the Third Moon). Shanghai: Min-chih, 1926.

Ku, Chung-hsiu. *Chung-hua-min-kuo k'ai-kuo shih* (中華民國開國史 A History of the Founding of the Republic of China). Taipei: Book World Co., 1962.

Kuo, Hsiao-ch'eng. *Chung-hua ko-ming chi-shih pen-mo* (中華革命紀事本末 A Complete Record of the Chinese Revolution). Shanghai, 1912.

Jansen, Marius B. *The Japanese and Sun Yat-sen.* Cambridge: Harvard University Press, 1955.

Landon, Kenneth P. *The Chinese in Thailand.* London: Oxford University Press, 1941.

Leng, Shao-chuan and Norman Palmer. *Sun Yat-sen and Communism.* New York: Praeger, 1960.

Levenson, Joseph. *Liang Ch'i-ch'ao and the Mind of Modern China.* Cambridge: Harvard University Press, 1953.

Li, Lien-fang. *Hsin-hai Wu-ch'ang shou-i chi* (辛亥武昌首義記 An Account of the Wuch'ang Uprising of 1911). Wuch'ang, 1947.

Lien, Heng. *T'ai-wan t'ung-shih* (臺灣通史 General History of Taiwan). Taipei: Chung-hua Book Co., 1955.

Linebarger, Paul M.W. *Sun Yat-sen and the Chinese Republic.* New York: Century, 1925.

________________. *The Political Doctrines of Sun Yat-sen.* Baltimore: Johns Hopkins University Press, 1937.

Liu, K'uei-i. *Huang Hsing chuan-chi* (黃興傳記 A Biography of Huang

Hsing). Taipei: China Cultural Service, 1952.

Liu, Lien-k'o. *Pang-hui san-pai-nien ko-ming shih* (幫會三百年革命史 A History of the Revolutionary Activities of the Secret Societies in the Last 300 years). Macao: Liu-yuan Publishing Co., 1940.

Lo, Erh-kang. *T'ien-ti Hui wen-hsien lu* (天地會文獻錄 An Account of the Heaven and Earth Society). Shanghai: Cheng-chung Book Co., 1948.

Lo, Hsiang-lin. *Kuo-fu chih ta-hsueh shih-tai* (國父之大學時代 The College Years of the Founding Father). Chungking: Independent Publishing Co., 1945.

MacNair, Harley F. *China in Revolution.* Chicago: University of Chicago Press, 1931.

Martin, Bernard. *Strange Vigour: A Biography of Sun Yat-sen.* London: W. Heinmann, 1944.

Miyazaki, Torazo. *Sanju sannen no yume* (The Thirty-three Years' Dream). Tokyo, 1926.

Powell, Ralph. *The Rise of Chinese Military Power, 1895-1912.* Princeton: Princeton University Press, 1955.

Purcell, Victor. *The Chinese in Southeast Asia.* London: Oxford University Press, 1965.

Restarick, Henry B. *Sun Yat-sen: Liberator of China.* New Haven: Yale University Press, 1931.

Saneto, Keishu. *Chugokujin nihon ryugaku shiko*(Draft History of Chinese Students in Japan). Tokyo, 1939.

Schiffrin, Harold Z. *Sun Yat-sen and the Origins of the Chinese Revolution.* Berkeley and Los Angeles: University of California Press, 1968.

Schlegel, Gustave. *Thian Ti Hwui, or Heaven-Earth League.* Batavia: Lang & Co., 1866.

Shang, Ping-ho. *Hsin-jen ch'un-ch'iu* (辛壬春秋 A History of 1911 and 1912). Shanghai, 1924.

Shao, Yuan-ch'ung. *Ch'en Ying-shih hsien-sheng ko-ming hsiao-shih* (陳英士先生革命小史 A Brief History of the Revolutionary Life of Ch'en ch'i-mei). Shanghai: Min-chih Bookstore, 1925.

_______________. *Chung-ko chih ko-ming yun-tung chi ch'i pei-ching* (中國之革命運動及其背景 The Revolutionary Movement of China and its Background). Shanghai: Min-chih Bookstore, 1927.

_______________. *Sun-wen chu-i tsung-lun* (孫文主義總論 Summary of Sun Yat-senism), Shanghai: Min-chih Bookstore, 1927.

Sharman, Lyon. *Sun Yat-sen, His Life and Its Meaning.* New York: John Day, 1934.

Stanton, William. *The Triad Society or Heaven and Earth Association.* Hong Kong, 1900.

Sun, Ching-ya. *Tui Sun-wen-chu-i che-hsueh chi-ch'u chih shang-ch'o* (對孫文主義哲學基礎之商榷 A Discussion of the Philosophical Foundation of Sun Yat-senism). Shanghai, 1925.

Sun, Yat-sen. *Memoirs of a Chinese Revolutionary.* London: Hutchinson & Co., 1927.

_______________. *Fundamentals of National Reconstruction.* Chungking: Chinese Ministry of Information, 1945.

Tai, Chi-t'ao. *Sun-wen-chu-i chih che-hsueh chi-ch'u.* (孫文主義之哲學基礎 Philosophical Foundation of Sun Yat-senism). Canton: Min-chih Bookstore, 1925.

T'ang, Leang-li. *The Inner History of Chinese Revolution.* London: G. Routledge, 1930.

———. *Wang Ching-wei, A Political Biography.* Peiping: China United Press, 1931.

Teng, Ssu-yu and Fairbank, John K. *China's Response to the West.* Cambridge: Harvard University Press, 1954.

Teng, Tse-ju. *Chung-kuo Kuo-min-tang erh-shih-nien shih-chi* (中國國民黨二十年史蹟 Twenty Years' History of the Kuomintang of China). Shanghai: Cheng-chung Book Co., 1948.

Ting, Wen-chiang. *Liang-jen-kung hsien-sheng nien-p'u ch'ang-pien ch'u-kao* (梁任公先生年譜長編初稿 Draft Full-length Biographical Chronology of Liang Ch'i-ch'ao). Taipei, 1958, 3 vols.

Ts'ao, Ya-po. *Wu-ch'ang ko-ming chen-shih* (武昌革命真史 True History of the Wuch'ang Revolution). Shanghai: Chung-hua Book Co., 1930.

Tse, Tsan Tai. *The Chinese Republic: Secret History of the Revolution.* Hong Kong: *South China Morning Post*, 1924.

Tso, Shun-sheng. *Hsin-hai ko-ming shih* (辛亥革命史 A History of the Revolution of 1911). Shanghai: Chung-hua Book Co., 1934.

Ts'ui, Shu-ch'in. *San-min-chu-i hsin-lun* (三民主義新論 A New Study of the Three People's Principles). Taipei: Cheng-chung Book Co., 1955.

Wang, Ching-wei. *Chung-kuo Kuo-min-tang shih kai-lun* (中國國民黨史概論 A Survey of the History of Kuomintang). Canton: Military Political Institute, 1927.

Wang, Yun-sheng. *Liu-shih-nien-lai Chung-kuo yu Jih-pen* (六十年來中國與日本 Sixty Years of Sino-Japanese Relations). Tientsin, 1933, 6 vols.

Ward, J.S.M. and Sterling, W.G. *The Hung Society, or the society of Heaven and Earth.* London: Baskerville Press, 1925.

Wei, Ta-fa-shih (The Venerable). *Chung-kuo pang-hui ching-hung han-liu* (中國幫會青紅漢留 Chinese Secret Societies– The Red, Green, and Han Liu Societies). Shanghai: Shuo-wen She, 1948.

————————. *Pao-ko pa-meng* (袍哥八門 Sworn Brothers' Society). Shanghai: Shuo-wen She, n.d.

————————. *Chiang-hu hua* (江湖話 Secret Society Language). Shanghai: Shuo-wen She, n.d.

Wen, Kung-chih. *Chung-hua-min-kuo ko-ming ch'uan-shih* (中華民國革命全史 Complete History of the Chinese Revolution). Shanghai: I-hsin Bookstore, 1929.

Williams, L. E. *Overseas Chinese Nationalism.* Chicago: Glencoe, 1960.

William, Maurice. *Sun Yat-sen versus Communism.* Baltimore: Williams & Wilkins, 1932.

Wu, Hsiang-hsiang. *Chung-kuo hsien-tai-shih ts'ung-k'an* (中國現代史叢刊 Series on Modern Chinese History). Taipei: Cheng-chung Book Co., 1960, 2 vols.

————————. *Sung Chiao-jen: Chung-kuo min-chu hsien-cheng ti hsien-ch'u* (宋教仁：中國民主憲政的先驅 Sung Chiao-jen: Forerunner of Chinese Democracy and Constitution). Taipei: Book World Co., 1964.

Wu, Tzu-hsiu. *Hsin-hai hsun-nan chi* (辛亥殉難記 The Martyrs of the Year of 1911). n.p., n.d.

ARTICLES AND PERIODICALS

Chen, Yi-sein. "The Chinese Revolution of 1911 and the Chinese In Burma," *Journal of Southeast Asian Researches,* December, 1966.

Chi, Ping-feng. "The Controversies between Revolutionists and Constitutionalists in the Late Ching Period," in Chung-kuo hsueh-shu chu-tso chiang-chu wei-yuan-hui (中國學術著作奬助委員會) *Synopses of Monographical Studies on Chinese History and Sciences,* III, Taipei, 1967.

Goodrich, B.W.F. "Secret Societies," *Malaya,* March, 1959.

Hackett, Roger F. "Chinese Students in Japan, 1900-1910," Harvard University Regional Studies, *Papers on China,* III, 1949.

Hao, Yen-p'ing. "The Abortive Cooperation Between Reformers and Revolutionists," Harvard University East Asian Research Center, *Papers on China,* XV, 1961.

Hsiao, Kung-ch'uan. "The Case for Constitutional Monarchy: K'ang Yu-wei's Plan for the Democratization of China," *Monumenta Serica,* XXIV, Los Angeles, 1965.

Hsin Shih-chi (新世紀 Le Siecle Nouveau), Paris, 1907-1909.

Hsin-min Ts'ung Pao(新民叢報 New Citizen's Journal), Yokohama, 1902-1905.

Hsueh, Chun-tu. "Sun Yat-sen, Yang Ch'u-yun and the Early Revolutionary Movement in China," *Journal of Asian Studies,* Vol. XIX, No. 3, May, 1960.

Hu-pei Ti-fang Tzu-chih Yen-chiu Hui Cha-chih (湖北地方自治研究會雜誌 Hupeh Self-government Study Society Magazine), Tokyo, 1908.

Huang, Hsing. "San-yueh erh-shih-chiu ko-ming chih ch'ien-yin hou-kuo" (三月二十九革命之前因後果 The Cause and Effect of the Revolution of March 29), *Ko-ming Wen-hsien Ts'ung-k'an* (革命文獻叢刊 *Serial Publications of the Collected Documents on the Revolution)*, Vol. I, No. 5, March, 1947.

Li, Shu-hua. "Wu Chih-hui hsien-sheng ts'ung wei-hsin-p'ai ch'eng wei ko-ming-tang ching-kuo" (吳稚暉先生從維新派成為革命黨經過 Wu Chih-hui, from Reformist to Revolutionist), *Chuan-chi Wen-hsueh* (傳記文學 Biographical Literature), Vol. IV, No. 3, March 1964.

Liu, Ta-nien. "Hsin-hai ko-ming yu fan-Man wen-t'i"(辛亥革命與反滿問題 The 1911 Revolution and the Anti-Manchu Question), *Li-shih Yen-chiu* (歷史研究 Historical Research), V, Peking, 1961.

Lo, Jung-pang. "The Overseas Chinese and Chinese Politics, 1899-1911: Some Historical Sidelights on their Political Behavior," unpublished paper presented at the 14th annual meeting of the Association for Asian Studies, 1962.

Min Pao (民報 Citizen's Journal), Tokyo, 1905-1907.

Schiffrin, Harold Z. "Sun Yat-sen's Early Land Policy: The Origin and Meaning of 'Equalization of Land Rights'," *Journal of Asian Studies,* Vol. 16, No. 4, August, 1957.

Shen, Chien. "Hsin-hai ko-ming ch'ien wo-kuo lu-chun chi ch'i chun-fei" 辛亥革命前我國陸軍及其軍費 The Land Army and Its Finance on the Eve of the Revolution), *She-hui K'o-hsueh* (社會科學 Social Sciences), Vol. II, No. 2, January, 1937.

Smythe, E. Joan. "The Tzu-li Hui: Some Chinese and Their Rebellions," Harvard University East Asian Research Center *Papers on China,* XII, 1958.

Su Pao (蘇報 Kiangsu Journal), Shanghai, 1903-1904.

Sun, Yat-sen. "China's Next Step," *The Independent,* New York, July 13, 1912.

Teng, Wen-hui. "Kung-chin Hui ti yuan-ch'i chi ch'i jo-kan chih-tu" (共進會的緣起及其若干制度 The Origin of the Common Advance Society and Its Various Regulations), *Chin-tai-shih Tzu-liao* (近代史资料 Materials on Modern History), No. 10, August, 1956.

Wang, Gungwu. "Sun Yat-sen and Singapore," *Journal of the South Seas Society,* December, 1959.

Young, Ernest P. "Ch'en T'ien-hua (1875-1905): A Chinese Nationalist," Harvard University East Asian Research Center, *Papers on China,* XIII, 1959.

UNPUBLISHED THESES

Cheng, Shelley H. "The T'ung-meng-hui: Its Organization, Leadership and Finances: 1905-1912," Ph.D. dissertation, University of Washington, 1962.

Chu, Ch'i-hsien. "A Study of the Development of Sun Yat-sen's Philosophical Ideas," Ph.D. dissertation, Columbia University, 1950.

Li, Ti-tsun. "The Political and Economic Theories of Sun Yat-sen," Ph.D. dissertation, University of Wisconsin, 1929.

GLOSSARY

Ai-kuo Hsueh She	愛國學社
Anhwei	安徽
Anking	安慶
Chang Chi	張繼
Chang Ch'i-yun	張其昀
Chang Chih-tung	張之洞
Chang Piao	張彪
Chang Ping-lin	章炳麟
Ch'ang Fu	長福
Chang Tseng-yang	張曾敭
Chang Yu-k'un	章裕昆
Chang Yung-fu	張永福
Ch'angsha	長沙
Chao Sheng	趙聲
Ch'aochow	潮州
Chekiang	浙江
Che-chiang Ch'ao	浙江潮
Ch'en Ch'i-mei	陳其美

Ch'en Ch'ien-ch'iu	陳千秋
Ch'en Chin-nan	陳近南
Ch'en Ch'u-nan	陳楚楠
Ch'en Po-p'ing	陳伯平
Ch'en Shao-pai	陳少白
Ch'enT'ien-hua	陳天華
Cheng Ch'eng-kung	鄭成功
Ch'eng Chia-sheng	程家檉
Cheng Lo-sheng	鄭螺生
Chen-nan-kuan	鎮南關
Cheng Shih-liang	鄭士良
Chi Sheng (Wang Tung)	寄生（汪東）
Chih-kung T'ang	致公堂
Chih-na Wang-kuo Chi-nien Hui	支那亡國紀念會
Ch'iang-hsueh Hui	強學會
Chiang-su Hu-nan Yu-hsueh I-pien	江蘇湖南遊學譯編
Chiao-yu Hui	教育會
Chien-kuo fang-lueh	建國方略
Chih Sheng	蟄伸
Chihi	直隸
Ch'inchow	欽州
Ching-shih Chung	警世鐘
Ch'ing-nien Hui	青年會

Ch'iu Chin	秋瑾
Chou Dynasty	周朝
Chou Hsien-jui	周獻瑞
Ch'ou Shih-k'uang	仇式匡
Chu Chih-hsin	朱執信
Chü Cheng	居正
Chu Ho-chung	朱和中
Chu Hung-wu	朱洪武
Chu Kwei-i	朱貴一
Chu Ping-lin	朱炳麟
Chu Shao-k'ang	竺紹康
Chuang Yin-an	莊銀安
Chun-chi Ch'u	軍機處
Chun Kuo-min Chiao-yu Hui	軍國民教育會
Chung Chen-ch'uan	鍾振川
Chung-hsing Pao	中興報
Chung-ho T'ang	中和堂
Chung-hua Ko-ming Tang	中華革命黨
Chung-kuo Chiao-yu Hui	中國教育會
Chung-kuo Jih Pao	中國日報
Chung-kuo Nu Pao	中國女報
En Ming	恩銘
Erh-shih Shih-chi chih Chih-na	二十世紀之支那

Fangch'eng	防城
Feng Tzu-yu	馮自由
Foochow	福州
Fu-jen Wen She	輔仁文社
Fukien	福建
Han Sheng	漢聲
Han-tsu Tu-li Hui	漢族獨立會
Hangchow	杭州
Hankow	漢口
Hanyang	漢陽
Ho Chang	何章
Ho T'ien-chun	何天炯
Ho T'ien-han	何天瀚
Hokou	河口
Honan	河南
Hsi Liang	錫良
Hsiao-chan	小站
Hsiao I-shan	蕭一山
Hsieh Liang-mu	謝良牧
Hsin Chung-kuo Pao	新中國報
Hsing-chung Hui	興中會
Hsu Ching-hsin	徐鏡心
Hsu Hsi-lin	徐錫麟

Hsuan Feng 選鋒

Hsueh Chun-tu 薛君度

Hua-hsien Jih Pao 華暹日報

Hua-hsing Hui 華興會

Huang Hsing 黃興

Huang Ming-t'ang 黃明堂

Huang-hua Kang 黃花崗

Huang San-teh 黃三德

Huangkang 黃崗

Hu Han-min 胡漢民

Hunan 湖南

Hu-pei Hsueh-sheng Chieh 湖北學生界

Hua-yuan Shan 花園山

Huichow 惠州

Hung Ch'uan-fu 洪全福

Hung Hsiu-ch'uan 洪秀全

Hung Meng 洪門

I-shu Hui-pien 譯書彙編

Jih-chih Hui 日知會

Jui Cheng 瑞澂

Jung Lu 榮祿

K'ai-chih Lu 開智錄

K'ang Hsi 康熙

K'ang Kuang-jen 康廣仁

K'ang-O T'ieh-hsueh Hui 抗俄鐵血會

K'ang Pao-chung 康寶忠

K'ang Yu-wei 康有為

Kao Chien-kung 高劍公

Kiangsi 江西

Kiangsu 江蘇

Kinhua 金華

K'o-hsueh Pu-hsi So 科學補習所

Ko-lao Hui 哥老會

Ko-ming chun 革命軍

Ku Chung-hsiu 谷鍾秀

Ku Ssu-shen 谷思慎

K'uaichi 會稽

Kuang-chih Shu-chu 廣智書局

Kuang-fu Chun 光復軍

Kuang Hsu 光緒

Kuang-hua Jih Pao 光華日報

Kung-chin Hui 共進會

Kung-ho Hui 共和會

Kung Pao-ch'uan 龔寶銓

Kuo Jen-chang 郭人漳

Kuo-min Pao 國民報

Kuomintang	國民黨
Kwangsi	廣西
Kwangtung	廣東
Kwangtung Tu-li Hsieh Hui	廣東獨立協會
Kweichow	貴州
Kweiyang	貴陽
Lee Ta-ling	李大陵
Li-chih Hui	勵志會
Li Chih-t'ang	李紀堂
Li Hsieh-ho	李爕和
Li Hung-chang	李鴻章
Li Shih-nan	李是男
Li Shu-hua	李書華
Li Tzu-chung	李自重
Li Yuan-hung	黎元洪
Li Yuan-shui	李源水
Liang Ch'i-ch'ao	梁啓超
Liang Chin-tung	梁敬錞
Liao Chung-k'ai	廖仲凱
Lin Shih-shuang	林時爽
Lingshan	靈山
Liu Ch'eng-yu	劉成禺
Liu Ching-an	劉靜安

Liu Ch’u 劉崛

Liu Kung 劉公

Liu Kwei-i 劉揆一

Lu Chih-i 呂志伊

Lu Pi-ch’en 陸弼臣

Lung-chi Pao 隆記報

Lung-hua Hui 龍華會

Ma Chun-wu 馬君武

Ma Chung-han 馬宗漢

Meng hui-tou 猛回頭

Min-chu Pao 民主報

Min-ch’uan 民權

Min-kuo Pao 民國報

Min Pao 民報

Min-sheng 民生

Min-sheng Jih Pao 民生日報

Ming Dynasty 明朝

Nan-yang 南洋

Nan-yang Kung-hsueh 南洋公學

Nan-yang Tsung-hui Pao 南洋總滙報

Nanking 南京

Ni Ying-tien 倪映典

Niu Yung-chien 鈕永建

Ou Chu-chia 歐榘甲

Pao-huang Hui 保皇會

Pei-yang Kung-hsueh 北洋公學

P'ing Kang 平剛

P'u-t'ien 莆田

San-ho Hui 三合會

San Min Chu I 三民主義

San-tien Hui 三點會

Shanyin 山陰

Shanghai 上海

Shao-nien Hsueh She 少年學社

Sheng-shih wei-yen 盛世危言

Shih-wu Pao 時務報

Shao-lin 少林

Shaohsing 紹興

Shensi 陝西

Shih Kung-chiu 時功玖

Shou Shan 壽山

Sih, Paul K.T. 薛光前

Su Pao 蘇報

Sun Wen 孫文

Sun Wen hsueh-shuo 孫文學說

Sun Wu 孫武

Sun Yat-sen	孫逸仙
Sung Chiao-jen	宋教仁
Ssu Huang (Ch'en T'ien-hua)	思黃（陳天華）
Szechuan	四川
Ta-han Jih Pao	大漢日報
Ta-t'ung Jih Pao	大同日報
Ta-t'ung School	大同學校
Taiping Rebellion	太平天國
T'an Jen-feng	譚人鳳
T'an Yu-ch'u	譚佑初
T'ang Erh-ho	湯爾和
T'ang Leang-li	湯良禮
T'ang Ts'ai-ch'ang	唐才常
T'ao Ch'eng-chang	陶成章
Teng Mu-han	鄧慕涵
Teng Sheng	鄧勝
Teng Tse-ju	鄧澤如
Teng Tzu-yu	鄧子瑜
T'ien-ti Hui	天地會
Tientsin	天津
Ting Hou-fu	丁厚扶
Ting K'ai-chang	丁開嶂
Ting Wen-chiang	丁文江

Ts'ai Chun	蔡鈞
Ts'ai Yuan-k'ang	蔡元康
Ts'ai Yuan-p'ei	蔡元培
Tseng Kuo-fan	曾國藩
Tseng Po-hsing	曾伯興
Tso Tsung-t'ang	左宗棠
Tsou Lu	鄒魯
Tsou Yung	鄒容
Ts'ui Shu-ch'in	崔書琴
Tsung-li	總理
T'u-nan Jih Pao	圖南日報
Tu Ch'ien	杜潛
T'u-ti kuo-yu	土地國有
Tuan Fang	端方
T'ung-meng Hui	同盟會
Tung-ya Wan-kuo T'ung-meng Hui	東亞萬國同盟會
Tzu-chih Hsueh She	自治學社
Tz'u Hsi	慈禧
Tzu-li Chun	自立軍
Wang Chih-ch'un	王之春
Wang Ching-wei	汪精衛
Wang Hu	王瑚
Wang Yen-chun	王延鈞

Wang Yin-fan 王蔭藩

Wen Kung-chih 文公直

Wen-hsueh She 文學社

Wu Chih-hui 吳稚暉

Wu Hsiang-hsiang 吳相湘

Wu Ch'un-yang 吳春暘

Wu Lu-chen 吳祿貞

Wu Yang-ku 吳暘谷

Wu Ying-yuan 吳英元

Wuch'ang 武昌

Wuhan 武漢

Yang Ch'u-yun 楊衢雲

Yang Ho-ling 楊鶴齡

Yang-kuang Jih Pao 仰光日報

Yu Lieh 尤烈

Yu Shao-wan 尤少紈

Yuan Shih-k'ai 袁世凱

Yuan Shu-hsun 袁樹勛

Yunnan 雲南

Yung Cheng 雍正

Yung Wing 容閎

INDEX

A

B

C

D

E

F

G

H

I

J

K

L

M

N

O

P

R

S

T

U

V

W

Y

ASIA IN THE MODERN WORLD, NO. 8

Paul K. T. Sih, Editor

Also in this series:

No. 1
THE CHINESE REVOLUTION of 1911
by Chin-tung Liang

No. 2
CHINA AT THE PARIS PEACE CONFERENCE in 1919
by Wunsz King

No. 3
CHINA AND THE WASHINGTON CONFERENCE, 1921-1922
by Wunsz King

No. 4
CHINA AND THE BRUXELLES CONFERENCE, 1937
by Tsien Tai

No. 5
CHINA AND THE LEAGUE OF NATIONS
by Wunsz King

No. 6
THE SINISTER FACE OF THE MUKDEN INCIDENT
by Chin-tung Liang

No. 7
THE KUOMINTANG: SELECTED HISTORICAL DOCUMENTS, 1894-1965
by Milton J. T. Shieh